Playing the Game

A Biography of Sir Henry Newbolt

Playing the Game

A Biography of Sir Henry Newbolt

Susan Chitty

Quartet Books

First published in Great Britain by Quartet Books Limited in 1997
A member of the Namara Group
27 Goodge Street
London W1P 2LD

A catalogue record for this book is available from the British Library

ISBN 0 7043 7107 3

Typeset by FSH Ltd, London
Printed and bound in Great Britain by WBC Bookbinders, Bridgend

For Peter and Marcia

Acknowledgements

I would like to express my thanks to two of Newbolt's grandchildren: Peter Newbolt who gave me access to the vast collection of Newbolt letters (copied by his wife, Marcia) and Theresa Whistler who allowed me to read a further selection. I also wish to thank the following suppliers of unpublished material: my husband, Thomas and his brother John, who gave me access to Chitty family papers; Anne Thwaite who enabled me to buy the letters of Henry Newbolt to Mrs John Buchan; the American Universities of Illinois and Hofstra which gave me permission to print extracts from Newbolt's correspondence with H.G. Wells; Charles Hodgson who gave me access to *The Book of the Omar Khayyam Club 1892-1910*, and John Murray, who allowed me to make use of the archives of his publishing house.

I would also like to thank Derek Winterbottom, author of *Henry Newbolt and the Spirit of Clifton* (1986), who made possible my warm association with Clifton College, the late Patric Dickinson, poet and editor of *Selected Poems of Henry Newbolt* (1981) who spoke to me most movingly about the poet just before he died, and the following among many, who also gave me help: D. & J. Aspinwall, Tony Davies, Arthur Duckworth, Robin & Suzanne Heath, John Heath–Stubbs, Richard Hough, Tim Jeal, M. V. Mahy, Paul Moynihan, Paul Pollack, Graham Tayar and Christine Winfield. My daughter, Miranda Barden, gave me critical and secretarial assistance.

Finally I must not forget the late Dr Michael Raymond who had the idea for the book, but, alas, did not live to see it published.

Playing the Game

A Biography of Sir Henry Newbolt

The sand of the desert is sodden red, –
    Red with the wreck of a square that broke; –
The Gatling's jammed and the Colonel dead,
    And the regiment blind with dust and smoke.
The river of death has brimmed his banks,
    And England's far, and honour a name,
But the voice of a schoolboy rallies the ranks;
    'Play up! playup! and play the game!'

CONTENTS

Abbreviations used in footnotes:

AHL: Letters of Henry Newbolt to Alice Hylton (unpublished)

CN I: CLIFTON COLLEGE TWENTY FIVE YEARS AGO, THE DIARY OF A FAG
  Sir F.G. Newbolt 1904

CN II: CLIFTON COLLEGE FORTY YEARS AGO, THE DIARY OF A PRAEPOSTER
  Sir F.G. Newbolt 1924

HGW Hofstra: H.G. Wells Papers, Hofstra University, U.S.A.

HGW Illinois: H.G. Wells Papers, University of Illinois, Champaign-
  Urbana, U.S.A.

LLL: THE LATER LIFE AND LETTERS OF SIR HENRY NEWBOLT
  Margaret Newbolt (ed.) 1942

McG I: SIR HENRY NEWBOLT AND ORCHARDLEIGH
  Michael McGarvie 1985

McG II: ORCHARDLEIGH HOUSE
  Michael McGarvie 1983

MR: THE MONTHLY REVIEW (1900-1904)

My Story: MY STORY: Unpublished memoir of Emily Newbolt

My World: MY WORLD AS IN MY TIME
  Sir Henry Newbolt 1932

NL: Letters written by Sir Henry Newbolt and his family

OFC I: CLIFTON SCHOOLDAYS 1879-1885
  O.F. Christie 1930

OFC II: A HISTORY OF CLIFTON COLLEGE 1860-1934
  O.F. Christie 1935

SP: SELECTED POEMS OF HENRY NEWBOLT
  Patric Dickinson (ed.) 1981

Whistler: IMAGINATION OF THE HEART, A LIFE OF WALTER DE LA MARE
  Theresa Whistler 1993

Introduction

Henry Newbolt has the misfortune to be famous for one poem,
the one with the chorus: 'Play up! play up! and play the game!'
Most people know only the chorus. Even Evelyn Waugh knew only
the first line, and found himself groping for the rest in his diary
for 1922. 'I went to a wine with Hill last night. My memories are
vague but I distinctly remember standing in the quad and trying to
quote Newbolt's "There's a breathless hush in the close tonight".
More recently, Perdita in Jilly Cooper's *Polo* had other problems
with the same poem in a school exam paper:

> '"And it's not for the sake of a ribboned coat
>   Or the selfish hope of a season's fame
> But his Captain's hand on his shoulder smote –
>   Play up! play up! and play the game!"

"Are Newbolt's views of team spirit outdated?"' was the first
question. 'Perdita wrote, "Yes," in her disdainful blue scrawl, "the

schoolboy in the poem must be an utter jerk and a poofter to boot to prefer his captain's hand on his shoulder to a season's fame and a ribboned coat.'"

Newbolt's ideals are inevitably ridiculed in our self-first-the-rest-nowhere society. A recent article in the *Sunday Telegraph*[1] described ours as the'Rottweiler Age' characterised by a return to the savagery of the early industrial revolution. That savagery was replaced by the Victorian ideal of chivalry, promoted by educationalists from the public schools down to the Boys' Brigade; the mediaeval knight became the role model. Newbolt's poetry was based on that philosophy. Many of the young officers mown down by German guns in the First World War carried his poems in their knapsacks.

Understandably, the popularity of Newbolt's poetry plummeted after that war. Those who came back from the trenches had had enough of the chivalry for which such a monstrous price had been paid. The embittered war poetry of Wilfred Owen and his comrades was now the rage, and the critics turned on Newbolt's 'huffing patriotic verses'[2] with their 'irritating monotony of metre'.[3] Newbolt dropped out of the anthologies, and before he died in 1938 he declared that, as far as the public was concerned, he had already been dead twenty years.

Then came the swing of the pendulum. First in 1938 John Betjeman declared that Newbolt 'wasn't half so bad a poet as Bloomsbury would have us think'[4] and added in 1962, 'I don't think any poet of the present century has written so many lines that are so easy to remember'.[5] (It is true Modern dictionaries of quotations contain columns of Newbolt.) He complained that Newbolt was now excluded even from school anthologies. 'The serious thirties, the frightened fifties, the sneering sixties would not include such unfashionable verse.'

Next came a new generation of poets who shared Betjeman's views; Philip Larkin and Kingsley Amis also turned away from Modernism in poetry. In his *Oxford Book of Twentieth Century English Verse* (1975), Larkin wrote that he would include 'no poems requiring a glossary for their full understanding.' He added that he

1. Jeffrey Richards, 6 May 1990
2. Vernon Scannell, *Not Without Glory*, 1976
3. Edith Batho, *The Victorians and After*, 1938
4. *Letters of John Betjeman* (1994), p.211
5. *The Listener*, 28 June 1962

wished to re-establish links with a pre-Modernist tradition of 'poetry about English subjects and places', a tradition that had been interrupted by a Celt (Yeats) and an American (Eliot). He included 'He Fell Among Thieves' in his anthology. Kingsley Amis chose the same poem and three others by Newbolt in The Amis Anthology (1988). He was particularly moved by the little-known lyrics. Of the love poem 'The Viking's Song', he wrote: 'Anybody who thinks that writing about physical sex cannot be genuine unless it is explicit should consider this poem'.

In 1981, Patric Dickinson, a BBC poetry editor and himself a poet, brought out a collection of Newbolt's poems with a biographical introduction. It is with radio audiences that Newbolt's poems have had most success in the last two decades. A few years ago, 'Drake's Drum' with its chorus: 'Capten, art tha sleepin' there below?' was regularly the most broadcast of any poem on Radio 4. In the first six months of 1996, 'Play Up!' was requested ten times.

I first became interested in Newbolt on New Year's Eve, 1990. We were sitting round a log fire when our host, (now, alas, dead) began to intone 'Clifton Chapel': 'This is the chapel: here, my son, your father thought the thoughts of youth . . .' At the end not an eye was dry, and the next day I opened Newbolt's autobiography, *My World As In My Time* (1932), for the first time. The book was in our shelves as he was related to my husband. It was a revelation. I had imagined a red-faced Colonel Blimp spluttering from his armchair. Newbolt was nothing of the sort. For a start, he was not a soldier and had never fired a shot in anger. He was not even a cricketer, being too slight to succeed at the game. He was not the scion of a great family, but was brought up in the blackest of Black Country where his father had been a clergyman. He wasn't even completely English, since his mother was descended from Jewish immigrants. I *had* expected him to be a man of deeply held convictions and this he was. I had not expected him to be a man of humanity, nor to be the man who brought T. S. Eliot to a wider public.

6. *The Amis Anthology* (1988), p 335

PART 1 CHILDHOOD 1862–1875

CHAPTER 1

Bilston

Henry Newbolt's childhood was inappropriate. He wrote of a father who called his son 'up from the terrace to ride', but there was no terrace, no horse and, after the age of four, no father. Young Harry first saw the light of day through the thick industrial gloom of Bilston, near Walsall, north-west of Birmingham. Bilston was one of the most heavily industrialised towns in England. It stood upon the Ten Yard Seam, a thirty-foot-thick sandwich of iron ore and coal. The coal powered the blast furnaces that smelted the iron. By the time Harry was born, there were forty-one blast furnaces, running day and night in Bilston. For twelve hours flames belched from the cone-shaped furnaces and then liquid iron ran off into sand beds, reddening the night sky. Living conditions for the working people were atrocious. Ramshackle houses faced each other across streets that were also drains, or stood around courtyards piled with filth. Only the privileged had clean wells to draw from. The rest preferred beer, with predictable results. Epidemic diseases were rife, particularly smallpox.

Harry's father was the Reverend Henry Francis Newbolt, a graduate of St John's College, Cambridge who had chosen to work in this place. 'We were never made for ourselves alone,' Henry Francis told his future wife. Henry Francis came of a nautical family. His father, Captain Charles Newbolt, had been a midshipman with Nelson's fleet. He died young of yellow fever, while in command of a merchant ship. The nautical tradition carried on into the next generation. Henry Francis's only brother Charles was a merchant seaman much afflicted by 'foul weather and light breezes',[1] but others said it was drink. After taking Orders, Henry Francis became a curate at Maidstone, where he married Mary Jane Newham of the Isle of Man. When she died, aged twenty-seven, he was left to bring up their daughter, Mary. For six years he was curate at St Matthew's Walsall and filled the two thousand pew-seats with his sermons. Emily Stubbs, still in her teens, first caught his attention when he started a bible class for Sunday School teachers. He looked, she wrote in her memoirs, like a sorrowing angel. She could hardly believe that she 'was loved and longed for by the man on whom the eyes and thoughts of many maidens of the parish were set'. She was to become his second wife and the mother of Henry Newbolt.

Emily's background was trade. The Stubbs family had risen by tanning leather. The men of the family were massive in stature and girth. 'In a tug-o'-war, our branch could always furnish a team of twelve men, heavier than the same number of any family in the county.'[2] Her father had resigned his post as Town Clerk after the passing of the Reform Bill, being seriously affronted when the Radical candidate was not elected. He remained retired from public life till his death 35 years later. Stubbses had been mayors of Walsall for as long as anyone could remember. They had married into the trade oligarchy of the town, adding each other's names to their own. George, Emily's father, was a Bradnock Stubbs; another branch was Heath Stubbs.

1. *NL*, HFN to EN, 11 Sept. 1865
2. Emily Newbolt, *My Story*, p.23; an unpublished memoir

Emily's mother was Eliza Solomon, and she came from a Jewish Hungarian family of pencil-makers who had settled in Birmingham at the beginning of the eighteenth century. Her father, Samuel Solomon, invented the famous quack remedy, 'Balm of Gilead.' Emily had the looks of her Jewish mother: she was small, dark and lively. Henry Francis compared her to a diamond 'so sharp and so bright'. Yet he compared her to a violet as well, and tried to put it into verse:

> 'I trembled for the varied white and blue
> Until I saw each coming spring renew
> The fragrant beauty of the little flower.'

Emily considered this sort of thing soppy. 'I know you will box my ears,' Henry Francis wrote at the end of a mildly sentimental letter. Emily had a stronger will than either her sister Eliza Jane Gordon, who was older than her, or her sister Selina Harrison, who was younger. The three girls had some education, and by the age of fifteen, Emily was at boarding school in Lichfield. She came top in everything. The problems of the three sisters began after they left school, when they found themselves once more at home with nothing to do but wait for husbands. While she was at school, Emily underwent conversion at the hands of a preacher in a country church (she was to retain a liking for country churches ever after). Now she decided, with her sisters, to teach Christianity to poor children. Not for the last time, Old Stubbs was displeased. He was, she wrote, 'a man who had all his life counted Money as the chief aim and end in existence.'[3]

Walsall society was amazed when this accomplished young lady fell in love with the luckless middle-aged curate. Stubbs would not consider him as a son-in-law. 'Stubbs nursed a belief, not uncommon among Victorian fathers, that his daughters were chattels, and if only they knew it, happier and better off with him than they would ever be in homes of their own making'.[4] Worse still, he particularly disliked clergymen. His excuse was that he was a Unitarian (although his family observed that he was never seen at the chapel). When Emily was twenty there was a frightful row and Henry Francis was forbidden the house.

3. *My Story*, p.7
4. *My Story*, p.19

The lovers now embarked on a secret correspondence and met secretly once a week in Walsall. Henry Francis finally secured the living of the newly-built church of St Mary's at Bilston, seven miles from Walsall. Bilston Vicarage was a stone building in the Tudor style, just off the centre of Bilston. 'Notorious' Bath Street ran in front of it and immediately behind was the railway. Beneath it was a disused coal mine, into which the Town Hall nearly descended on one occasion. A different fate awaited the vicarage. It was demolished in 1968. At the back of Barclays Bank in Bilston there is a plaque which reads:

Sir Henry Newbolt
Poet
1862–1938
Born near this place

Henry Francis moved into the large vicarage, 'almost too large perhaps', and decided not to furnish it properly till Emily should be at his his side. He blamed this lonely period in Bilston for the decline of his health. 'Something is wrong, and I don't like either to go to a doctor or physic myself. Perhaps a little starvation would be a good thing.'[5] He fought depression and a sense of exclusion. Occasionally, he reminded Emily that his family were of nobler descent than hers. He tried to establish his connection with the Knowles Newbolts, whose pedigree was of 'curious antiquity'. He had visiting cards printed with a crest.

Meanwhile, he had the drunkards of Bilston to quell. He told Emily how he was on his way home one night 'when the coachman shouted out, "Mr Newbolt, get out! Here's a dead man" and there in the middle of the road, lying exactly under the wheel of a wagon with one hand holding the wheel, was a man not dead but hopelessly drunk. We pulled him out and at last bullied him awake. It was a perfect miracle, the three horses were all quite fresh and had they dragged the wagon a bit he would have been killed or terribly injured.'[6] Henry Francis also provided adult education in the form of cottage lectures on the poets of the day (Tennyson, Browning and Longfellow). 'His situation in Bilston was much like that of a missionary in Africa,' wrote Emily. 'In some ways he was

5. *NL* HFN to EN, n.d. 1859
6. *NL* HFN to EN, 17 Aug. 1860

swallowed up and lost in the heart of the Black Country.'[7] There were now two other members of the Henry Francis household. His eight-year-old daughter Mary, and his cousin George, the eighteen-year-old son of Colonel Newbolt of India. (The Colonel was one of the many brothers and sisters of Charles Newbolt of Nelson's fleet.) George, alas, was no companion to Henry Francis. His pleasures were 'of the butterfly sort'. Henry Francis complained to Emily. 'If only he could play chess.'[8]

Henry Francis and Emily were married on 5 December 1860, when Emily reached her majority. Henry Francis was 37. The ceremony took place without Stubbs at St John's in the Pleck, a poor part of Walsall. Even when the bridal party had left the house for the church, 'the inscrutable old man sat still by his December fireside, and his daughter was given away by her gentle and indomitable mother'.[9] Henry Francis hesitated to ask his own grand relations to 'such a wedding as I feared mine would be', but in the end Colonel George Newbolt came, bringing with him an escritoire as a present.

At last the couple were together in the half-furnished vicarage. They gladly faced what Henry Francis called 'that great work that you and I have to do.'[10] Henry Francis and Emily had been married for eighteen months when the author of 'Drake's Drum' was born. Only a few days before the day of his son's birth on 6 June 1862, one of the most frightful accidents ever known in South Staffordshire, the Millfields Ironworks Disaster, occurred in Bilston. The eight-ton top of a boiler was blown high into the air and twenty-seven men were killed.

Young Harry quickly set about establishing his position in the household. By the time he was a month old he was ready to be taken to Walsall to be presented to Grandfather Stubbs. The rift between Emily and her father was never officially healed, it was simply 'overlooked'. 'She came and went in her father's house, as if she had never left it.' Henry Francis, however, was conscious of his continued exclusion from the Stubbs circle. He was not quite without company during Emily's visits to her parents and her married sisters, however. His daughter Mary was now eleven, and

7. My Story, p.20
8. *NL* HFN to EN, 11 May 1860
9. *My Story*, p.7
10. *NL* HFN to EN, 17 Nov. 1860

did her best. She helped organise Emily's Sunday School of twelve girls, 'putting everything out ready'. She also contributed suggestions for her half-brother's diet. 'We found Harry so very fond of salt,' he wrote, 'and so resembling his mother in this way that Mary suggested he might resemble her in other things also, and it was perhaps our duty to supply him with a large quantity of cayenne as well as salt – will you let us know whether we shall let him have it or not?' Emily's tendency to go on visits was somewhat abated by the birth of Frank, a year after Harry. He immediately became 'Mary's property', Henry Francis wrote. Milly arrived two years later. Her full name was Emily. 'Something about her makes you take notice of her,' said Henry Francis.

Henry Francis's health had continued to deteriorate. Bilston did not agree with him. It was decided that a temporary exchange of living might help, and the family spent six months in the vicarage at Coalbrookdale, not far to the north of Walsall, which they loved for its hill walks, its garden full of roses and the River Severn nearby. It was while staying at Coalbrookdale that Harry received his first letter from his father, who had gone back to Bilston to assist the curate. He was all of two years old at the time. 'My dear little Boy. Did you ever have a letter before – I thought I would write you one and tell you such a lot of things – Papa is at home in his own house – Mamma's ferns are green and well, though small – The wind has been blowing so hard today that the leaves have been blown up into this room and they went whirling and twirling about in the air just as if they were at play – was not that funny? Papa went for a walk today to Portobello where the young men were playing cricket – I wonder whether Harry will be fond of cricket.'[11] In a letter to Mary, Henry Francis wrote, 'Harry is growing such a queer little fellow, so good and oh so naughty. The other day he was naughty and I said Harry I shall send you upstairs. "Oh," said he, "then I had better go at once."' By this time, Mary had been sent away to a boarding school at Sydenham. She was now 'a great girl' of twelve and a half. In the letters she wrote to her father, Mary showed herself to be independent-minded, if not downright difficult. When she went to stay with her great-uncle, Henry Francis advised her against hoop trundling in the park. 'If you were walking out with Uncle ... and none of the rest of the children were

11. *NL* HFN to HN, 30 Aug. 1864

with you, the hoop should be left behind, as most gentlemen are more particular than Papa in such things, who would willingly help you trundle your hoop in the Park itself, if there were no danger of its getting under the horses' legs and causing an accident.'[12] There was an almost psychic link between father and daughter at times. When Mary was only seven, Henry Francis told Emily of a dream he had had when she was about to visit her aunt, Mrs Newham, in the Isle of Man. 'I could not think of anything else but Mr Newham's cranky boat and I could not get the feeling out of my mind how horrible it would be if Mary were upset in it. And even now when I pass her little room an unpleasant feeling comes over me.'[13] Mary was to die at sea at the age of seventeen.

By Christmas 1865, the family were back in Bilston and Harry was 'more amusing than ever.'[14] By now his cot has been moved into his parents' bedroom because the night nursery was damp. This sharing of his parents' bedroom is one of Newbolt's earliest memories, indeed, one of his only two memories of his father. 'I was sleeping in a cot of mahogany with high cane sides – and being very thoroughly awake I was climbing over one of these sides with a view to an excursion round the room. My mother saw me when it was just too late – I was actually straddling the fence. She was standing on the opposite side of her big bed and could only cry hastily for help. My father stepped instantly from his dressing room ... caught me in the act to fall, replaced me, and said seriously, "You must never do that again," and then with a lighter tone, "You might dash your little brains out"[15] Harry's other memory of his father was connected with the study. His parents were entertaining a friend to supper by the fire. 'I was about three and allowed to stay up. I listened to my father's talk. He was making a smiling complaint of some minor troubles, "And then in comes Mr So-and-so and borrows a book", pointing to the shelves over his shoulder. I was curious about his name, which I had never heard before: and afterwards I asked my mother who was the bad man called Mr So-and-so.'[16] Henry Francis's library made a deep impression on his son. There was a 'whole wall covered with books.

12. *NL* HFN to MN, 16 Nov. 1863
13. *NL* HFN to EN, 9 July 1860
14. *NL* HFN to EN, 28 Feb. 1865
15. *My World*, p.2.
16. ibid.

Stone-coloured ranks of the *Quarterly Review* and many yellow and blue numbers of the *Edinburgh Review*.'[17]

Newbolt's early memories of the outside world were of an industrial landscape. The trains went past his nursery window. 'When one went by, my brother and I used to run across to enjoy the sight of the gigantic toy moving past of its own accord.'[18] When he went out, his pram was pushed by his nurse, Old Emma, 'by black canals and among huge slag-heaps where no grass could grow, where the sun rarely shone, where at night a man could read his newspaper by the glare of the blast furnaces, luridly reflected in the dense low sky. There was not much to choose in those days between the dingy town and the dingy landscape outside it, except that the town abounded in stirring people while the country showed hardly a sign of life and was apparently inhabited by an underground race.' The mine pumping stations stood around the town. They looked like 'half buried letter N's.' The child thought they were giants asleep with their knees in the air. 'The horror of them was fascinating'[19]

Harry's days at Bilston were numbered. His father was wasting away. Dr Best diagnosed an ailment 'of the bladder and prostate gland'. (Henry Francis probably had cancer of the prostate.) Finally, the decision was taken to give up the living at Bilston and return to Walsall, that paler 'shade of smokeland'. In 1866, the family moved into 6 Doveridge Place, in a small terrace of houses at the top of the town, near St Matthew's Church. Henry Francis already knew Doveridge Place, he had lived there as a curate. In March he preached a sermon at St Matthew's, Walsall, part of a Lent series. It was his last professional engagement, although almost to the end he tried to find a new church appointment. In May he was removed to Ilfracombe on the advice of Sir James Paget, but only survived three weeks there. Back in Walsall, Harry was unaware of the gravity of his father's condition. Now four, he dictated his first letter to his mother. He reminded her that Papa had promised him a toy water pump and he gave news of Milly: 'It looks so pretty to see her todling [sic] about.'[20]

Henry Francis died at Ilfracombe on 24 May 1866, aged 42. The burial took place in St Matthew's overcrowded churchyard, Walsall.

17. *My World*, p.6
18. *My World*, p.2
19. *My World*, p.7
20. *NL* HN to EN, 6 July 1866

Since the cholera epidemic of 1849, the gravediggers had had to drive rods into the ground to find space for fresh burials. Henry Francis, however, had a space waiting for him at the back of the church where the ground falls gently towards Cannock Chase. A seven-foot-high tombstone was in place, bearing a list of names including those of his mother, his first wife and their son who had died in infancy. As usual, Mr Stubbs was missing from the procession. His place was taken by a crowd of poor people who had walked over from Bilston. In Henry Francis's church at Bilston, his 'deeply attached people' subscribed to a tablet commemorating him as an example of Christian charity. The inscription can still be read on the rare occasions when the church is not locked: 'His sun has gone down while it is still day.'

CHAPTER 2

Walsall

Doveridge Place was to be Harry's home for the next ten years. The little terrace is a turning off Sandwell Street, where there is now a plaque in his memory. The Newbolts lived in the house at the far end, number 6, looking south over open country. A pall of black smoke in the valley below marked Bilston. At the age of four, Harry, although dressed in black, was too young to grieve for his father. He was not, however, too young to realise that 'we were in a new way the centre of attention among our friends. "So this is the little fatherless boy," they would say.' Upon him was placed the burden of his mother's grief. For two years Emily 'never knew a happy hour.'[1] She would not admit that Henry Francis had gone. 'She seemed literally to be still living with her husband.'[2] Newbolt

1. *My Story*, p.9
2. *My Story*, p.8

wrote in his autobiography: 'We children always went to her room in the morning, and I was allowed to stay and see her breakfast. There I constantly heard the same tale, "I had such a wonderful dream last night – I saw your father quite clearly, and he spoke as if he had never gone away."' Harry's sense of loss was yet to come. 'It persisted and grew with the years, a proof of the power with which my mother succeeded in transfusing my personal life with her own.'[3]

Number 6 Doveridge Place no longer stands. It was an early nineteenth-century doll's house tacked on to the end of a row of Georgian ones. It had four rooms each on the ground and first floors and four attics for the servants. The principal room was Emily's sitting room. (One resembling it can still be seen in the Jerome K. Jerome Museum in the town.) The chairs, tables and sofas from Bilston had been squeezed into it, and any spare corner was filled with ferns. Besides ferns, Emily was addicted to woollen tapestry work, and gradually coated her chairs, stools and firescreens in rich reds and blues. It is hard to imagine how even a quorum of crinolines could have fitted in among all this. Emily was an assiduous hostess, and gentlemen were never permitted to run out of churchwarden pipes, or ladies of bread thinly-spread with home-made strawberry jam. But she was also out a great deal, doing God's work. She opened the first Mother's Meeting ever held in the town and collected sixty members. At home, she was often at her sewing machine. 'She sewed and mended and contrived and economised so that the little boys and girl should always look neat and properly dressed.'[4] Henry Francis had left nothing, and her father had told her to name a sum on which she could live. On principal she had named a low one.

The children were kept upstairs with Old Emma. They chiefly saw their mother when she came to take tea with them. She would then read to them the works of two living authors, Hans Andersen and Mrs Sewell (the mother of Anna, she wrote improving ballads for the drinking classes). Old Emma was assisted by the two housemaids, Ann and Elizabeth. The fourth servant was Fanny, who was both cook and housemaid. Fanny was so zealous in the cleaning of the outside windows that she was often in danger of falling into the garden. She was less enthusiastic in the kitchen, and things were inclined to go wrong if Emily was not at home. Nor was Old Emma's

3. *My World*, p.9
4. *My Story*, p.11

11

supervision of the children's religious upbringing all that it might have been. They were expected to say grace before meals, but on one occasion Mrs Newbolt appeared in the nursery when it was Milly's turn. 'Something was not right and she asked the child to repeat the grace. "Nees nors nurses, nors nose nays nays." There was a pause, almost a gasp, then, "You are too big a girl to say it like that – now say it again for me. For these the Lord's mercies the Lord's holy name be praised." For years afterwards, "Nees nors nurses" remained our private name for grace.'[5]

Fortunately, the two small boys and 'fat, jolly Milly' had plenty of opportunity to escape from the rule of women. There was a large garden at Number 6 where things actually grew, unlike the vicarage at Bilston. Each child had a plot which it tended (occasionally). 'We have been diging (sic) in our little gardens today,' Harry wrote to Mary, 'But we don't dig in your garden and when I see pussy go on it I send her off again.' Mary's garden, like Mary, was contrary. It was all grass, with bluebells in the middle. Harry was fond of the cat and was delighted when she had kittens. He was also deeply attached to a small flock of pigeons, spending hours watching the young ones. There was a smallholding nearby, and every morning some 'delightful ducks' passed in procession along the muddy path at the end of the garden. 'One of them made a habit of coming across to peer at us through a gap in our hedge. We made a point of being there at the right time to return the salute of "Usual-duck"'[6] The three little Newbolts longed for a farm of their own. Old Stubbs owned Fulbrook Farm, which they occasionally visited. It stood just south of Walsall in water meadows, now buried under the M6. 'We children had planned to live [there] when our time came to "to retire".'[7] But the nearest the Newbolts got to their own holding was the stableyard at Doveridge Place. They kept rabbits in the loose boxes. 'The children have made a sad wilderness of the yard,' kind Miss Eliza Windle at Number 4 told Mary.[8]

Young Harry was fascinated by books. At the age of five he committed the sacrilege of kneeling in front of one. 'I had gone with [my mother] to Bilston to see an old friend of hers: and to keep me quiet during the visit I was given a book to look at. It was

5. *My World*, p.13
6. *My World*, p.11
7. *My World*, p.23
8. *NL* 19 May 1866

a large illustrated edition of Don Quixote, and its weight made it necessary to lay it on a sofa. I kneeled down to bring myself within range of the pictures. I soon became aware that our hostess was speaking to my mother about me, and that my attitude was the cause. Happily I also heard my mother reply, to the effect that she was sure no irreverence was intended.'[9] The neighbours at Doveridge Place encouraged Harry's interest in books. Mrs Windle and Miss Eliza Windle asked the three children to tea once a week and allowed them to gloat over the horrors of *Struwwelpeter*. But it was the humourous old gentleman next door who taught Harry to read. 'Before I was six I had been so well coached in Mr Blyth's parlour that I read aloud to him a passage in *The Times* [about] the Abyssinian campaign.'[10]

Now the gates of knowledge were wide open, but there was not much in Emily's theological library that could enter them. 'I learned from *The Land and the Book* that the Baptist's edible locusts were really insects and not merely beans; and that butter could be made (though with difficulty, I found out on trial) by shaking milk in a leather bag.'[11] This practical approach to religion met with less success when Harry attempted to walk on water. 'I waited till the time of evening church, when no one was likely to be about, and then filled the large earthenware basin in which our pigeons took their bath. My attempt was made with good faith, but only resulted in wet shoes and socks.'[12]Harry frequently dreamed he was rising from the ground with a slight effort and floating down the staircase. The feeling of reality was so vivid that one morning he determined to use his flying powers by daylight, and went so far as to launch himself down a short flight of stairs. Fortunately, he broke no bones. Sometimes, however, Harry's dreams were of a more frightening nature: 'I remember that going to bed in summer was often a trying experience. When the light of the summer evening faded I generally found that sleep was not to be had. Then as I lay in deepening twilight I became aware that the ottoman in the opposite dark corner of the room was the lair of a wolf who lay crouched upon it with his eyes fixed on me and his low growl becoming gradually louder and louder until the

9. *My World*, p.12
10. *My World*, p.13
11. *My World*, p.6
12. *My World*, p.12

moment came for him to make his spring. At that moment I always woke to find myself alone and safe.'[13]

Mary continued to play an active part in the children's lives, although she was now sixteen. 'In the holidays we children never left her if we could help it.' It was only at this stage that Harry discovered that Mary was not his full sister. 'We knew nothing of the grade of "half-sister", and I remember running home one day to my mother, telling her with hot indignation that Mr Blyth had laughed at me for speaking of Mary as my sister. "She's only a half sister," he had said. This mystified me. Mary was twice my size. How could she be a half-person?'

The Newbolt children were taken to see Mr and Mrs Stubbs twice a week. The old couple lived in the end house of a terrace called St Paul's Close, opposite the church of the same name. (The terrace has now made way for shops, and the neo-classical church has been replaced by the present neo-gothic structure.) In the meadows behind St Paul's, Stubbs hung out his hides. These fields had been even more extensive before his father, Joseph, had sold part of them to St Mary's Grammar School at £400 an acre, a modest price for what is now the town centre.

Harry saw his grandfather as a Johnsonian figure: 'His bulky form gave all his movements a slow dignity. His left hand holding his snuff-box, his right hand uplifted to carry a pinch, while in measured words he cross-examined me. Thus he ruled the town from a chair beside the fire.'[14] When Harry first knew him, Stubbs could still fire an arrow from his longbow. 'Of all grandfather's possessions his two longbows were for me the most coveted.' Another source of interest was the contents of his desk drawers, full of 'quill pens in bundles, penknives with which to cut them, inkpots filled with bird shot [and] a tall ivory-handled seal.'[15] Grandfather was at his most inspiring at the head of the table at Christmas, whence 'he not only presided but ... carved every dish with his own hand. With sixteen at table, this took some time, and the more because my grandfather kept faithfully to the old provincial etiquette. As each portion was carried to the guest for whom it was carved, the courteous voice followed, "Cousin Partridge, have I sent you what you like?" And the formula

13. *My World,* p.11
14. *My World,* p.14
15. *My World,* p.15

14

came in reply, "Thank you Sir, an excellent cut."' Cousin Partridge was a poor relation and sat at the bottom of the table. Emily afterwards confided to Harry that Cousin Partridge was 'the best man in the room, whatever the rest might think of him.' He had made the mistake of taking Orders and had but a poor living.

Grandmother Stubbs was more approachable. Like Emily, she was small and active, with a nose that declared her a Solomon. Her appearance was completed by the addition of a black wig. Harry particularly enjoyed her still-room 'with its cakes of several kinds, Elvas plums, almonds and raisins [and] moulds of damson cheese.'[16] Her drawing-room was formal. 'Everything in it was "best". We would never have entered there at all if it had not been for grandmamma's golden harp, and the brand-new musical box which she had bought in Birmingham to save herself the trouble of playing the harp. Tea in the parlour was always a feast. Even the youngest and most dangerous, that is to say, Milly, drank out of superb old Derby china, and we were each given a whole round of loaf spread thick with jam. "You will make them ill," my mother used to say, and grandmother's invariable answer was that jam was as wholesome as good butter.'[17]

One day Harry found his way to the least suitable book in the Stubbs's library, Eugene Sue's *The Wandering Jew*. The plot concerned a collection of people on their way to Paris to collect an inheritance. Few it seems arrived. 'My recollection is that there are in it some forty murders.' When his grandmother discovered that Harry was reading this calendar of crime, she replaced it with *Burke's Peerage*. At the time, the boy could make little of the substitute. The pictures were all coats of arms, and the language heraldic. Eventually *The Wandering Jew* returned to its old place, but how changed! 'My grandmama had taken her embroidery scissors and cut out every passage which described murder or sudden death.'[18]

Throughout his ten years at Walsall, Harry was aware that his mother had a 'secret friend'. 'We meant by "secret" anything beautiful or rare which belonged to our most private feelings.' The friend was Sister Dora, Walsall's own Florence Nightingale, whose statue stands in the central square. Sister Dora was the daughter of a Yorkshire hunting vicar. Her brother, Mark Pattison, was a

16. ibid.
17. *My World*, p.16
18. *My World*, p.13

distinguished Oxford scholar. Inspired by Miss Nightingale's association with the Deaconesses of Kaiserwerth, Dora joined a fairly permissive Anglican Order and came to run the Cottage Hospital at Walsall when she was in her late twenties. She was a striking figure, tall and handsome, dressed all in black, her firm jaw emphasised by the starched cap that did not quite hide her splendid auburn hair. She could pick up a hefty drunken miner and dump him into a bed as if he were a baby. Nor had she lost her sporting instinct (she had been a fearless rider to hounds in her youth). Her favourite entertainment was chasing sewer rats up the hospital stairs. 'She would snatch up a poker and set to work while the men, from their beds, called "Give it to them , Sister Dora".' Emily met Dora the year before Henry Francis died. Dora had recently fallen heavily in love with the young surgeon at the hospital. When she renounced him she suffered a hysterical knee joint and, for some time, was semi-paralysed. More commonly, her affection was lavished on her nurses and on young married women. Emily was one of these. When Henry Francis died, Dora wrote to Emily: 'My Dearest, I've only just been told of your great trouble. Oh, my darling, would that I could come, and tell you *how* I feel for you.'

Years later, Harry was affected by the directness of Dora's letters of uplift. 'All through my childhood I shrank from any spoken expression of piety. Dora was the exception and could express religious feelings as naturally as any other.' He recalled his first meeting with her at the hospital. 'I was about five years old and I remember that she picked me up with a sudden movement and tossed me to the ceiling.'[19]

In 1875, the year before Harry left Walsall, there was another terrible blast furnace accident, this time at the Burchills in Walsall. It gave Dora her place in history. A torrent of molten metal exploded over men working the base of the furnace and killed eleven instantly. Seventeen more died of burns in Dora's hospital. The smell of decaying flesh in the wards nauseated even her doctors. Only *she* never left their bedsides, day or night. She herself died of breast cancer three years later, at the age of 44, suddenly unable to believe in God or to find the courage that the least of 'my men' had shown in his last agony.

19. *My World*, p.24

CHAPTER 3

Mary

When Harry was six, Mary, now a lanky 16-year-old (her friends called her 'Long Saturday') was sent to a finishing school in Germany for a year. The correspondence between her and Emily during 1869 provides a lively picture of the Newbolt family at that time. Dr Schwalb's regime at Neuweid was tough. The girls were up early to swim in the Rhine (Mary, being 'delicate', was excused this) and had done lessons for two hours by breakfast time, 'while *you* are still in bed, dear mama.' There were fearsome penalties for speaking any language but German, but Mary, as usual, showed no undue respect for authority in this matter. She was not excessively in awe of Emily, either. She refused to take singing lessons, declaring, 'I can't sing a bit now.' In the matter of economy she tried to be co-operative but, all the same, complained: 'The mohair is awfully short. I look a queer guy in it. All the girls [here] have as many dresses as if they were going to be married.'

Female friendships blossomed at Neuweid: 'We have such a fuss here this week, two girls, great friends, slept together or at any rate went to each other's beds all night and Frau Doctor [sic] found out.' Mary herself had a crush on Mlle Olga, the French governess who was half Russian. She was plump and eighteen, and played the piano like an angel. Mary grew pale for the love of her. In spite of all this, she made excellent progress in German. Occasionally, she succumbed to the temptation to read an English novel. Emily gave her tempting glimpses of the progress of *Edwin Drood* in serial form.

Mary's love of 'the three chicks' back at home was unfeigned. She constantly urged Emily to have 'likenesses' made of Harry, Frank and Milly. Harry seems to have been her favourite. She wrote him letters which were seldom answered. Emily. however, wrote faithfully. She emerges a cheerful, busy person with a network of friends and relations. She was particularly close, not only to her sister Selina Harrison, a doctor's wife at Penn Fields just outside Walsall, but also to Eliza Jane Gordon, her older sister, married to a clergyman near Lichfield. The three sisters, with their families, spent summer holidays together in North Wales or occasionally at Whitby, always travelling by train in a 'saloon carriage with tables and sofas'. Emily also corresponded with a variety of Solomons and Newbolts. Young George Newbolt, now in India, seemed to spend all his time on leave in the hills and was married. He had grown 'dreadfully fat and cross'. However, Emily always returned to the subject of her younger sister, Selina Harrison. She had had a sixth baby, 'such a fat, soft, dear little pet'.

Penn Fields became a second home to Harry. There was 'a fishpond full of perch and pike', he wrote in his autobiography, 'and an avenue where sparrows could be catapulted.' Dr Alfred Harrison could reel off entire Ingoldsby Legends from memory. His assistant was a gangling young man called Tom Webb, who rode a 'boneshaker' with wooden wheels. 'Its weight made it formidable both to those who rode it and those who were ridden down by it. My brother and I admired it quite as much as our grandchildren now admire motors and airplanes.' Tom could also string bows and do all sorts of things for a chap that Mama could not do. He later became rather famous for his relations. His brother was the first man to swim the Channel and so became 'the most popular man in the world'. He perished trying to do the same thing at Niagara Falls. Tom Webb's son was to marry the novelist Mary Webb.

Emily's life was rich in social occasions. In summer there were picnics with croquet and archery at Penn Fields and other local country houses. Emily was particularly proud to know the Barnetts at Park House, Rugeley. The Barnett children played with the young Newbolts: Maud Barnett had a pony of her own. In winter there were dinner parties, concerts, panoramas at the Agricultural Hall, and Mr Bellow reading the Trial Scene from *Pickwick* at the Town Hall. Visits to factories to see the wonders of modern technology were popular; Harry learned the secrets of glassblowing. Tom Webb often came on these visits. He also took the boys to the circus in Birmingham ('Harry loved the clever monkeys') and to the Wolverhampton Exhibition, where Harry was very anxious to see King Theodore of Abyssinia's clothes.

But above all, Emily had good works on her mind. There were the Monday Working Parties for Sister Dora's hospital. On one occasion, Emily and her friends cut out nine shirts while Miss Henrietta lectured to them on her work with the 'heathen' women of India. Emily also joined a choir which met at the home of Dr Drewing, the Poor Law Medical Officer. They did not confine themselves to the *Messiah* either. 'We had some music from *Macbeth* with the most peculiar words, we were laughing all the time.' Emily eventually became a soloist with Dr Drewing's group.

At home Emily was economical to the point of meanness: she bought china cut-price at the factory gate, even her beloved ferns were only replaced by the kindness of friends. 'Tom has brought me a large harts' tongue and two prickly ones. The old ones were much withered.' Little Milly inherited her mother's carefulness. Years later, Harry wrote a poem about his sister, entitled 'The Frugal Aunt'.

> She dined upon a cold poached egg
>   Saved from the breakfast table.
> Contrast her lot with ours, I beg,
>   She dined upon a cold poached egg:
>   While we were munching mutton-leg:
>   As thick as we were able,
> She dined upon a cold poached egg
>   Saved from the breakfast table.

Emily loved her garden. When winter seemed interminable, she told Mary of plans for the spring, 'with many thoughts of her who I hope will see them blossom. Sown in hope to be gathered in joy like those who have left us.'[1] Emily seldom mentioned Francis in her letters, but there remained a well of loneliness in her. Harry continued to be Emily's confidant and friend. Every year, on 24 May, he went with his mother to visit 'him so dearly loved' in St Matthew's churchyard. On that day there always arrived through the post a few uplifting words from Colonel George Newbolt. That year, mother and son planted a clematis by the stone.

Harry was now showing extraordinary promise in every field, if Emily is to be believed. Her letters to Mary contain the following observations:

> 'Has already a very good idea of swimming.'
> 'Quite taken up with his music.'
> 'Played in the game of croquet wonderfully well.'
> 'Is playing chess with Frank.'
> 'Is reading your old school books.'
> 'His memory is perfectly amazing.'
> 'He improves every day.'

On 6 June, the prodigy celebrated his seventh birthday. Unfortunately, he was not well, having over-exerted himself in the garden the day before with a girl called Nellie Brace. He did, however, rouse himself sufficiently to open his presents. He had a real telescope from Mr and Mrs Stubbs, a bow and arrow from Mary ('he is very much delighted') and Kingsley's *Heroes* from Tom Webb. ('He is acting it out in his play and talking about it continually.') He also admired the warriors of Mrs Pinnock's *Greece*. Among them he found a new hero, Epaminondas. (Epaminondas, it will be recalled, directed his troops to victory although mortally wounded, at the battle of Mantinea, on the plains of Arcadia.) The theme of a heroic death had impressed Harry at an even earlier age. On one occasion he was out with Old Emma and another nurse in Walsall when he saw 'a small detachment of troops in scarlet, marching over a wooden bridge.' Emma turned her head away, and the other nurse said, 'Why don't you look?' Her reply was, 'I don't like to see them – they're dressed like that to go to

1. *NL*, EN to MN, 1 March 1870

20

their death.' The theme of death in battle reappeared a year later, when Harry was taken by his mother to see the *Victory*. A Newbolt cousin, Captain Roberts, took them round. In the *Victory*'s cockpit, Harry was shown the place where Nelson had died, and Captain Roberts suddenly took him by the shoulders and made him lie full-length in the exact spot. He never forgot it.

Harry and Frank started school together at Mrs Schofield's up the Birmingham Road. Within a month, Harry was given 'an excellent character'. He was also given scarlet fever, a disease which in those days often proved fatal. Fortunately, the case was a mild one and Emily took the only steps then available – 'isolation and carbolic soap'. Callers sat on chairs in the garden and talked through the window. Only the Windles, 'always friends in need' dared enter the house. As for Harry himself, 'he reads and sews and is almost merry sometimes!'[2] (Emily taught all her children to sew.) To amuse Harry, Tom Webb drew cartoons of himself on a bicycle running over 'a street child'.

When he had recovered, Harry went on a rumbustuous holiday, without Mama, to Aunt Eliza Jane Gordon's house near Lichfield, where she was raising a family of seven boys and seven girls in the rectory. 'At Hammerwich I revelled in a life more free and unconventional than I had known elsewhere. My uncle was a genial boyish man. He made us wooden stilts and ran and jumped ditches on them himself.' On one occasion, 'the graveyard being temporarily desanctified, we discovered the bones of our Heath ancestors, who had lived in Hammerwich in the seventeenth century.' From his uncle, Harry acquired a love of fishing. Robert Gordon 'cared nothing for the stream, the trout or the fly. He was all for pools and pike and perch.' He fished the Minster Pool in which the Cathedral spires are mirrored 'a scene, when twilight is falling, unlike any other I had known in England.'[3] The period with his Gordon cousins had a startling effect on Harry. 'He is so much more romping and boylike,' Emily declared. He no longer obeyed every order she gave. He refused to write to Mary at all.

Old Mrs Stubbs now died suddenly (but not before a deathbed conversion to Christianity). Mr Stubbs remained alone at the Close, as helpless as a stranded whale. 'The children must wear

2. *NL*, EN to MN, 8 Sept. 1869
3. *My World*, p.30

deep mourning.' Emily told Mary. '*You* need only wear second mourning when you come back.' So, for the second time in three years, Harry was in black. He always remembered the day his grandmother died. He was planning to play marbles with a friend in the stableyard. 'I had to go and tell him I could not play. I said simply, "I can't play today – Grandmamma has died," and he replied. "What a pity!" The inappropriate phrase revolted me. I never played with him again.'[4] But there were consolations. Mrs Stubbs had divided her jointure between her three daughters, and the year 1869 ended with a move to a large, sunny house, 85 Birmingham Road, now demolished. There were new chintz covers for the chairs, and acres of wallpaper went up. It was Mary who had discovered the place before she went abroad. (She needed a room to herself.)

Emily did not leave 'dear Doveridge' without a backward glance. 'It is haunted by so many scenes in my life, she wrote. The strangest scene was surely the last to be enacted there, never referred to by her son. She had become engaged. Nothing is known of Angelo Solari, except that he lived in Birmingham. (There are no Solaris now in the Birmingham telephone directory.) He called one day at Doveridge Place when Emily was out. When she returned, she discovered that he had given the children rides on his pony, 'but Milly tumbled off and in trying to save her, Emma fell flat down in the yard making them all roar with laughter. They wish the pony would come again but I should think he had better not,' Emily wrote to Mary.[5] Mr Solari persisted, and soon Emily was in love with him. She saw him as 'spoiled all these years by a life in solitude, uninfluenced by the good a woman may do every man if she is herself a true Christian.' It was Mary who persuaded Emily to give him up. She threatened never to return to Walsall if the wedding took place, but to make herself a burden instead on her mother's relatives. To make matters worse, she had to spend Christmas in Germany 'exchanging little hand-stitched presents with weeping girls'. And her adored Mlle Olga had just left. On 1 March 1870, Emily wrote to say that she had given up Solari. 'But I shall always think of him with regret. It has been a very strange experience and I trust you, my darling, will never know the same, for it is enough

4. *My World*, p.18
5. *NL*, 9 Nov. 1869

to turn one's hair grey, which it seems rapidly to be doing to mine.'

Mary was to die without knowing the 'strange experience' of falling in love with a man. The signs of consumption had been there for some time, in the form of coughing and headaches, but no one recognised them. 'How is it you are always tired on Sunday when you write your letters?' enquired Emily. Mary herself made light of her symptoms, declaring that the doctor was 'half an old woman' and that Tom Webb, who ventured an opinion by post, was 'the greatest goose I know'. Soon she was confined to a small room at the top of the house with a high fever. On 15 May she wrote her last letter to Emily. She had been delighted by a photograph of Harry: 'I am so pleased with Harry's likeness, only he screwed up his forehead so much, dear little fellow.' Then she described a tour of the garden. 'It was dreadfully tiresome getting down the stairs but Herr Doctor helped me on one side, and one of the girls on the [other]. Then they helped me upstairs again, laid me on the bed, and I slept for two or three hours.' When Emily received this letter she panicked. All thought of economy was gone. Mary must come home at once. It was arranged that Dr Schwalb's daughter and Mary's friend, Marie Thiel, should bring her by sea. There had been no time to book private accommodation, and the three women spent the first night in the public saloon. The next morning, two English ladies gave up their private cabin for them. 'We asked Mary,' Marie Thiel wrote, 'if she liked better to try to walk or if she like to be carried with the bedclothes. She preferred the latter. But this operation must have been too much for her. It was in carrying her from one room to the other that she fainted. After the swoon she began to sink fast. Fraulein Schwalb tried several times to call her attention to the very serious moment, but Mary only opened wider her eyes, looked a moment round, but did not know us.' Mary died that day, 28 May 1870. She was two months short of her eighteenth birthday.

CHAPTER 4

Caistor

Back at 85 Birmingham Road, little Milly waited for Mary. Her words, wrote Emily, were oft repeated: 'Where is my sister Mary?' 'She ought not to stay so long.' 'How many weeks is it till she comes?'

At last Emily had to admit to the children that Mary had gone to her Heavenly Home. It was only when they were pulled out of bed in the middle of the night to sign papers connected with her that they realised that they were her sole next of kin. 'So she was a real sister after all.'

It was Emily who suffered most from Mary's death. Had she loved her enough? Should she have let her go to Germany? Should she have brought her home sooner? What about the effect of the Angelo Solari affair on her? Mary's aunts, Inman and Ridgeway, assured Emily that she had done all she could. 'You know how wilful she was. I said to her one day, "How *does* Mamma manage you?" Mary's reply was, "I'm never wilful with her. Her loving eyes look so sorrowful if I am, but I like to astonish Uncle Inman and Uncle Ridgeway.'" Emily now came as near as she ever did to a breakdown, and the children had to be sent to stay with neighbours for six weeks. Fear that she might have forgotten his eighth birthday impelled Harry to write the first letter in his own handwriting to be preserved. Dated 6 June, it ran as follows: 'I hope you will soon be well again, only think today is my birthday I am so very glad are not you I remain your loving son Henry John Newbolt.'

Up to the age of ten, Harry's education seems to have been strangely neglected. It is true that Emily now employed a governess, but Miss Green was for the younger children, and took tea with them *upstairs*. Harry, although only a year older than Frank, took tea *downstairs*. Yet it was from Miss Green that he picked up his first scraps of Latin. He found them disappointing. He could not see how *mensa, mensa, mensam* had anything to do with Lars Porsena of Clusium. Eventually he was sent to Queen Mary's, the local grammar school, a fact which he obscures in his autobiography. Queen Mary's was founded by Bloody Mary in 1554. Needless to say, the Stubbs family had had a hand in the school: Joseph Stubbs had sold it part of his tanning yard on which to build. By the time Harry became a pupil at the school, it had been occupying a site a mile north of the city centre on the Lichfield Road for twenty years. The buildings were (and are) formidable. An endless facade of red brick confronts the visitor. The largest room in the building was Big School. Here the Revd Irvine, headmaster, used to sit enthroned and, like Jupiter Olympus, thundered when he heard a false quantity. Irvine was a notorious flogger and the standard of education at the school was not high when, in 1868, the famous T. H. Green inspected it. The boys, he declared, 'enter in a state of ignorance, and scarcely stay three years.' He added, 'their social status is not generally high. The more genteel people of the place seldom use the school.' And this in spite of the fact that the grammar school was carefully segregated from a commercial school housed in the same building. The boys of the two schools had fights and the Commercials, although outnumbered, usually won.

It is hard to imagine how the delicate little Newbolt survived in such an atmosphere. (He was a year younger than any other boy in the school.) Without Mr Bamber he probably would not have. The Revd William Bamber was the school's second master. He had been educated at Giggleswick, and was soon to become head of the grammar school at Appleby. Newbolt never denied his debt to Bamber, who virtually gave him private tuition during his year at the school. 'He taught me Latin, English, Mathematics, besides the beginnings of Greek and I never had a tutor with a clearer idea of what he was teaching,' wrote Newbolt to Marshall , a later head. 'I make this point in order to justify myself for accepting your kind proposal to describe me as having been educated at Walsall.' This backhanded compliment was extracted in 1921 at Marshall's request, when he wished to inscribe the name of Henry Newbolt on the school Honours Board. It was Marshall's ambition to turn Queen Mary's into a public school, complete with houses, caps and an Officers' Training Corps. He failed. The school has now abandoned its premises to the girls of Queen Mary's High School, established next door in 1893. Walsall Grammar School now inhabits modern premises towards Bilston and has indeed finally become a public school.

Harry's happiest hours were spent at home. 'The boy with the short, crisp, gold hair entered quickly by a side door, tossed his cap on the hall table, and turned into the dining room. It was empty, as he had expected: the children would of course be in the schoolroom, upstairs, and his mother busied elsewhere. The French window was illuminated at this moment by a pale gold sunset. Against the glass on one side of it hung two transparencies, presenting coats-of-arms, whose mediaeval designs and rich colours produced a solemn and almost dignified effect, not common in suburban villas. This afternoon was for the middle ages.'[1] What he was intent upon was painting the family coat of arms. With deep concentration, the boy filled in the bar azure and the lions or. Percival, the hero of Newbolt's autobiographical novel *The Twymans* was, of course, Harry. The novel, which concerned a disputed inheritance, followed Harry's own life story fairly closely from the age of ten until his marriage.

At this stage, it was decided that Harry must be sent somewhere

1. *The Twymans*, p.21

that would implant enough Latin in him to get him to Eton. Mr Bamber, who had by now become Emily's friend, had declared himself unable to add the task to his other duties. So a solemn conference of the elders was called in Emily's drawing room to decide on a preparatory school for Harry. A small establishment at Caistor on the Lincolnshire Wolds was chosen. It was run by the Revd Anthony Bower, a Cambridge mathematician. There was a good reason for selecting Bower. He had been Harry's father's tutor at Cambridge. Caistor was also a grammar school. It was housed in a fine old stone building opposite the church, and had been for generations a local day school. Bowers had changed all that, handing over the sons of tradesmen to the lower master and creating a special division for public school candidates, of whom he had fifteen. Most of these boys boarded in Bower's own home, Grove House, above the town, and walked behind him to school every morning.

Bower, known to the boys as 'Nix', claimed to get his boys into Eton or Winchester, or, failing that, Clifton or Rossall. Success depended on Latin in painful quantities. For four hours every morning Bower stood behind a tall desk with his pupils around him in a semi-circle. He appeared a genial man, but he was convinced that the only way to instill the rules of grammar was through 'swishing and thwacking. The cane always lay ready to his right hand, and the moment his wrath was roused by what was said or unsaid or mis-said, the blows rained like hail upon the offender and generally upon his neighbour too'[2]

Harry quickly discovered that the path to popularity was through food. 'I gave the boys some (apples) last night and they gave me some cheese. And another boy named Danby brought an enormous pork pie, nearly half a yard across without exajeration' [sic].[3] Order of precedence among the boys was decided by fights, and these were their source of entertainment. Harry, though a lightweight, was a quick-moving boxer. His last antagonist was Fred Koe (Andy McKay in *The Twymans*): 'McKay came on, towering over Percy, and whirling his arms like a windmill. Presently Percy's head cleared, and he began to see what was happening: he was striking too low, and his opponent was striking too high – the result of their unequal

2. *My World*, p.37
3. *NL* HN to EN

27

stature. Next time he reached the enemy's nose, and a stream of blood followed that refused to be staunched.'[4] After that Harry had only to observe the etiquette, 'which bade him refrain from cheeking his superiors, to avoid fights.'

Gang fights were another matter. Fighting with the 'town cads' was a favourite sport. There was a snow fight on Percy's (and probably Harry's) first day. As the scholars emerged from the school yard they were met with a volley of snowballs 'as hard as turnips' The leader of the cads was Jakes, 'a youth with the figure and head-dress of a coal-carter. For an instant Percy was all defiance as he stood alone and fired his two shots at the enemy; then Jakes moved irresistibly towards him and his heart stopped. Another instant, and he was running, as he had never run in his life before!' Finally Jakes was felled in single combat by Craig (the head boy). 'He submitted to having his face rubbed with snow. But when Percy came forward with a handful of snow, the victim's sense of fairness revolted. "Look 'ere," he said, "what's yon cocksparrow got to do wi'it?" Percy knew he had fallen below even Jakes's standard of chivalry.'

Organised games at Caistor were unknown, although Mr Letch (Letchworth in *The Twymans*) occasionally organised a football match. Emily advised Harry against it, after he wrote, 'One of the strongest boys was running and he caught his knee in my chest and over I went backwards head over heels, and one of the boys thought I had broken my neck'.[5] Emily wrote back at once: 'I hope you will keep out of the way of the boys when they are running.'[6] Newbolt was later to be tolerant of Caistor's lack of organised sport. 'I have never undervalued games', he wrote, 'But I am sure we gained greatly by our informal wanderings in that wild and idyllic landscape.'[7] After school the boys were literally let loose. With George Bower, the headmaster's son, Harry roamed Pelham Woods and the Sandbraes and climbed dangerously high in search of rooks' eggs. 'For me there had always been a unique charm about a wild bird's egg. [An egg] is intangible life, inaudible song, the greatest of wonders in a tiny fragile form.' He never forgot seeing his first egg at the age of five. 'I was with my mother staying in a country house outside Walsall when I was called into the back hall to see the keeper, who had come

4. *The Twymans*, p.80
5. *NL* HN to EN, Feb. 1873
6. *NL* EN to HN, 20 Feb. 1873
7. *My World*, p.37

in carrying a clutch of rooks' eggs in his cap. I instantly desired them. My fingers closed over the nearest egg and I was away with it to the other end of the house. At night I rolled off to sleep with it in my hand. I woke in the morning to find a sticky ruin.'[8]

On another occasion, it was George Bower who paid the price. Nix had driven the two boys to a church ten miles away where he was to take evensong. 'Bower and I were allowed to spend the hour of service in the garden, but under a most emphatic injunction not to touch birds' nests. We promised. But George, who had courage equal to any risk, filled the recesses of his Glengarry cap with eggs. His father, as we mounted the high dog-cart for the return journey, asked us lightly, "You've taken no eggs?" "No, Father." We drove along in silence for some way, then he remarked, "Georgie, your cap's not straight." and with his whip hand he crushed it hard down upon his head. Not a word was said on either side, nor did George venture to wipe away the streams of egg-yolk which dripped down his hair and neck as we drove home.'[9]

Not long after that, Harry joined the church choir headed by Letch with Stuart Craig at the organ. In winter, only the chancel was lit and the boys sang to the dark nave. There were presences down there. As the young voices rose, other voices were heard. One of a deeper tone moved him more than all the rest. It was, Percy knew, the voice of Sir William de Gandon, who lay carved in stone. He clothed the sheep-cropped wolds with romance. His manor house stood near Caistor. Tennyson was another weaver of spells. At the beginning of Harry's first summer term, the school usher led all the boys to the highest point of the wolds and showed them the spires of Clixby, Claxby, Somerby and Saxby, 'where Tennyson's people live.' Tennyson's people! It took only a small leap of the imagination to re-enact the deeds of Arthur in the deep woods at his feet. For the most part, however, Harry behaved like a happy savage. He spoke in a broad Lincolnshire accent to the local gamekeepers and heard jokes that would have made his mother blush. 'The country humour was Rabelaisian, the facts never concealed by the language.' With Fred Koe, he plotted to 'renounce modern civilisation, with a saving clause in favour of a double-barrelled gun apiece',[10]

8. *My World*, pp.30–31
9. *My World*, p.44
10. *The Twymans*, p.56

Harry's first year at school ended with the funeral of Mr Stubbs, who died on 13 December 1873. The old man had become ill before Harry went back for the autumn term. 'I was taken to say good-bye to him in the late afternoon. In the sombre firelit room he lay in a huge four-post bed, rigged with an arrangement of pulleys by which he could raise or lower his massive form. He called for his purse, the long green silk purse, out of which I had had so many six pences and shillings. This time it was the gold end.'[11] The funeral was a grand affair. The drawing room table was laid with boxes full of black gloves. 'We drove in a long slow procession to the new cemetery, much delayed by the great weight of the huge lead coffin.' The poorer sort were less concerned. They cursed Old Stubbs's soul for robbing the poor of the Penny Dole. (He had converted the Moseley Dole into alms houses in 1824, but they remained convinced that he had kept the gold and carried it to the bank in a wheelbarrow.) Harry was allowed to lay claim to Stubbs's set of *Waverley* novels bound in blue leather, but what he secretly longed for were Fulbrook Farm and Mr Stubbs's hunting lodge at Blymhill. When these two properties were sold, he felt he had been cheated of his inheritance.

It was Emily who chiefly benefited under the will of Mr Stubbs. He left her half his 'secret wealth'. Unfortunately, she believed that the money was a sacred trust for the good of others. As well as trying to save fallen women, she opened a Temperance Coffee House called 'The Lifeboat', which sank when the family left Walsall. No 'Temperance Beverage' could hold its own there. It was too near Burton, as a triumphant publican remarked. A fellow fighter in the war against the Demon Drink was Edward Fitzgerald, the curate at St Paul's. Nor were Henry, Frank and Milly exempted from good works. Emily and Mr Fitzgerald had recently started a branch of the Mission Army in Walsall. They tempted the children of the poor into church halls with tea parties and singing, and then Mr Fitzgerald addressed them. Frank had been appointed a Mission Army collector, and the Newbolts seemed perpetually to be owing each other small sums of money for the Army.

The first Christmas home from school was a good one. Emily had saved a box of fireworks for Harry's return. In many ways she was a

11. *My World*, p.21

boy at heart. She read all the boys' magazines, and was delighted when both 'H.J.N.' and 'F.N.' won prizes for correctly solving puzzles in *Good Things for the Young of All Ages*. She enjoyed a game of cards too. Harry preferred marionettes. 'I am glad Milly liked the marionettes,' he wrote when the Christmas holidays were over, 'but I am afraid there was a dreadful smell during the transformation scene'(Nov. 1874) (This was almost certainly caused with gunpowder.) He also preserved a wren's wing for Milly's doll's hat. During the following summer holidays, a church cricket team was formed. 'Shall I bring my cap home with me?' he enquired, 'or is there a straw hat that I could wear?'[12]

In the autumn of 1874, Harry's second year at Caistor, Frank joined him, He had begged his mother to let him go and she had finally agreed, while declaring that her heart would break with no boys in the house. Her distress would have been greater had she known that, soon after his arrival, her second son came close to losing an eye in a mock Battle of Agincourt. He was hit by an arrow on the temple, a fact also carefully concealed from Nix. Frank only lasted a year at Caistor on account of a 'delicate disposition'. It must have been trying for him always to take second place to his brother. His letters to his mother were, in fact, better written (and spelt) than those of Harry. In one, he describes the excitement of receiving a hamper from home. 'There was something in it I wanted more than anything and it *was* there – O wonder of wonders and joy of joys – Harry said it could not and would not come, but I trusted implicitly in your love for me and then I got it and regularly jumped into the 7th heaven of delight for you can't think how much I wanted it and actually prayed for it.' What 'it' was, we shall never know!

Meanwhile, Harry was becoming Nix's favourite. 'Harry is my ideal of a boy. I could fill sheet after sheet with unalloyed eulogy.'[13] 'I think he would do anything for me,' remarked Harry smugly of Bower.[14] Many years later, Mr Letch wrote to Harry to remind him of a scene from *King John* they had acted together. Letch had played the king, in his death throes from a deadly poison. Harry as Prince Henry had said, 'Oh that there were some virtue in my

12. *NL* HN to EN,16 June 1875
13. *NL* Bower to EN, 1876
14. *NL* HN to FN, 20 Feb. 1873

tears that might relieve you.' Letch kept a photo of the frail, golden-haired boy on his mantelpiece for the rest of his life.

On 6 June 1875, his thirteenth birthday, Harry, in his mother's opinion, became a man. She worked a gold chain for him to wear and prayed earnestly that it would protect him from the temptations ahead. 'I feel sometimes as if my spirit must hover around you. I know that the angels are there, fathers of the fatherless.'[15] The best protection, she declared, would be confirmation. She was not a parson's wife for nothing and her head was full of proverbs. 'Go forth,' she wrote to him, 'as Christ's faithful soldier armed with the shield of faith and the sword of the spirit'. And if Harry could not always keep to these high principles, she reminded him of the hymn: 'What, Fall'n Again? Yet Cheerful Rise!' Then she started on a series of 'heart-to-hearts' She probed Harry's conscience with intimate questions. She said she was convinced that the laying on of the bishop's hands would produce a spectacular change in her boy. She reminded him of Mary. '*She* was a changed girl after her confirmation.'[16] Emily barely disguised her hope that both her boys would take Orders. Harry was confirmed at Easter at Lichfield Cathedral in the presence of many friends and relations. It was the cathedral itself, rather than the bishop, that impressed him. 'Beneath the vast symmetry of these aisles, the peace of ages answered him.'

Sexual temptation did indeed come Harry's way when he was thirteen, but he disguised himself as Percy to tell the tale. The setting was the annual Sheep Fair at Caistor when 30,000 sheep were folded 'on one great sweep of the Wolds. Great was the chorus of their bleating and their multitudinous odour under a Mayday sun.' A shepherdess who spoke in 'slow deep Lincolnshire' lay on a bank, 'looking out with a dreamy softness from under the shadow of her little cloth cap. Shyly, Percy sat down on the turf at her side. Without leaving her lazy mood she leaned a little farther back and looked up at him.' Suddenly something, or someone, warned him of approaching dishonour. It was Sir William risen from his tomb in Caistor church. 'The ghostly hand lay heavy as steel upon his shoulder.'[17] The boy scrambled to his feet and ran to join a schoolboy companion.

15. *NL* EN to HN, 4 Mar. 1875
16. *NL* EN to HN, 25 Jan 1876
17. *The Twymans* p.78

The scholarship examination was now approaching and Harry must come under the lash. Until now Nix had desisted from bringing undue pressure on the boy. 'I should have pushed him towards still more – had I not been aware of his delicate constitution. The boy's pluck and spirit for work were enough to tempt any Master,' he confided to Emily.[18] Now, however, he showed no pity. Clifton, rather than Eton, had finally been selected, chiefly because Nix was on to a winning streak with Dr Percival, the new headmaster. Harry still failed to shine at Latin. 'I knew my Ovid when I had to say it this morning,' he wrote to his mother; the implication was that often he did not know it. Much of Nix's teaching was by rote. Whole pages not only of Virgil, but of the Latin Primer, must be learned by heart. 'I shall have to press a little for the Clifton Examination,' Nix warned Emily, 'but not beyond what I think the boy can bear.' He miscalculated, for the boy was not his cheerful self by Christmas 1875. Confined to his room at home with a pile of books while others had fun, he became peevish, and even rude. He also started to suffer from sick headaches (possibly migraines). The last summer at Caistor was a hell of 'gerund grinding', as Letch called it. The grinding was in vain. Harry did not win a scholarship. Nix broke the bad news. Harry had not done himself justice in classics or maths, 'on which I had very much relied'. He wished Harry. 'Better luck old fellow next time!'

Newbolt insists in his autobiography that he won a scholarship to Clifton. He writes that he was fishing in a local pond with Mr Fitzgerald, when the news arrived. 'We were quite annoyed to hear suddenly the noise of horses and wheels approaching. Then into the quiet of our paradise there came a festive little procession, my mother and sister in front, my Uncle Alfred Harrison behind, someone waving a newspaper and someone else an official notice. I was in the list! I think it gave me more satisfaction than any other success that ever fell to me.' He proceeded to elaborate. He was in the Clifton 'scholarship list' and this involved 'a small emolument'. There is no mention of a scholarship for Henry John Newbolt in *The Cliftonian* records for 1876. He was, however, awarded an internal scholarship a year later.

18. *NL* Bowers to *EN*, 25 Jan. 1876

PART II CLIFTON 1876–1880

CHAPTER 5

New Boy

Harry heard Clifton before he saw it. He became aware of 'the sweet crack of bat on ball' as the cab took him to the entrance examination. He described its effect on Percy: 'In front lay a wide green sward, flooded with low sunlight, and covered in every direction with a multitude of white figures. Something broke over his spirit like a wave, a glimpse behind the mere beauty of the white young figures, of the long descended discipline they symbolised.'[1] What Percy was observing was a batch of house matches. As many as six of these could be accommodated on the expanse of grass, known as The Close, that lay in front of the school.

Clifton College, like Harry, was but fourteen years old when he

1. *The Twymans*, p. 80

35

arrived in 1876. It was one of a rash of public schools that broke out from 1840 onwards, far outnumbering the mediaeval and Tudor foundations they aped, intended to convert into gentlemen the sons of the new middle class. It was conceived by a group of prominent citizens (including the physician father of the author John Addington Symonds), and was built on the downs above Bristol. By Newbolt's day, the march of villas towards it had already begun. Tall Victorian Italianate houses encroached upon outlaying playing fields. The school fought back by putting up Gothic boarding houses which were even uglier. When Harry looked across The Close that first time, he would not have seen the unbroken line of educational pink Gothic that we see today. At that time there was only Big School, built on the massive lines of a mediaeval hall, and, set back from it, a two-storey building with the library above and cloisters below. The chapel in front was not yet linked to the main buildings.

Newbolt's first memory of his time at the school was connected with Clifton chapel. 'That September day in 1876,' he wrote, 'I had no friends. When the bell ceased ringing I walked alone into the chapel and just stood inside the entrance watching the stream of the school pouring in and settling into the long rows of seats.' (The seats in Clifton chapel face each other, like those in a choir.) 'Up and down the aisle a singular figure was moving – the School-Marshal, a tall and terrific man in a long black gown, with red eyes and the drooping whiskers of an old-fashioned dragoon. He directed many to their places with commanding gestures, but by some chance he overlooked me as completely as if I had been a very small black beetle.' No doubt, in his short black jacket and cap, Newbolt resembled such an insect. 'When the service began I hastened to sit down in the nearest place immediately under the stall of the Headmaster. In fact (unknowingly) I took the lowest seat of all. Outside I was jostled be a scornful young scholar who had been watching me. "Where did you think you were? Right under Jumps's nose!" All was eventually explained by Mr Dunn, the German teacher. "Go up higher," he advised. "We nominate you to a swanship: and you take a place among the ducklings."[2]

Harry made a better impression in the Lower Fifth. He came top of an arithmetic paper set on the first day of term, beating 'not a few of the classical scholars from higher up the school.' He was so

2. *My World*, p. 54

good at Latin unseens that he was accused of cheating, when in fact he merely knew the *Aeneid* by heart. He was sent up to Percival's room to explain. John Percival was Clifton's first and greatest headmaster. He resembled a piece of classical statuary. 'His face was finely chiselled, his general air marmoreal,' (Percival's bust translated into real white marble can now be seen in the East Cloister.) Percival had been educated at Appleby Grammar School, going on to take honours and Orders at Oxford. He had then taught at Rugby, and it was on the precepts of Dr Arnold that Clifton was modelled. Sunday after Sunday, Percival thundered Arnold's message from the pulpit: 'The whole is greater than the parts.' Percival put the Christian message over less forcefully, in spite of the fact that he would one day be Bishop of Hereford. He only occasionally attempted to transfer the boy's allegiance from pagan heroes to Arthurian ones, but personal religion embarrassed him.

Percival surrounded himself with a circle of masters described by some as 'a noble band' and others as 'an eccentric bunch'.[3] These men he encouraged to befriend, rather than dominate, their pupils, to form a team 'running together after the irregular verb.'[4] George Wollaston was one of the greats. He was housemaster of Newbolt's house, North Town, one of the two houses for day boys. Wollaston was the main reason for the success of the day-boys system at Clifton. He showed that it was possible to make a day-house as 'real' as a boarding house, although its only walls were those of his drawing room. Harry saw him as the knight to whom well-born squires were sent, 'from whom they learnt the arts and exercises of social life'.[5] On second thoughts, Harry decided that 'Woolly Bear' was more a figure from the sagas. 'His huge frame, his blue eyes and fair beard, his bluff sincerity and the sudden thunders of his utterance gave him a strange Norse air.'[6] (He was said to throw boys into cupboards when roused.)

Wollaston's hospitality to the boys of his house was limitless. [7] In 'unbuttoned' moments he would lie on the hearthrug talking of Dante, Milton and William Morris. When he was answering letters

3. OFC II
4. *The Twymans*, p.90
5. *My World*, p. 48
6. *My World*, p. 78
7. *FN* II

at his desk he would read out 'some stirring anecdote' from a far flung Old Cliftonian (O.C.) 'so that we came to feel we were living in a world of heroes.' Bug hunting (as it was scornfully called at Clifton) was Woolly Bear's passion. He spent his summer in the Alps, dressed and talking like a native, chasing the wild elusive butterfly. Frank was to catch the infection from him, and spent much of his pocket money on 'lethal jars and cabinets'.[8]

Sydney Irwin, classics master of the Upper Fifth, was another of Clifton's greats. Although 'pale, menacing and satirical,'[9] he had a liking for Harry, and used to invite him home in the evenings to read the *Odyssey*. They read fast, having no need of dictionaries, revelling in the story, 'its caverns welling with the fresh springs of Romance'.[10] Sometimes Irwin's eyes would close and he would throw back his head and recall his own adventures in antique lands. But it was when they turned to the poetry of Virgil that Harry heard the distant drums of romance. There was, in 'those pathetic half lines' of Virgil 'a feeling of mystery, of the underlying significance of things' that was sadly lacking in the Clifton curriculum.

Harry's education remained remorselessly classical as he went up the school. Every day began with an hour of repetition and there was construing ('doing con') to take home every night. He studied Maths and German with some success for a time, but these too had to give way to classics. English Literature was barely touched, although one master insisted on a brief exposure to Chaucer. As for English Language, a weekly essay was set, but only three pages were demanded and the boys began low on the first page and ended high on the last. Poetry writing was not encouraged. One master, it is true, was a poet. T.E. Brown, the famous Manxman, used to allow boys in his class to offer verse as an alternative to the essay, but Brown was master on the Modern Side.

Fortunately, Harry continued to be a voracious devourer of books. He claimed to have read Shakespeare 'through and through' before he was fourteen, and Scott, of course. His reading of poetry was somewhat undiscriminating. 'If I had had a director, he would have saved me from trudging so many miles through Southey's long–dead forest.' At night it was Irwin who introduced

8. *FN* I p.42
9. *FN* II, p.11
10. *The Twymans*, p. 113

him to the Metaphysical poets, and Wordsworth he met on a holiday in the Lake District. 'We spent the August of 1879 in Ullswater, where my mother joined with Mrs Cookson and her five boys next door and took the tiny hotel, which exactly held us all. The Cooksons, being related to Wordsworth, 'were provided with a complete edition of his works, and an almost equally complete knowledge of all the local allusions they contained.' Byron was not to be found in the Newbolt home. 'So at least I believed. But some years afterwards I discovered that a locked drawer in my mother's knee-hole table contained two articles of unconditional contraband – one was a copy of the *Roman Missal,* which had been of interest to my father, the other was a parcel tightly tied up and containing the fine 1810 edition of Byron's shorter poems in three columns with their covers carefully torn off.'[11] The Newbolts were vaguely related to the Byrons, a fact firmly suppressed by Emily. 'It was embarrassing even to be cousin's cousin of a monster'.[12] It happens there was also a Byron to whom it may have been even more embarrassing to be related: H.J. Byron was a popular playwright, and in Frank's opinion his connection with 'an immoral stage' was more appalling to Emily than were the doings of Lord Byron. If creative writing was not encouraged in class, a certain amount of comic verse was produced unofficially. Harry was by now sixteen and near the head of the form, sitting apart with three friends. 'While we appeared to be taking notes we were in fact taking turns at filling a notebook with pages and pages of a narrative poem in the style of the *Ingoldsby Legends.*' He did however, write one serious poem at this time. It consisted of eight lines and was entitled 'E.N.'s Dislike of Bells, 1878'. In it, Emily tells Harry that he too will one day feel the sadness she felt whenever she heard the bells of St Matthew's at Walsall ring.

> 'Thou too shalt hear beside that shore
> The sweet sad bells of Memory chime
> The requiem of the golden time
> That passed long since for evermore.'

Harry's school friends were not memorable; they were often boys who he happened to be placed next to in class. His particular

11. *My World,* p. 75
12. *My World,* p. 76

friend at Clifton was a certain Reggie Wood, 'a most graceful cricketer.' Harry was allowed to sup with Wood whenever he liked at Wood's boarding house, a rare privilege granted by Edward Oakeley, a progressive housemaster. When Wood died young by drowning, Newbolt remained silent about feelings 'too deep for words'. There were boys at the school who were to grow up to be famous, but Harry did not number them among his friends. Only later did he come to know Douglas Haig, who had an undistinguished career at the school. Harry recalled only his Scottish accent, although he insisted later that he made a 'fine figure in The Close with his resolute chin, clear eyes and placid brow'[13] Perhaps more surprising was Harry's failure to make a friend of Arthur Quiller-Couch, the Cornish author. Harry only mentions him once, on the occasion when Couch defeated him in the English verse competition. They had been rivals all through their school years. It was only when Quiller-Couch read *The Twymans* years later that he discovered how much they had in common. 'But was it *you* or was it I, who heard the crack of bat on the ball and caught his breath at first sight of the Close?'[14] Frank Younghusband, the Tibetan explorer, also became a friend only after both men had left the school.

Percival believed in games. Games were the cement that bound his state together. Games also maintained the moral health of the individual. He was aware that some thought that there was too much playing of games at Clifton. But he knew that there were few who would not have bartered away all chance of intellectual distinction for a place in the Cricket Eleven. Cricket was the king of games. 'One's real interest in life was cricket,' wrote O.F. Christie, Clifton's historian.[15] From early March till the 'first week of the Autumn Term one played it almost continuously when not actually in class.'[16] Sometimes boys played in two cricket matches at once. On one occasion, at least, Frank played in three. This was possible because of the multiple occupation of The Close. This had its perils. It was a 'test of nerve while fielding at point to your own game, to be standing in the position of square leg to a neighbouring game.'[17]

13. *My World*, p.61
14. *My World*, p.6
15. OFC I, p.254
16. OFC I, p.256
17. ibid.

Good Form was demanded when playing cricket. It was Bad Form to wear a flannel shirt. Correct togs were an evening dress shirt and a top hat (for protective purposes). It was Bad Form also to applaud at a cricket match (although it was permissible for athletics). A dropped catch required a letter of apology to the captain. 'I am so thoroughly disgusted with myself because it spoilt your hat-trick,' wrote one boy.[18]

Frank, already 6ft 3ins by the age of seventeen was, the cricketer in the Newbolt family. He recalled the thrill of being selected for the school Eleven. 'When I saw the 11 enter the pavilion for a formal conclave I confess I got very excited. After a suitable interval, the great men strolled leisurely up to the parapet, and one gave me a quiet wink, while another simply shook my hands without saying anything. I was now of the company of Valhalla.'[19] The great 'foreign match' of the year was the Cheltenham Match. In 1883 Frank was almost the last man in. The 'sweet evening hour' had come, and 24 runs had still to be made. 'However, [Frank] Newbolt hit three boundaries and compiled 14, leaving 10 for Harland' – which Harland mercifully made.[20] The joy of the Cliftonians knew no limit. The assembled 663 awaited the return of the triumphant team. 'As they saw us they gave one tremendous yell, the horses were taken out, and with my name dizzying me, I was snaught up to heaven, and the whole company began carrying me towards Worcester Crescent.'[21]

For Harry, it was enough to know such men. 'We went about our own work and play in a proud obscurity, content to know that we belonged to a great and famous fellowship.'[22] 'I was myself always unreliable and second rate as a cricketer. In my single week of glory I captained my House XI for the first and last time, and led them to a very unexpected victory. After that a few happy knocks in country matches make up my record.'[23] Harry would have liked to excel at football too but, according to *The Twymans*, he was not solid enough for the wear and tear of the game, which had changed little since the 'bloody and murthering' days of

18. F.N. II, p.24
19. F.N. II, p.116
20. F.N. II, p.128
21. ibid.
22. *My World*, p.63
23. *My World*, p.46

Shakespeare. According to Frank, Harry tended to make one 'brilliant run' in each game, and then fizzle out. No one, anyway, could win against the enormous Will Threlfall of South Town House 'who shook us off like a lion would shake off terriers'.

Emily's first task on arrival at Clifton had been to buy a house in Worcester Crescent, almost within sight of The Close. Living so near to the school had advantages. At the end of the school day Harry had only to slip through a loose paling and be in the quiet room set aside by his mother. Thus he was spared much of the brutality of school life, and even his duties as a fag were lightened. Frank tells us that Clifton fags anyway 'had none of the fascinating duties about which we had read in *Tom Brown*, and, indeed, I cannot recall that they did anything much for their masters.'[24] The masters did, however, perform one useful function:they helped their fags with homework. Emily was a poor substitute.

The house in Worcester Crescent (which still stands) was, in Emily's words, modest, but roomy. It was modest because it was semi-detached, being the right-hand one of a pair. It was roomy because it had three spacious floors, a long flower garden running down to the front gate and a wider one at the back. It stood in a horseshoe rather that a crescent, with three similar pairs. Here, says Emily, 'the boys lived and worked and grew to youth and early manhood and were happy and good.'[25] So, as a matter of fact, did the girl.

Milly was a lanky schoolgirl now and went to the school round the corner. She was given to passionate friendships with other girls but she was still 'a good chap' and had been honoured with the title 'Newbolt III' or 'Terts.' Her duties were those of a real fag. According to *The Twymans*, 'she attended the boys on their return from school with slippers, buttered toast, and consolation for the troubles of the day. In the holidays she bowled and fielded for them. In the wilds of North Wales she kept them supplied with newspapers, chocolate and other unprocurable commodities.'[26] In real life Frank remained her favourite.

From Frank's diary, we have a vivid picture of how the young Newbolts spent an Easter holiday. They did the following:

24. FN I p.43
25. *My Story*, p. 12
26. *The Twymans*, p. 125

Played cricket, lawn tennis, croquet.

Fenced.

Played hockey on the landing because it was raining.

Bought walking sticks and went for walks.

Projected catching fish (but there was an East Wind).

Shot arrows on the Downs (until turned off by the Rangers).

Painted cards.

Arranged albums.

Lounged.

And, of course, they read books. They did not only read books, but they acted them. The hairy black hearthrug in the dining room was the source of an excellent moustache for the hero of *Verdant Green* by Cuthbert Bede. Verdant Green was a fictional undergraduate whose archly humourous misadventures delighted the Newbolt boys. Frank's literary style was never, alas, to deviate from the example set by Cuthbert Bede.

Street life in Worcester Crescent was not lacking in entertainment. There was Harry's old enemy the fish boy, who had the unpleasant habit of commenting on the Newbolts' prowess at tennis through the railings. Frank related the story of his undoing with glee. 'We had lost some balls and at last concluded that he had stolen one. Harry in his best manner sent me to fetch his new hornbeam, and, white with suppressed fury, gave the wretched errand boy his choice between producing a ball from his person and receiving condign chastisement. The lout chose the safer course.' On another occasion, Harry and Frank gave the house maid and the cook a terrible fright. They came to the back door dressed as beggar women and demanded alms in the roughest of accents.

Frank's passion was science. He was now specialising in physics and chemistry, and Harry assisted him with experiments in the basement. There was the 'amazing exploding pickle jar'. Rather less successful was the attempt to boil sulphuric acid. The house filled with choking fumes and Frank fled to his bedroom, leaving Harry to explain. Harry himself now became interested in physics. He installed an internal telephone system and illuminated his mother's dining–table 'with a light of rather feeble candle power.'[27]

27. *My World*, p.75

CHAPTER 6

Praeposter

Percival left Clifton for an Oxford headship at the end of Harry's first year in the Sixth. It seemed inconceivable that the school could survive. It was Harry who, as the senior member of the Sixth Form present, led the cheers when 'the departing Ancestor made his last appearance. He mounted the stone staircase as far as the first landing, turned to look down upon us, and removed his trencher cap. Suddenly the silence was broken by a staccato voice – "Three cheers for the Headmaster!" I heard the words with no realisation that I had uttered them myself.'[1]

No man is irreplaceable and Revd James Wilson all but replaced Percival in Harry's heart. Tall, thin Jimmy Wilson was barely forty when he came to Clifton from Rugby. In these respects he resembled Percival. In others he could hardly have been more different. Newly

1. *My World*, p. 67

bereaved, 'he was human to the core. His emotional nature was aptly symbolised by his flowing beard, and at any moment of intense feeling his voice would crack suddenly with a heart-shaking effect.'[2] 'The Jimmy' took Newbolt on holiday with him to his native Isle of Man and recited T.E. Brown to him on the leeward side of the funnel going over. He was an active man, and the episode of the hen was much enjoyed when Harry returned to Clifton. The couple were waiting for a train when a countrywoman dropped a basket full of fowls. Harry set off in pursuit and caught all but one 'powerful old hen who was making a bee-line for the wood. I was nearer her than Wilson, but he ran by with enormous strides and by the time the train drew up he had hurled himself bodily upon her.'[3]

As a Sixth Former, Harry automatically became a praepostor. The prefectorial system had been brought from Rugby by Percival, so it was boys who did the flogging, boys who dressed and behaved like men. Frank was impressed by Harry's promotion, Emily less so. The following family conversation (adapted from *The Twymans*) ensued:

Frank: You know, Mother, Harry's an awful swell now. He can do anything without leave from anybody. He could go up to London if he liked.

Emily: [Decidedly]. I'm sure he won't do that. The return fare's nearly a pound.

Frank: And he can thrash anyone in the school. He could thrash me if he chose.

Emily: [Revolted]. I should write to the headmaster at once if he did anything of the kind

Harry: [With patience exhausted]. I will thrash you this minute if you don't shut up.

Harry now discovered a talent for the lonely sports, those of running and rifle shooting. He knew that neither could compare in the eyes of the school with cricket or football. Indeed, wrote O.F. Christie, 'not only did shooting not count, but gaining shooting colours actually labelled a boy an outsider.'[4] The full title of the School Corps was the Rifle Volunteer Corps, commanded by

2. *My World,* p. 68
3. *My Story* p.73
4. OFC I, p. 244

45

Col. Edmund Plant of the 2nd Gloucestershire Engineers. Plant was always assisted by a school volunteer, a position held by Harry, but Harry was in fact no volunteer. 'I was conscripted. At the end of one term I was arbitrarily promoted Sergeant, and soon afterwards Lieutenant. By the summer of 1880 I had advanced sufficiently as a marksman to win the Regimental Challenge Cup for Officers and to take the school eight to compete for the Ashburton shield for public schools at Wimbledon. In the following year, my last, I shot again at Wimbledon, and by this time I was Captain of the School Corps,'[5] Thus began and ended Harry's only spell in uniform.

Frank did not fail to tease Harry about his shooting. Frank was the gargoyle on Harry's cathedral, ever ready to pour ridicule. He referred to the school marksmen as 'shooters' and suggested that the cadets might just as well drill with hockey sticks as their old Sniders, which were no better than blunderbusses. Shooting did, however, win a House Cup for North House. Harry scored 58 at 500 yards. 'That night Frank and I dined with the Wollastons. The Challenge Cup was placed in the centre of the table. Wollaston, quaffing the victory ale, was reduced to a kind of Viking language. He talked in riddles and exulted gloriously.'[6] Harry was even inspired to write a house song:

> 'We'll shout for the House we love
> Its star shall never go down
> The North Star shines above
> The old North Town.'[7]

The Long Penpole, a ten-mile race across Durdham Downs, was a Clifton tradition. The course was gruelling, but a vast crowd awaited the winner. A final burst of speed was expected as the runners came down off the downs. Harry now ran his first Long Penpole. He came in five minutes after the two winners, 'very much exhausted, his head wagging'. He did better a year later in the Short Penpole, a seven-mile race, all but defeating Frank Younghusband.[8]

5. *My World*, p.77
6. *My World*, p.78
7. OFC I
8. *My World*, p.61

'Mile after mile we measured road and grass.
Twin silent shadows, till the hour was done.
The Shadows parted and the stouter won.'[9]

It was over short distances that Harry excelled, collecting prizes in the quarter-mile hurdles and the one hundred yards. 'He was essentially a sprinter,' wrote Frank. 'He ran as the linnet sings, because he must.' But running was not cricket and he knew it didn't count. 'A match between two teams is a battle, with attack and defence, prolonged hand to hand fighting, visible tactics.'[10] A race is not.

The social life of the adolescent Newbolts was equally strenuous. The stately mansions of Clifton with their billiard rooms were full of parties, and there was much dancing of the polka with chaps' sisters. Fancy dress parties were popular. Frank describes his best friend, the magnificent cricketer Brain, choosing his costume for one of these occasions. 'On a Wednesday he showed himself to be a Neapolitan Fisherman, complete with net. Next day he made his final selection and appeared as a Hungarian Hussar. White satin tunic, pink silk knicks.'[11] Brain was so keen on drama that he even attended meetings of Harry's Bard of Avon Society, founded for the reading of Shakespeare. Clothes in general were a subject of immense interest to the young men at Worcester Crescent. Frank described his outfit for a trip to London: 'A black bowler hat, a suit of light grey cloth, stick-up collar. Tie to match.[12] (Stick-up collars were frowned on by the school authorities and Frank was careful to remove his on the way home.) In a school debate proposing dress reform, Frank opposed the motion. The cylinder hat, he pointed out, had saved lives.[13] Most of all, he despised a ready-tied cravat. It was not easy for the Newbolts to find money for clothes. A greatcoat ordered from a Bristol tailor had to take the place of a birthday present for Harry.[14]

Wollaston provided much of Harry and Frank's social life, and gave parties where they could meet the very occasional young lady.

9. Excerpt from 'Epistle To Colonel Francis Edward Younghusband', *SP*, p.98
10. *The Twymans*, p.109
11. FN II, p.23
12. FN II, p.105
13. FN II, p.100
14. ibid.

Clifton was hard on girls. In chapel the womenfolk were seated in the gallery[15] and heaven help the owner of the eye that strayed there. 'There could hardly have been a *cleaner* school in England,' wrote Quiller-Couch.[16] Yet Harry did get to know a girl. Or at least Percy did. In *The Twymans*, Percy develops a crush on Nellie Egerton, with whom his sister was having one of her 'electric friendships'. One summer night he walked her home. At her garden gate the couple paused. 'They looked into the wells of darkness which they knew for each other's eyes, and without perceptible movement they leaned towards one another for a kiss. The moment of trance was broken by a sound of footsteps. A long elastic stride passed their bower without stopping: but a gruff voice came back to them like a stone flung into a pool. "Good-night, Miss Egerton," it splashed. "Goodnight, Percival."[17] The voice was that of the fictionalised Wollaston.

Emily did not get invited to parties. It could have been otherwise, she said. 'If she had elected to spend her income on a carriage and pair, and live in one of the more pretentious houses close by, she might have had plenty of society and have been courted and flattered by some of those who now, while never failing to invite her boys to their parties, left her out in the cold, to sit beside a dying fire, to wait for the return of the lads who were enjoying the fun and festivity she was still young enough to have enjoyed with them'.[18] The presence of Colonel George Newbolt, living in Guthrie Road behind the school, had encouraged Emily to come to Clifton, but he proved socially useless because of his strict evangelical opinions. Frank and Harry regarded him as a bit of a joke. 'He and two other retired officers were known in Clifton as the three holy colonels, chiefly remarkable for having married between them eight wives, and having 33 children.'[19] Instead of socialising, Emily concentrated on good works. She started her own charity 'for rescuing clergymen who had fallen into poverty.' She tells us in her memoir how she collected and sorted old clothes for them. A large packing room was set up, known to her children as 'Mother's Old Rag Shop'.[20] The boys were also embarrassed by

15. OFC I, p.88
16. *Arthur Quiller-Couch, Memories and Opinions* (1944), p.62
17. *The Twymans*, p.150
18. *My Story*, p.12
19. FN II, p.66
20. *My Story*, p.14

her Walsall habit of serving high tea. Frank recalled how, when five members of the Liverpool XI 'tea'd *mecum*', there was no afternoon tea available. 'I found the table laid in the dining room, and a soused mackerel awaiting my attention. After agonies of explanation I persuaded the cook to bring a tray into the drawing room, with tea and bread and butter for six, but I had that uncomfortable feeling that in the eyes of these men of the world, I was as young and innocent as David Copperfield when Steerforth called him "Daisy".[21] In his last December at Clifton, Harry went to Balliol to try for the scholarship (the peak of public school ambition). Three friends went with him: Nash, Jose and Boas (a noted cricketer). The results were devastating. Jose took the second scholarship, Nash and Boas both won exhibitions and Newbolt won nothing. Norman Moor, his form master, made enquiries. It seemed Harry had missed an award by a hair's breadth. He had quoted from Tennyson's *In Memoriam* in an essay on biography. This source was considered unorthodox.[22] In the event, Harry did not regret his second choice of college, Corpus Christi.

21. FN II, p.11
22. *My World*, p.81

CHAPTER 7

Headboy

Although he had secured a place at Oxford in the autumn, Harry had two terms left at Clifton. The first of these was far from idle, for he became acting head of school in place of Nash. The story of Nash is a tragic one. A brilliant scholar and organist who could bring tears to a thousand eyes at a school concert, his scruples were too delicate to cope with high office. He was often at Worcester Crescent examining his conscience with Harry. The captaincy of football (which came automatically with headship) worried him particularly. He had fears that he might be crippled if he played with the team, or, worse still, let Clifton down. After the Balliol examinations he became severely depressed and later at Oxford he ceased to speak and finally died. Fortunately, Harry's overlords were anxious that he should not suffer a like fate. He was excused from much of the routine work of the Sixth. As Cock of the School, his relationship with the new headmaster, Wilson, became close and Wilson now often dined at Worcester Crescent. After the meal the two of them would retire to discuss school matters, the bearded sage paying careful attention to Harry, now 'a lanky youth, responsive and bright-eyed, but thin and rather sombre of countenance.'[1]

Harry's supervisor in the Sixth was a pale, keen-faced young man called Norman Moor who is barely mentioned in the autobiography. Yet this Norman was none other than 'Norman', the adored schoolboy of John Addington Symond's secret homosexual memoirs – the boy who combined physical beauty with spiritual emptiness. 'He had a face made to be cast in bronze (and) a storm of dark hair laid in heavy masses'.[2] As a small boy, Moor had been 'ravaged' by a member of the Harrow XI, now he only cared for boys younger than himself. In a letter to Symonds he confessed, 'I regarded every small boy as a possible spoon.' But especially, he loved young cricketers. 'What could be more erotic than a sight of a lithe lad dressed all in white, a lock of hair falling carelessly over one eye, spurning the green sward to catch a high ball, his body arched backwards like the bow of a Grecian archer?' (The highest term of physical praise known at Clifton was to describe a boy as 'a graceful cricketer'.) As a master, Norman Moor had more influence on Harry's literary development than Harry was willing to admit. One winter's evening, Percy was at home translating English verse into Latin hexameters. Two lines of Keats's 'The Eve of St Agnes' struck him forcibly:

> 'And they are gone: ay, ages long ago
> These lovers fled away into the storm.'

'There they were now, those lines, under the lamplight of a January evening, in the handwriting of the sixth-form master, reproduced in the bilious violet ink peculiar to the copying machine.'[3] 'The boy read on, following the poet through the sleeping house. Why was he so affected by it? Who were the lovers and why were they fleeing? He had to go at once to the house of the master, Mr Smith, to find out.' 'Smith' was none other than Norman Moor. Newbolt now, according to Frank, began to spend

1. *The Twymans*, p.103
2. J.A. Symonds, *Memoirs* ed. Phyllis Grosskurth, p.193
3. *The Twymans*, p.116

hours in his study writing Arthurian ballads. Two of them, heavy with nostalgia, appeared in *The Cliftonian*.[4] over invented initials (as was the custom), 'Cadbury Castle', was signed N.B. (New Bolt). 'The Ballade of Tintagel' appeared two years later, when Harry was already up at Oxford. In his last six months at Clifton, he made an attempt on the school prize for English verse. The subject set was 'The Fall of Athens', but Quiller-Couch won it.

Frank, meanwhile, was developing as an artist and etcher. He was largely self-taught, art at Clifton being the province of Colonel Plant of the Corps. 'Boys who had heard of Botticelli thought it was a cheese.'[5] By the time he reached the Sixth Form, he was drawing landscapes and copying illustrations from Emily's magazines. Frank first saw his work reproduced in the *Ladies Pictorial*.[6] There was another boy, younger than Frank, at Clifton who later made his name in the art world: his name was Roger Fry.

Harry's last term at Clifton ended in triumph. He beat the great MacTier in the quarter-mile.

> 'He saw the School Close, sunny and green,
>   The runner beside him, the stand by the parapet wall,
> The distant tape, and the crowd roaring between
>   His own name over all.'[7]

It was an equally thrilling moment for Percy. 'In thirty yards he had shot past two of his three opponents, in thirty more he had drawn up to the right shoulder of the third. No need of any backward glance to tell the challenged that the challenger was there. For five desperate strides he held his own. Percy knew that for himself, too, that breaking-point was all but here. But then the calm, remote inexorable power that was riding his heart at will, drove both spurs home and sent him in one terrible rush across the line.'[8]

The last days at Clifton had come. They were 'an uprooting, a painful wrench'.[9] Harry's memories of Clifton were entirely happy, he declared. Unlike Frank, he had always been an optimist. He would have happily lived his Clifton days over again. And in a sense

4. OFC II, p.349
5. Winterbottom, p.23
6. FN II, p.10
7. 'He Fell Among Thieves', S.P., p.61
8. *The Twymans*, p.110
9. *The Twymans*, p.137

he did not leave Clifton, since he still lived in the area, and continued to join in school events and school debates during the university vacation. The Old Cliftonian Society was already active, and he became a keen member. Commem was the time for the great annual gathering of O.C.'s. The massive chapel now came truly into its own. Even the aisle was packed. Twenty years later, in his poem 'Commemoration',[10] he wrote:

'I sat by the granite pillar, and sunlight fell
    Where the sunlight fell of old,
And the hour was the hour my heart remembered well,
    And the sermon rolled and rolled
As it used to roll when the place was still unhaunted,
    And the strangest tale in the world was still untold.

And the School passed; and I saw the living and dead
    Set in their seats again,
And I longed to hear them speak of the word that was said,
    But I knew that I longed in vain.
And they stretched forth their hands, and the wind of the spirit took them
    Lightly as drifted leaves on an endless plain.

10. S.P., p.31

PART III OXFORD 1881–1885

CHAPTER 8

First Year

Harry arrived at Oxford accompanied by his mother. She at once embarrassed him by bargaining with his scout over some furniture for his rather dark rooms in the Founders Tower. Then she called on Percival, now the Master of Trinity, and put her foot in it again. She referred to the Trinity quad as 'your front yard', and suggested it needed tidying. When she left, she extracted a promise from Harry to writer to her daily about everything he did and thought. She did, however, settle a sum of money on him which would provide him with a modest income. Even after Emily had returned to Clifton she remained on Harry's conscience. Her letters to him at Oxford were full of complaints about exhaustion. He did his best to soothe her. 'You are overdoing yourself about this bazaar,'[1] he wrote in one letter; in another: 'You must take a temperance pledge limiting exertion generally.'[2]

Once Emily was gone, the peace of the ancient college descended. Corpus Christi, in Merton Street, is Oxford's smallest, and possibly prettiest, college. It has everything a college should have, but scaled down: quadrangles, a chapel and a dining hall, all in little space. Harry never forgot his first dinner in Hall. As the junior scholar present he was expected to say the long Latin grace, and he remembered the appearance of the hall as he waited to begin it that night. Shields bearing coats of arms glowed below each light bracket and 'the quiet eyes of great men looked down from their portraits.'[3] Harry was suddenly filled with a longing for a past that he felt certain had been his own personal past. He knew he had been there before:

> 'Ages past the soul existed,
> Here an age 'tis resting merely,
> And hence fleets again for ages.'

Browning's 'Christina' expressed it perfectly. One of Harry's first acts at Oxford was to have his family coat of arms painted on a shield. Percy did the same. 'He entered with the intention of buying the shield of his college, and while doing so it occurred to him that he might have his own arms painted to match.'[4] Colonel George Newbolt, head of the family, seems to have made some objection, for Harry wrote: 'I am going to see Uncle George on Saturday and will explain to him.'[5] Harry felt the need to lay claim to landed forbears. Indeed, the plot of *The Twymans* depended on this issue: young Percy Twyman is cheated of his inheritance, but finally recovers it. He who was deemed 'plated goods' is proved 'solid silver'.

Naturally, Harry was eager to play games. But games at Oxford were not like games at Clifton. 'True, college played college at football, but how much did it matter if we lost to Balliol?' Ardent loyalty remained attached only to the College boat, 'on which we

1, *NL* HN to EN, 14 March 1882
2. *NL* HN to EN, 21 Feb. 1882
3. *The Twymans,* p.181
4. *The Twymans,* p.159
5. *NL* HN to EN, 14 Nov. 1883

concentrated all our patriotic feelings.'[6] Harry painted the scene when the Corpus Torpids (second eight)came Head of the River (by the traditional method of bumping the boat ahead). 'Water sparkling, flags flying, ladies on barges, rattles, bugles, bells and yells.'[7] Wilder still were the celebrations in the quad that night. There is a description of the midnight football match in *The Twymans*: 'Someone threw down a football, and a mad game began, a game played on gravel with only one principle, that everyone was against the man with the ball. Percy found himself dribbling, kicking, charging, collaring, with extraordinary success, running swiftly like a shadow, for it was a cloudy night and no faces were distinguishable, nor did shocks or bruises seem for the moment to produce their usual effect of pain.'[8]

On his arrival at Corpus, Harry had himself volunteered for the college boat, but at nine and a half stone, he had not 'the beef' for an oar (the average weight of a crew member being twelve stone). Yet he was too heavy to be a cox. He did cox a four once, but was dismissed immediately as the cause of his boat's defeat. Harry appears to have done little running during his first year at Oxford, perhaps because the college already had a brilliant 100-yard sprinter in Laugham Carter. He did enjoy a little competitive sailing, and was victorious in one race. 'With a stiff breeze behind, we tore through the water, one side buried in the waves,' he told Emily.[9] He won because all the other boats capsized. Years later, he still remembered the 'cool, delicious gurgle beneath the boat, like the ghost of a drink satisfying the memory of a thirst.'[10] Of cricket there is no mention. Because he did not play games, Harry found himself dubbed an Intellectual as opposed to a Heavy. The most distinguished of the Intellectuals was the literary Oliver Elton, who was dubbed a Disloyalist by the Heavies for not cheering the college boat on one occasion. He was besieged in his ground-floor rooms by 'a knot of full-flavoured rowing men, determined to drag him to the pump to expiate his supposed lack of riverside patriotism',[11] and was only just rescued in time by his fellow Intellectuals.

6. *My World*, p.94
7. *NL*, HN to EN, 22 Feb. 1884
8. *The Twymans*, p.191
9. *NL*, HN to EN
10. *The Twymans*, p.176
11. *My World*, p.96

Arthur Sidgwick, Harry's classical tutor, a man of refined appearance, had strong connections with Clifton, being a close friend of John Addington Symonds, who had been deeply in love with him. Sidgwick in turn had a restraining effect on Symonds, · persuading him to excise the more explicit homosexual fantasies from his poem 'Eudiades'. Sidgwick immediately admitted Harry to his inner circle, and it was he who took the shy undergraduate to a meeting of the Browning Society at Lincoln College. There Sidgwick read a paper, 'tilting his head a little back, and casting his eyes down so as to show the eyelids almost closed. This effect, combined with the flowing of his silver beard, gave him a very classical appearance. The paper flowed on from one point to another and at every pause, low murmurs of admiration came from the obscure corners of the room. The Society was responding to a skilled player'.[12]

The Browning Society was a revelation to Harry, partly because it was still rather dashing to prefer Browning to Tennyson and partly because one-third of the Society's members was female. Harry was painfully aware of Rhoda Broughton's 'roseate arms emerging from a low-cut mauve dress'[13] as she recited a dramatic monologue. She was the author of romantic novels which, in her own words, circulated fast at Mudies' Library by reason of their large type, wide margins and plenitude of titled names. Mark Pattison, Rector of Lincoln, also came to the Browning Society. His habit of seducing blue stockings there was revealed in Rhoda's best-selling novel *Belinda*. Harry could hardly believe that Mark Pattison was Sister Dora's older brother. 'I looked vainly for a likeness – there seemed to me to be nothing in common between this silent shrunken old gentleman and the smiling Demeter.'[14]

Browning's love poems deeply impressed Harry. His women were no Ladies of Shalott; they were made of flesh and blood. Yet their love was no transient episode, but lived on from age to age in fresh incarnations. Harry came to regard the reading of *The Ring and the Book* as a turning point in his life. The tales of Pompilia and her murdered husband Count Guido caused his interest in King Arthur to go into temporary retirement. 'I had first strayed into

12. *My World*, p.89
13. ibid.
14. *My World*, p.89

the dim-rich City of Camelot at the age of 12,' he wrote. 'Then came the discovery of *The Ring and the Book*, and a great part of Camelot fell into ruins.'[15] The streets of Ghent were now preferred to the windless valley of Avilion. Perhaps it was appropriate that one of the last of Harry's Arthurian ballads was entitled 'A Fair Death'. In it he compares his father to King Arthur. His fellow undergraduates praised the long poem so extravagantly that he had it privately published in booklet form in 1882, at Robinson of Walsall's Steam Printing Works.

15. *My World,* p.91

CHAPTER 9

Second and Third Years

At the beginning of his second year, Harry moved into three of the most beautiful rooms in Oxford. They were on the first floor of Staircase Two of the Fellow's Building (now the Bursar's office). They had recently been vacated by Ruskin himself. (Ruskin, now very old, lived in the Woodstock Road.) Harry, being an admirer of Ruskin, was enchanted. The view through the tall windows was of Christ Church Meadows, 'held in the embrace of the Thames and the Cherwell. I had never at any time been at home in a scene of such ancient peace and beauty.'[1] He took to reading Cicero on a punt drifting slowly down the Cherwell. The wolds of Caistor and downs of Clifton now faded before the riverscapes of Oxford, 'my paradise for life'[2]Long punting expeditions were made with friends out into the countryside.

1. *My World*, p.108
2. *My World*, p.98

Harry obtained a First in Mods at the beginning of his second year, along with his Corpus stable companions, Cholmeley, F.S. Boas, Anthony Hawkins and Nash. (Anthony Hawkins later became well-known as the novelist Anthony Hope, author of *The Prisoner of Zenda*.) Harry now started the philosophy section of his degree. His tutor was Tommy Case, a lover of good wine, good talk and football. Case felt an irresistible urge to tease the somewhat serious young man. He assured Harry that Herodotus was 'completely reliable as a geographer', that the work of T. H. Green, Professor of Moral Philosophy, was 'all rot' and that Aristotle and Plato alone needed to be studied, 'and them not yet. Have you read any novels?' he asked. When Harry mentioned Scott, Dickens and Thackeray, Tommy roared with laughter. 'Those are hardly novels! I should call them studies in Ancient History. What about Fielding and Smollett?'[3] When Tommy Case could be induced to discuss philosophy, he limited the subject severely. 'Again and again,' wrote Newbolt, 'I remember coming to a point where a philosophical inquiry led straight to the borderland of religion. At the frontier I was always stopped. "I don't think we need go into that."' Only Professor Müller, was willing to talk about God. In the garden of his North Oxford home he waved an arm towards the Parks: '"If you say *that* all is not made by Design, then you are not in the same world with me."'[4]

There was another don at work on the loosening up of Harry, the 'Beaky Bachelor' of *The Twymans*. Perhaps he never existed, but the aesthetic decadence he represented certainly did. The following dialogue (slightly abridged) took place between the Bachelor and Percy.

> *BB:* Whist or waistcoats? Have you made your choice yet? You Downton [Clifton] men always take to one or the other. You lace the ego up so tight at school, you must begin by a little outburst. I was quite glad when I saw your friend Quiller yesterday, looking self-conscious in a crimson plush vest.
>
> *Percy:* Well, I confess to a waistcoat: I ordered one today.
>
> *BB:* Bring it to me to see then, at lunch on Thursday. *(At this moment someone on the opposite side of the table invited Percy to a game of whist.)*

3. *My World,* p.115
4. *My World,* p.116

BB: Twyman doesn't play.

Percy: Not well, but I will come.

BB: I said waistcoats or whist. What are you doing with both?

Percy: (Rising from the table.) Ah! Perhaps I laced my ego tighter than the rest!

Newbolt did indeed buy a waistcoat at Oxford, and more: 'I had myself one of silvery corduroy, which I wore with an old rose tie and a sage green suit.'[5]

A further unlacing of the stays occurred now that Harry had his new rooms. One hot summer, when the nightjars were whirring in the Meadows, Harry and his friend Cholmeley, a whimsical Irishman, felt ancient stirrings in them. 'We had discovered that through the windows of Professor Nettleship's rooms we could get down into the locked Fellow's Garden at night, and thence carefully manoeuvre ourselves over the spiked iron railings and into Christ Church meadows. Here there was always a constable on night duty, but he carried no lantern and was quite helpless in the deep shadows of the Broad Walk. Cholmeley and I played with him one night at a game of blind man's bluff, first making enough noise to set him hunting, and then running just ahead of him along Dead Man's Walk, and down the river path. When the round was nearly finished we made a silent spurt, reached our railings well ahead and were over them and in our garden in time to hear the pursuer go panting by. My own belief is that there was in us in those years a haunting from the Middle Ages – the undergraduate of the Thirteenth Century was born again in us.'[6]

Oxford was as sociable a place then as it is now. 'My letters were little more than a list of those who entertained me at breakfast or dinner, and those who dropped in to a lunch ordered from the kitchen in my own rooms'.[7] His friends were numerous, many of them Old Cliftonians. Some were invited to stay at Clifton during vacations, provided the house was not filled with what Harry described as 'broken-backed' relations. At the beginning of Harry's second year, Frank had come up. He went to Balliol, but without a scholarship. There are occasional references to him furnishing his rooms or giving dinners. Before he went down he announced his engagement to Miss Bright. Harry's involvement with girls was less

5. *My World,* p.135
6. *My World,* p.108
7. *My World,* p.94

drastic. The young ladies of Oxford were mostly the daughters of dons, and well-chaperoned. Alice Liddell (lately of Wonderland) and her sisters had recently married, but there were Miss Percival, Miss Arnold and Miss Legge. Miss Legge was a beauty: 'She might have anticipated Zuleika Dobson.' Her father was James Legge, Professor of Chinese. 'For us, at any rate, she was the Queen of Bohemia. Whenever she rose in our sky the meaner beauties of the night were effaced.'[8] But it was a German, Beatrice Müller, who captivated Harry in the summer of his third year. Beatrice was the younger daughter of Professor Max Müller. Magical indeed were those lamp-lit evenings at Norham Gardens, when she sang 'with untiring enjoyment' Schubert's songs, accompanied on the piano by her sister, Mrs Conybeare. The words of the songs were by her grandfather Wilhelm. On these occasions, Harry was so filled with emotion that he could hardly lift his eyes to meet those of her father across the room. Harry also sang (though he does not admit it in his autobiography). At Clifton he had obliged at Colonel George Newbolt's gatherings, and at school smoking concerts.[9] After he met Beatrice, he had a piano moved into his rooms and sent home for sheet music.[10] Now his voice could mingle with hers in duets.

In Max Müller, Henry found another hero-father. Müller was a polymath. Born at Leipzig, he had edited the Hindu *Veda* by the age of twenty-three. He was now Oxford's first Professor of Comparative Philology, yet he had retained the openness of a child. Mrs Müller was a handsome woman, 'one of the most competent and commanding I have ever met'. She kept a close eye on Harry and Beatrice. 'She knew that attachments between young people of the undergraduate age were as likely as they were untimely, and she took pains to keep the fun so open and so loud as to avert perils.' Yet she was a stout friend 'to any man who was thoroughly in love', and if she found his disease incurable she would 'embrace his cause with the most loyal and inconsistent fervour.'[11] Mrs Müller's idea of loud and open fun took the form of picnics up the river, not in a boat, but in flotillas of boats. On the way home everyone sang, Beatrice taking the lead.

Commem Week was the high season for girls at Oxford. Eager

8. *My World*, p.115
9. *NL* HN to EN, 2 Dec. 1884
10. ibid.
11. *My World*, p.119

mothers brought them down from London for college balls and private dances. (Balls went on until 4 a.m. whereas dances ended at midnight.) 'The town filled suddenly with unfamiliar beauties, crossing and recrossing before the set background of cloisters like the groups which pass over the stage when the curtain rises.'[12] In 1884, Harry arranged for Emily to bring Milly to Oxford to join in the fun. The very thought of a ball made Emily feel tired, but her presence was required as a chaperone. The week went well and Harry and Milly were invited everywhere. Harry danced the Highland Fling so well with Miss Arnold that Ruskin asked him to do it again. 'As we pranced around the room we saw the great little man beating time to our step, with his head thrown back and his eyes half closed in a kind of ecstacy.'[13] There was an even more alarming presence at another private dance, held at All Souls – none other than Percival himself. 'I saw in a queer dream Dr Percival looking on with his marmoreal smile. I danced – yes, danced – before his eyes – with his daughter Bessie. He was not amused by our giddy revolutions.'[14]

Harry himself gave a dance that summer. He felt he owed it to his rooms, he said, but no doubt he intended to sit out a dance or two with Beatrice in the Fellow's Garden. That garden, by day the setting for energetic games of tennis with Arthur Sidgwick, became an enchanted place by night, heavy with the scent of jasmine. Dick Peile, a close friend, was Harry's co-host, which was decent of Dick, considering he couldn't dance. Harry had first to ask permission from Tommy Fowler, the college ''am and heggs' scoffing president. Fowler replied:

My dear Newbolt.

We have no objection to you and Peile giving a dance in your rooms providing you will keep the party within moderate limits, and bring it to an end by 12 o' clock.

I understand that the dance is to be confined to your own personal friends, and would therefore advise you to keep your intention of giving a party as secret as possible. There is no limit to the rapacity for invitations of the *mères de famille.*

Sincerely yours
T. Fowler[15]

12. *The Twymans,* p.200
13. *My World,* p.114
14. ibid.
15. *My World,* p.113

Harry found the rapacity in fact came from his fellow undergraduates. As for 'moderate limits', there was no problem there. By the time space had been set aside for supper-room, band and sitting out, there was barely room for 25 couples. The dance went well, although Milly may have been disappointed by the high proportion of Old Cliftonians among her partners. Emily had her own photograph taken at the end of Commem Week. There is a look of resignation in her face, not to say exhaustion.

Harry and Milly were now close friends. She was 'upon the upward slope towards 18', tall and graceful, according to her mother, with 'large dark eyes like those of her father'.[16] But for Harry she was still 'a child he could command at will'. Milly had been 'alarmingly ill' during the previous winter, and Emily had taken her to a London doctor, but now she was once more the 'jolly Molly' of *The Twymans*, popping the balloons of her family's pomposity and even referring to her older brother as 'an old stick'. She studied history at home. Harry recommended Froude and Huxley to her, but when he suggested Ebers and Mimmsent she revolted. Harry felt strongly the injustice of women being barred from the university, and in 1884 he attended the Convocation at the Sheldonian, at which women were admitted to public examinations. The building was crammed, he said, and the right side won by 143 votes. He immediately brought forward a motion of satisfaction at the Union.

The long vacation of Harry's third year was spent largely at home, partly because he was short of money and partly because Finals were only just over the horizon. He had made an attempt to stay up at Oxford to work, but it had proved unbearable. 'No one who has not tried it can imagine the sense of desolation. Every street was empty of the familiar figures. As evening came on it got worse. All the college gates stood wide open, but the lodges were unlit and the quadrangles soundless.'[17]

16. *My World*, p.13
17. *NL*, 8 Sept. 1884

CHAPTER 10

Fourth Year

Harry returned for his last year full of intentions to work. (He was now living in digs at 47 The High.) It was assumed that he would get a First. Frank was absolutely sure he would and Emily had been assured of it on good authority.[1] But first there was Divvers to be dealt with. The divinity exam was compulsory. It was not difficult and was indefinitely retakeable. All the necessary biblical facts could be crammed from one book, if one could be bothered. 'I can't be bothered,' wrote Harry to Emily. 'If I am ploughed I shall swear. And if I swear you'll be vexed, so I suppose I shall get through.'[2] All went well until he was called for a *viva* at 3.00 one afternoon, the very time he was due to run a 100-yard sprint. Frantic at the thought of missing his last opportunity to beat Savigny, a Blue, he walked up to the examiners' table and asked

1. *NL* FN to HN, 1 Aug. 1885
2. *NL* HN to EN, 15 Nov. 1884

permission to change the time. They refused. He bowed himself out and went directly to the Iffley Running Ground. As a result, he was deemed to have grossly insulted a University Board of Examiners and, but for the intervention of Tommy Fowler, would not have been allowed to sit the exam again. The incident ended satisfactorily. Harry licked Savigny. He does not explain why he took up athletics in his last year, having not partaken in his first.

Harry now made a determined attempt on high office in the Union. He was aiming at the position of librarian, which carried with it the Vice Presidency. He was well fitted for the post, as he had already spent many happy hours compiling a subject index for the library. To strengthen his position he set about being elected to one of the University's political clubs. It didn't seem to matter which. He was put up first for the Russell, whose members, he assured Emily, were really Liberals. When the Russell blackballed him, he immediately put up for the Palmerston. 'The Conservatism of today is far different to that of the last generation. Even if there be a Conservative Party when I stand for the House, I shall certainly have no sympathy with it. Once a Liberal, always a Liberal.' Harry anyway took little notice of Emily's political opinions. 'You know you always end up by agreeing with me.' He also began to speak more frequently. In February 1884, he spoke in favour of enlarging the Navy and won a substantial majority. Now he had to find someone to nominate him. He was proposed by E.H. Spender (father of the poet), and was chosen as the Liberal. But when the elections came round, Vidal, the Conservative candidate, got in. Then it was discovered that Vidal had been canvassing before his election, which was again the rules. He offered to resign, but the Union officials wouldn't accept his resignation. Once more, Newbolt had found an honourable reason for his failure.

The heady delights of an Oxford summer mixed ill with 'grinding like a black' for Finals. On 6 June, Harry celebrated his 23rd birthday with a picnic on the upper Cherwell, but the river gods did not favour him as they did Mrs Müller. It rained and he could only afford one boat. In the end, the distinguished company ate lunch in the boat house and Max Müller made a speech from the landing stage. The last Commem at Oxford was due to start the day after Finals ended. Thoughts about whether Milly could wear last season's pink ball gown to the Conybeare's dance chased through his head as he took his eleventh and last paper in the Old Divinity School. That same day Emily and Milly arrived. 'By nine we were in Corpus Hall, where we danced to the hour of sparrow chirp. After our guests had left us, we ran improvised hurdle races in the garden and some went down to the bathing place, until it was possible to get breakfast, and prepare for another round of the clock.'.[3] The last week in the City of Delight passed 'like an opium-dream'. To add to the sense of unreality, 'Glimpses of our old life' kept appearing. 'On one occasion Mr Fitzgerald from Walsall and Uncle Robert [Gordon] from Hammerwich, turned up for lunch in Hall and vanished again like wraiths.' Indeed, looking back, Harry felt the whole time at Oxford had had a dreamlike quality. 'The sense of time did not exist. The seasons, it is true, flitted round in their accustomed circle, and a very gay dance they made of it. Among them too the iridescent wings of Cupid flashed continually in and out. The whirl was unresting, but it never seemed to move, as full of mad pursuit and wild ecstacy as the men and maidens on a Grecian Urn, their loves forever unfulfilled.' And so the farewells were said, the china packed, and the train caught for Bristol. It was halfway through the long vacation that Harry received a letter from Frank, who had read the Oxford First Class list through ten times before he had been able to believe his eyes. Harry's name was not in it. He had got a second.

3. *My World*, p.132

PART IV MARGARET 1886–1895

CHAPTER 11

The Law

Newbolt spent the next fifteen years in a profession he grew to dislike increasingly. Why did he choose the law, and having chosen it, why did he stick to it for so long? At the time there seemed to be few alternatives. The failure to get a first at Oxford 'was more than a disappointment, it was a catastrophe.'[1] Newbolt found reasons for it. The Ancient Greek History paper had all been set by the very professor whose lectures he had skipped on Tommy Case's advice. Whatever the causes, the effects were unavoidable. Without a first there was no hope of the junior academic post that he and most of his more gifted fellow graduates aimed at. Clifton would probably have offered him a teaching post. He spent part of the Christmas vacation of 1883 correcting Latin papers for Oakeley, but he was not

1. *My World*, p.140

tempted to stay on. 'I will *not* be a pedagogue!' he told his mother. Two tutorial posts were also turned down, one coaching young George Howard of Castle Howard for his Oxford entrance examinations. Emily still 'hoped, yet scarcely dared to hope that he would take Orders', but not unless 'he were impelled by irresistible longing for the life.' Harry had no such intentions. He had been too heavily dosed with Victorian piety as a child. Any idea of making the army a career had been abandoned by the age of eighteen. A post-script in a letter to Emily, written while he was still at Oxford, simply says, 'Please sell my Corps uniform.' Business, of course, was out of the question for a gentleman. (Frank's adored Brain entered the family firm in Bristol, but redeemed himself by getting killed in the First World War.) Journalism, the career chosen by Rudyard Kipling, was not considered either. Apart from the Church, the law was probably the only career that would have been acceptable to Emily.

In the autumn of 1885, Newbolt took a temporary post with his cousin Heath Stubbs in Bloomsbury Square. In Stubbs's chambers he was apprenticed to an equity lawyer for whom he attempted to draft cases. Now, like Percy, Newbolt was to spend the hours of daylight in the 'dingy Pupil Room among companions whom he must one day leave behind. It was humiliating to come down so suddenly from Oxford into the dark warren of the Inns of Court.'[2] He was depressed by the impersonal nature of the law. It was a world of 'knowledge without beauty, possession without mystery. Property, property, property, that's what the work seemed to say. Land ceased to be any part of the inhabited earth, any part of historic England, it became a fee simple, or a dominant tenement.'[3]

Newbolt took rooms at 11 Portsea Place, near Marble Arch. He chose the street because five Corpus men were living there already, and he made sure that he had a spare room in which he could put any other Corpus men who might be passing through. His walk to work took him the whole length of Oxford Street, but central London held few charms for him. Like Percy, he constantly compared its 'sordidly grandiose and mechanically decorated buildings' to the graceful ones of Oxford.[4] During his wanderings

2. *The Twymans*, p.335
3. ibid.
4. *The Twymans*, p.384

in London, Newbolt took the opportunity to visit the College of Arms, 'a charming little red building squeezed almost out of existence between two huge meaningless blocks.'[5] Years later, Newbolt followed a gentleman called Rouge Rose Poursuivant to 'the hushed and reposeful library' where he was shown his own pedigree.

Once settled in London, the young lawyer lost no time in attempting to recreate the social life he had known at Oxford. He left calling cards with people to whom he had introductions, and invitations materialised. At a ball he was introduced to no less a trio than Gladstone, Lord Acton and Oscar Wilde. 'I remember best the voice and manner of Wilde. He was dressed with ruffles to his shirt and a high rolled collar to the back of his coat; he stood at the hither [end] of the room and discoursed to groups of ladies on the splendours of the less-read Elizabethan dramatists. His quotations seemed to bear out all that he claimed for them, and I noted the names that I might study them at my leisure. But when I searched the plays afterwards I found not a word of any of the lines.'[6]

Yet, despite a lively social life, Newbolt felt deeply alone. 'I could dine, dance and play tennis at many houses, but these people were themselves dispersed among the vast crowd, and I felt like a waif and a stray as I wandered from one to another.' He longed for a home of his own, where he could entertain, but 'I had no college kitchen at my service – I had come into an exile where [the young] go in droves up the stairs of others and eat the bread of [those] they hardly know.'[7]

There was one family with whom he felt at home. The Walronds, related to the Max Müllers, were always hospitable. Young Arthur Walrond was one of the few do-gooders that Newbolt could admire. 'He is *not*, as you imagined, a clergyman,' Newbolt inform-ed Emily. Walrond ran a boy's club in Notting Hill Gate. 'It is quite in the slums,' Newbolt told Emily, 'and the boys are little Street Arabs.' It was Newbolt's task to lecture to them. Eventually, Walrond built a swimming pool. Here there occurred a scene of metamorphosis: 'In two minutes the boys had thrown off their rags and, to my great surprise, I saw that, though I had thought them

5. *The Twymans*, p.234
6. *My World*, p.157
7. *My World*, p.155

ugly and half-starved, they were in reality well-made and well-nourished.' A public bathing area of some sort was a feature of many clubs at this time. Regrettably, some of the pools were regarded as public spectacles. At a club patronised by Baden Powell, the secretary noted, 'the youngsters objected to be looked upon as something in the nature of performing animals by too curious visitors.'[8] Newbolt certainly saw these boys as more than animals. He admired them for their manliness and independence at an age when he would still have been at prep school. They gave back to him that sense of corporate life, 'that I was always looking for. They enlarged my idea of patriotism.'[9]

The theatre was a blessed place of escape. Newbolt admired the new operettas of Gilbert and Sulivan at the Savoy, but for the stirring of deeper emotions, he preferred Henry Irving as Mephistopheles at the Lyceum. He was assiduous in attending concerts with mixed parties of young friends. (Hans Richter, the Hungarian conductor, was all the rage in London at the time.) Nor were the visual arts neglected. Like everybody else, Newbolt attended the Summer Exhibition of the Royal Academy, but he also admired the more old-fashioned style of Holman Hunt's 'The Light of the World' and 'The Scapegoat'. Reading, however, remained his chief solace. During the first Christmas holidays at home from London, he read Rabelais (in French) and Rossetti's *Shadow of Dante*. On 29 December he spent the whole day comparing Goethe's *Faust* and Marlowe's *Dr Faustus*.[10] He was shocked to discover how much Irving's stage version had left out. Throughout this period, Newbolt was also writing. 'I am writing several things as hard as may be.'[11] However, whatever he wrote at this time, he does not appear to have kept it.

Newbolt had soon left his cousin, Heath Stubbs, and obtained a place as pupil in the chambers of Thomas Methold of Lincoln's Inn. Methold was a man after Newbolt's heart. 'He taught me not only to draw up a will but to shoot red-legged partridges.'[12] When the year with Methold was finished he went, in October 1886, for six months into the offices of Thomas Willes Chitty, a Templar and

8. Tim Jeal, *Baden Powell* (1922), p.90
9. *My World*, p.154
10. *My World*, p.151
11. *NL* HN to EN, 12 Mar. 1886
12. *My World*, p.145

a man he already knew. Chitty was six years older than Newbolt, and descended from formidable legal ancestors. His grandfather and great-grandfather, both called Thomas, had been leading barristers. Cousins and uncles had published collections of cases that are studied by law students to this day. Tom Chitty himself was a compulsive worker. 'When I started as a junior at the Bar,' he wrote, 'I worked from ten in the morning till 7.30 and again at home from 10 o'clock until two or 3 o'clock in the morning.' He boasted that the only exercise he took was running from case to case.

In 1887 Emily moved to Addlestone, a mile from Weybridge, and Newbolt bought a season ticket to Waterloo and became a commuter. But he never liked Addlestone. It was 'not quite in the country', in spite of the woods at the back of the house. He referred to the place as 'Addlepate'. Another powerful lady was causing an upheaval that summer. 1887 was the year of Queen Victoria's Jubilee, and the nation was celebrating her fifty years on the throne. Newbolt saw the procession enter the Abbey 'under a sky of blue and gold. Again and again we heard waves of cheering roll over the city.' To add to his joy, a few days later he was all but run over by the queen, on foot, as she left the Victoria and Albert Museum. 'I was held up by the passing out of a miniature procession, the principal figure in which was a short but dominant old lady in black, who looked, at the first glance, to be exactly what she was – the most powerful and popular of the world's rulers. She came on with a force and dignity which seemed as if it must sweep us all from her path: but to my surprise there was just room for me to survive, and she passed me as though I were invisible.'[13]

Newbolt made progress in Tom Chitty's chambers. 'I passed my examination in March 1887 [and] in May I was published a Barrister. In June I received my first briefs [and] in July I earned my first fees in Court. I had no doubt that I was on the path which would take me to the top.'[14] The time had now come for Newbolt to set up in his own chambers. He moved four doors down from Chitty to 14 Old Square, which he was to share with Rowland Whitehead, a school friend, for the next ten years.[15] Conveyancing

13. *My World*, p.156
14. *My World*, p.161
15. *My World*, p.207)

rather than pleading, in fact, took up the greater part of his time. Briefs were thin on the ground, and he joined the staff of a new series, devised by Tom Chitty and intended to rival the official Law Reports. 'On them I spent a good deal of weary time in Court with little profit. It seemed to be very seldom that a really good new case arose.' Soon he was spending more time in the courts as a reporter than as a barrister.

When the long vacation came around again, Newbolt set off for the Archipelago. By Archipelago, he meant those islands of hospitality supplied by country hostesses throughout the British Isles. The house-party reached its zenith in the nineties. A young man with the right introductions and a railway ticket could find lodging even in the most remote corners of the country. The average length of stay was a month. In Scotland Newbolt found a replacement for Beatrice Müller, who by now seems to have faded from his horizon. His Oxford friend, John Mitchell, had invited him to stay at Blairgowrie, near Perth, and here he was surrounded by members of the best Scottish families. 'The strangest of their characteristics was their massive pride in absolutely nothing. I was told that Sir John Kinloch claimed a shoemaker as his cousin.[16] The charming and lively Beatrice Burn-Murdoch did not discourage his attentions. They played tennis all day and they danced half the night. Before the end of the visit, Newbolt came to 'believe that our agreements were for life.' He was wrong, but he continued to pursue Miss Burn-Murdoch through two London seasons before giving up.

Another year he visited the Koes in Tipperary. Fred Koe was away with the marines, but his parents were at home and so was Fred's uncle, Captain Smethwick. Ireland was a dangerous place at this time. The Parnellites were in, the priests had forbidden tenants to pay their rents and the Koe shooting party had an unpleasant experience. 'From the hill above we saw men signalling vehemently to us as they ran down in our direction. "They'll have heard of your hammerless gun," said my host. They came down, out of breath and full of purpose [and] demanded to see the new gun. "The only new gun here," said my host, belongs to this gentleman. "He is a visitor to Ireland." The tension in their voices paralysed me. At last the leading hillman said energetically, "We'll not be taking it," and at the same moment put his hand out and took the gun from me. It was handled

16. *My World*, p.143

and admired, and a few minutes later given back. Few scenes have ever made a deeper impression on me.'[17]

Ireland continued to haunt Newbolt, and on 17 September 1898, he contributed a sad poem to the *Saturday Review*. The first verse ran:

'Down thy valleys, Ireland, Ireland,
Down thy valleys green and sad,
Still thy spirit wanders wailing,
Wanders wailing, wanders mad.'[18]

Not everybody liked the poem. Roger Casement considered it patronising to the Irish and parodied it:

'Up thy chimneys, England, England
Up thy chimneys black and sad
Goes thy smoke-wrapped spirit, paling
Goes pale-aleing – feeling bad'[19]

The Chiltons of Guildford were Newbolt's favourite hosts. Being childless, they devoted their ample means to making other people's grown-up children happy. Their William Morris style house, Orange Grove, stood on the boundary of Losely Park (an Elizabethan mansion now famous for yogurt production). An old-fashioned life-style was pursued within. Newbolt always remembered his first visit. 'We found Mrs Chilton, a matron of imposing bulk, sitting alone in the deepening twilight, and playing a complicated game of Patience. Conversation and game proceeded together until lights were brought, and the Revd George Chilton came in from woodcutting. The room was alive with a ghostly company of cats – in all seventeen.'[20] There was also a dachshund and an aged and exacting (not to say smelly) Scottish terrier. Every summer the Chiltons migrated to Sinai Villa high above the sea at Lynton in North Devon. There 'they maintained a continually changing party of eight or ten, who rambled, hunted, fished, made verses, sang and picnicked with an energy that made them known all over Exmoor.'[20] Eager to be involved, Newbolt rented Seawood Cottage nearby and

17. *My World*, p.148
18. *S.P.*, p.71
19. Quoted by Brian Inglis, *Life of Roger Casement* (1973), p.111
20. *My World*, p.139
20. ibid.

installed his mother and his sister. He wrote a poem about Mrs Chilton.

> 'Her ample brows were crowned with sober felt
> And useful string supplied a homely belt.
> Oft in the van, to rearward oftener placed,
> She gave the word – and all obeyed in haste.'[21]

Two summers later Harry and Milly Newbolt were to be of the official party. They joined the Krambambuli train at Woking. (Krambambuli was the name by which Mrs Chilton's tribe were known.) The Chiltons always took two compartments, one being reserved for servants and animals. When the train stopped at Yeovil, Harry's life changed.[22]

21. *My World*, p.144
22. *My World*, p.166

CHAPTER 12

Margaret

On the platform at Yeovil, waiting to join the train, was Miss Margaret Duckworth. She wore a straw hat trimmed with a lilac satin ribbon and was carrying a basket full of purple grapes. Mrs Chilton welcomed Miss Duckworth on to the train as her adopted niece. Margaret was serenely, almost coldly, deliberate in her responses. She refused luncheon, but offered her own grapes to the company. 'She seemed to be sitting in the centre of a circle, and we around her at some little distance,' wrote Milly that night. 'She's lovely, but doesn't want to be. When you speak to her you find she has left a kind message, but she is not at home.'[1]

Within two hours of their meeting Newbolt was in love with Margaret. His first letter home was light-headed: 'The air has got into our heads already, rain and sun in alternate half hours and the sea all colours at once.'[2] There was a masculine element in

1. *My World*, p.165
2. *NL* HN to EN, 31 Aug., 1887

Margaret. Her friends called her a boy in petticoats. She rode fast horses, was president of the Krambambuli Club and could walk stride for stride with any man across Exmoor. Only once did she allow herself to be assisted: when they waded across the confluence of the East and West Lyns, she hitched up her skirts and permitted Newbolt to carry her on his back. Following her out hunting was a hair-raising experience for Newbolt, who was not a keen rider of horses. 'We went tearing over the moors at a mad rough-and-tumble gallop, one minute up to our horses' knees in bog, and next tearing over sheets of heather.' Althea, the heroine of Newbolt's autobiographical novel, *The Twymans*, was based on Margaret. She was all but a boy, the twin of her utterly charming brother, 'with his upright carriage of the head, and soft auburn hair, her grey eyes were as unflinching as his, her voice had the same rich tones.'[3]

Margaret not only acted like a boy, she though like one. Science and philosophy interested her as much as music and art. She was a fine violinist. Her scientific studies had already brought her into collision with her father, the Revd Arthur Duckworth, owner of Orchardleigh, a large estate near Frome in Somerset. Her mother, a religious fanatic, imposed ever more severe restrictions. Edina Duckworth was the youngest daughter of Lord Campbell. Her piety was extreme and her children hid at her approach, to avoid being taken aside to say a little prayer. Even her husband did not escape. She was horrified when she discovered that he had been reading *Curious Crimes* on a train. She was also a little disappointed at his lack of enthusiasm for High Church ritual, and observation of eves, saints' days and fasts. Her letters were always dated by the name of a saint. On one occasion, she cut out an article by Darwin from a magazine so that Margaret should not read it. As a result, her daughter was obliged to get up early to study in secret. This habit eventually brought about a nervous breakdown through lack of sleep.

Newbolt was attracted by the boy in Margaret. In future he would address her in his letters as 'Dear Lad'. On their long walks together, he treated her like a fellow undergraduate. They talked about books and concerts and the Summer Exhibition at the Royal Academy (she was also a talented watercolourist). He told her of Clifton and Oxford, of his ambitions to succeed at the bar. But he was too shy to

3. *The Twymans*, p.203

speak of love. Nevertheless, by the time the house-party at Lynton broke up, he decided he had come to an agreement with Margaret and informed Mrs Chilton. Mrs Chilton was delighted and started up the marriage machine. She would take a letter from Newbolt to Orchardleigh to be presented to the Revd Arthur. She had little doubt that Newbolt would immediately be invited to join the house-party there. Meanwhile, he retired to the Clifton Downs Hotel and awaited a summons. It came in the form of a telegram. The Duckworths would meet him in the Pump Room at Bath and inspect him. There, Newbolt found a man in a black beard and a fur coat, the Revd Arthur himself. 'We conferred for some time on matters of [family] business and then he took me out to meet Mrs Duckworth who was shopping in the town. She also was very nice, though rather odd in her manner and appearance. Between them they encouraged me very much and invited me to go down tomorrow and stay with them.'[4] Mr Duckworth's diary of 13 October 1887 gave his version: 'Met Henry J. Newbolt at Pump Room. His means = 0. Prospect of £8,000 at his mother's death, £300 per annum allowance during her life.'[5] Meanwhile, Wollaston had received (with shouts of laughter) a letter from Mr Duckworth, asking for information about Newbolt's character. The next day a telegram arrived from Mrs Chilton. It was all off. It seemed that in these negotiations nobody had thought of consulting Margaret.

When Margaret was informed of her parents' plans for her future, she politely but firmly declined them. She had a reason for this. She was in love with someone else, her cousin Ella Coltman. Ella was a year or two older than Margaret. She was a beautiful and serious young woman, the Grisel of Walter de la Mare's novel *The Return*. He called her 'the loving friend'. Hers was 'the still, listening face', hers the 'white muslin shoulders and dark hair, the eyes that seemed to recall some far-off desolate longing for home and childhood'. Ella's passion was literature, and she could be a devastating critic of the literary attempts of her friends. Had she lived in a more enlightened age, she could have headed a university English department. Her background was similar to Margaret's: wealthy middle-class, recently promoted to the ranks of the landed gentry. Her father, Frank Coltman, was a lawyer who rented Lorbottle Hall in Northumber-

4. *NL* HN to EN, 14 October 1887
5. McG I, p.6

79

land for the grouse shooting. Her mother was the daughter of one of Wellington's generals, and had something of the Iron Duke in her. She was known as the 'Duchess'.

Margaret had spent her summer holidays at Lorbottle Hall with Ella since she was a child. As they grew older they fell in love with each other. Lorbottle was a romantic place for two romantic young people. It was built of grey stone, solid and square, standing beneath a grim rampart of basaltic cliffs. Above the cliffs were the moors 'where the rain-blown grouse were hard to bag'. On a corner of the house was a tower room where, according to Theresa Whistler, her grand-daughter, the two girls always slept. When storms rattled the windows they lay locked in each other's arms, dreaming of Porphyria's lover and the 'sullen wind' which 'tore the elm-tops down for spite'. When the sun rose the next morning they saw from their casement window, not the moors of Otterburn, but the Appenines of Browning.

Ella was a member of the Grecians, a club consisting of young women who studied Greek together. Their leader was the poet, Mary Coleridge (a great-great-niece of *the* Coleridge). They studied under William Cory, a famous classics master at Eton, who had been sacked for the usual reasons and had changed his name to Johnson. The sage lived in Hampstead (carriages to be left around the corner) and his disciples sat at his feet, construing Plato's *Phaedo*. 'It is as if Socrates were in the next room', exclaimed one follower. The wine was heady. Mary Coleridge, Ella Coltman and a third young woman, Violet Hodgkin, had all seen their brothers go away to school to study classics while they stayed at home with a governess. Now they were breaking into the men's secret world.

This brotherhood of women denied their favours to men. They regarded themselves as men and gave each other male names: Ella was Fidus Achates, Virgil's loyal bearer of weapons. Mary Coleridge was the leader of the Grecians, and was in love with each of them in turn. Her fiercely sensuous love poetry was invariably addressed to women, young and faithless:

> 'Her yellow hair is soft, and her soft eyes
> Are as the doves for meekness. Only feel
> The softness of the hand in mine that lies!
> The sheath is velvet but the sword is steel'[6]

6. Mary Coleridge, from 'Beware!' *Collected Poems* (1954), p.161

Violet Hodgkin was barely seventeen – 'warm, impulsive, gay' – when Mary met her. Violet's defection to a husband, John Holdsworth, caused Mary intense pain and resulted in a haiku.

> 'Ah no!
> When from thine arms, not from thy heart I go,
> May there be no book wherein to read
> The rapture of my soul, her bitter need!'[7]

It was Ella Coltman who had introduced Mary Coleridge to the Duckworth girls. Mary immediately fell in love with *two* of them: Margaret, 'the dearest of all'[8] and pretty Helen, her younger sister. Mary had a considerable glamour for Margaret. She had met Browning, that is to say, she had peeped at him from behind the piano. Her father, Arthur Coleridge, frequently received famous people in his drawing room at 12 Cromwell Place in South Kensington.

Newbolt now had to begin his courtship all over again, this time by letter. Mr Duckworth recorded Newbolt's letters in his diary:

Oct 17: HN replies to Margaret in a touching manner, and she stays away from dinner.

Oct 19: Miss Milly Newbolt suggests that Margaret is so young, may she not relent?

Nov 4: Margaret is firm. HN must wait in order to win.

Dec 5: HN quite understands he has no chance now.[9]

When the Duckworths opened their house in Bryanston Square the following Easter, Newbolt hastened to call on them. Mr Duckworth wrote: 'Met H. Newbolt near our door – come to fetch the MSS of the Krambambuli Club! He looks wretchedly thin and is lame (he had been injured in a football match)'. Duckworth encouraged Newbolt to call and he immediately responded. 'I lunched, I dined, I attended evening parties. The house seemed to be full of a great number of people, all related to one another, and I felt like a foreigner.'[10]

One of the people Newbolt met at Bryanston Square was Ella

7. ibid., 'Ah No!' p.253
8. ibid.p.45
9. McG I
10. *My World,* p.70

Coltman, Margaret's bosom friend. He was aware that his future depended on her. Margaret would only accept him if Ella was intimately included in their married life. Fortunately, he was charmed by the serious young woman in the ornate Renaissance gown. She in turn admitted that he was worthy of her friend. He came to an understanding with Margaret a month later, when a friend arranged for him and Margaret to be included in a group attending an Oxford ball. 'We danced, and I went to my room at sparrow-chirp with a feeling that my plans for the autumn were no longer so indefinite.'[11] Mr Duckworth was displeased by the informality of the arrangement: 'Like a servant, she has a follower but is not engaged. I advised complete separation for a year.'[12] Now he had doubts about Newbolt's character. Newbolt was said to have 'such a quick temper that he was advised to prefer Chancery to Common Law.' Even poor Milly came in for disapproval: 'rather provincial, like a bullfinch.' But always it came back to money. The young man had made only £30 since October. He was so desperate that he was prepared to 'fall back on teaching if the worst came to the worst.'

It was August again before Margaret was once more waiting on the platform at Yeovil. As before, the dogs, cats and maids descended from the train at Lynton and went in procession to Mount Sinai. But now everything had changed. Harry and Margaret met in the hall early the next morning. 'We went out to the rocks overhanging the sea near the Castle Rock and never thought of coming to breakfast.'[13] They were engaged! Within two hours Newbolt had written to Emily: 'a year all but eight days since we met! It seems like ten years, and yet I could believe that we had never left Lynton at all'.[14] Five days later he added 'we are happier and happier' Milly gave a slightly different picture: 'Harry has not yet reached the stage of placid enjoyment which I was looking forward to for him. He is still at concert pitch, harmonies and discords follow like patches of sun on an April day. He's always sweet and contented with Margaret. Mrs Clinton feels she has lost him,and he never seems to want anything she can do. It is a rather sudden descent and she feels it.'[15]

11. *My World*, p.172
12. McG II, p.8
13. *My World*, p.172
14. *NL* HN to EN 22 Aug. 1888
15. *NL* MN to EN, 1888

CHAPTER 13

Orchardleigh

A visit to Orchardleigh for Newbolt was at last in order. Now he saw Margaret the countrywoman in her natural setting. Her home was a great house perched on the side of a valley. An avenue of elms commenced at the side of it, and down this Margaret cantered every morning on her favourite hunter, raising a spray of dew. Behind her followed some rather undisciplined dogs. Margaret loved Orchardleigh as one can only love a childhood home. According to Newbolt, she was 'filled with devotion to the soil of her birthplace and would as soon kill a friend as change the name of the smallest of its fields.'[1] Now she could show Newbolt the secret places in the woods and the unknown lake-islands. Together the lovers spent long days, 'sometimes riding through the greenest and most peaceful country that the world contains, sometimes floating on a sheet of smoothest gold enamelled with a million

1. *The Old Country*, p 20

water lilies.'[2] In a letter to Emily, he described swimming alone early in the morning 'as Adam had swam. Glassy water, kingfishers, trees full of blue mist, sunlight on everything and silence everywhere.'

At Orchardleigh, Newbolt was haunted by a sense of the past. It seemed to him that the place was still inhabited by people who had lived there hundreds of years ago: 'Are there no voices but ours in these old mossy woods and sunlit gardens, no steps but ours by this lake?'[3] Later he was to write a novel, *The Old Country*, about the owners of Orchardleigh (renamed Gardenleigh) in the Middle Ages. Aubrey, the androgynously named heroine, was a version of Margaret.

The actual house at Orchardleigh was brand new. The old house had stood by the lake. The new one had been built by Margaret's grandfather, William Duckworth, a Manchester lawyer, 'rock jawed and iron-headed',[4] who had made a fortune in conveyancing by discovering the slightest flaws in title deeds. He had employed the architect Thomas Henry Wyatt (famous for elaborate lunatic asylums), to design the great stone double-gabled mansion. Wyatt had provided the building with the latest in technology. It had a fireproof frame of wrought-iron girders 'tested by hydraulic pressure at the Butterley Works', not to mention hot water pipes throughout and *en suite* bathrooms. The Duckworths were unanimous in their condemnation of the old house by the lake. Mr Duckworth called it a 'hideous tumbledown' in his diary. 'It was ruinous and costly – a patchwork of inconveniences, with its narrow fourteenth-century yard [and] a great Queen Anne front out of all proportion. Frogs were traditionally reported to have come in troops to serenade the drawing room windows'[5] It was, of course, the old house that Newbolt resurrected in *The Old Country*.

Shooting was the chief occupation of the house-party, and Newbolt delighted in the wildfowl. As the days shortened, the returning mallards, coots and pochard enlivened the scene and furrowed the water of the smaller lakes, 'hardly visible through the leaves of the trees that overhung them.' [6] Although partridges were

2. *The Old Country*, p61
3. *The Old Country*, p.20
4. *The Old Country*, p.8
5. *The Old Country*, p.122
6. *The Old Country*, p7

not plentiful that year, Newbolt bagged two and a half brace.[7] (That is to say, more than Campbell Duckworth, Margaret's brother.) The party were out seven hours that day, 'our first long separation!' Margaret had been left at home to write letters. Unfortunately, she was rather tired. There were so many relations to be written to, and anyone who was not informed of the engagement might be offended for life. 'I am scrawling this in the schoolroom,' Newbolt told Emily 'where M. is asleep – a picture of loveliness – on the sofa.'[8] One day, Frank came over from Bath. Milly also stayed, and there was an embarrassing visit from Aunt Eliza Jane Gordon. Her husband had given up the living at Lichfield and they had settled regrettably close to Orchardleigh. Three of their twelve children were still in the schoolroom. They arrived in an old pony carriage at the wrong time of day 'and stayed a fearful time'.[9]

On the whole, Newbolt got on well with Mr Duckworth, an old Etonian. He had trained as a clergyman and had even held a living until his brother was killed in the Crimean War. He then moved effortlessly into the role of squire, entertaining lavishly. He was at his best at the head of his table. Newbolt described his 'frank and almost boyish manner' as he told the amusing (but never improper) stories that he carefully recorded in his diary for such occasions. After dinner as many as four varieties of port might be handed round. Sometime, these feasts had dire consequences for Newbolt. On the morning after one, he wrote to Ella in a low state; 'I ate all the wrong things for dinner last night and stayed up too late playing billiards'.[10] Nevertheless, he considered that Duckworth was a true heir of the ancient family of Champney, that had held Orchardleigh for many generations. Like them 'he had drained and sown, administered the king's peace, and handed on the place unimpaired.'[11]

But, there was a skeleton in the family cupboard that Newbolt does not mention. Theresa Whistler possesses a photograph of Margaret and her sisters as young women, all dressed in black with white frills round their necks. With them are two boys. The taller

7. *NL* HN to EN, 3 Sept. 1887
8. *NL* HN to EN, 1 Sept. 1888
9. *NL* HN to EN, 1 Sept. 1888
10. HN to EC, 18 Sept, 1890, Private Collection
11. *The Old Country*, p.20

is Campbell, the heir. But who is the younger? He is Herbert who, according to Theresa Whistler, contracted syphilis from one of the maids as a boy, and was locked away in a bedroom. Peter Newbolt disputes this, insisting that Herbert was not ostracised, but admits that he led the secluded life of an invalid, first, at Orchardleigh and later at Chiswick, where he died in 1918. He was said to be Margaret's favourite brother.

It was now Margaret's turn to visit Newbolt's mother. He was chiefly worried about the food. Stodgy roasts would not suit Margaret, and he himself was too much in love to eat much anyway. 'May I suggest that we should have always fish for dinner and *never* soup which M. does not take? Oh! I can hear you and Milly howling with laughter. Still let's be brave and also propose an unusually large supply of vegetables and fruit to which I am becoming greatly addicted.[12] The visit seems to have gone well. 'Mrs Newbolt does not come down till after breakfast,' Margaret wrote to her mother, 'so we four have it alone together. You can't think what a happy quartette we are. Frank and Milly are tremendous allies always together. It amused me very much, seeing old photos of Harry and hearing stories about his childhood from Mrs N. She has given me such a pretty old-fashioned brooch which belonged to Harry's great-grandmother. After dinner Mrs N. played some accompaniments. Then I watched Frank preparing a plate for his etching.'[13]

Mr Duckworth believed in short engagements and Harry had only one more year to wait. In the meanwhile, Frank's wedding to Professor Bright's daughter took place in November, and Milly was married to Tom Chitty in December. 'The children had outrun me again!' declared Newbolt.[14] In the spring of 1889 the couple set about house-hunting. They had their eye on South Kensington, which was cheaper than Mayfair, and had become quite fashionable since the extension of the Metropolitan Line to Gloucester Road. Also it was 'in the centre of all our friends'. It was Julia Stephen, the mother of Virginia Woolf and the original of 'Mrs Ramsay' in *To the Lighthouse*, who eventually found them a house. She 'carried us off on a tour of inspection among streets

12. *NL* HN to EN, 9 Sept. 1888
13. *NL* MEN to ED, 21 Sept. 1888
14. *My World*, p.173

that we had not thought of before, and by evening we were persuaded that 14 Victoria Road was the one spot in all London where we could live and flourish.'[15] Victoria Road, with its low stuccoed villas, is one of the prettiest streets in London. At first sight, the 'bright, quiet road' appeared like an avenue, so low were the houses and so abundant the trees. To add to its rustic charm, it was closed at one end and debouched upon Kensington Gardens at the other. 'It is not a thoroughfare to anywhere,' Newbolt told his mother.[16] The house stood on the west side of Victoria Road (the number has now been changed to 53). There were steps leading up to the front door, thus allowing the servants a semi-basement and the family French windows on to the garden at the back. There were three bedrooms on the upper floor. Emily was now invited to 'help make this doll's house pretty and comfortable enough for anyone – even the Princess.' (Margaret was the princess.) Emily did little to help and the home was not ready by the wedding day.

On the fifteenth of August, Harry and Margaret were married in the island church of Orchardleigh. It is said that there were a hundred and twenty people in the little chapel. Old Mrs Wren, widow of a head groom, was perched in the pulpit. Owing to nerves, Newbolt's memories of the ceremony were sketchy, but others kept a record. Mr Duckworth conducted the ceremony 'and advised Margaret to be meek, gentle, and cheerful.'[17] Emily was delighted with 'the longed and dreaded wedding'.[18] Margaret had come to her 'so lovingly before Church. I could not be sorrowful while you are so glad,' she told Harry. Afterwards,45 people sat round the luncheon table at Orchardleigh and 300 tenants had tea in a tent.[19] Newbolt ate little. He had been suffering from indigestion for some weeks. He and Margaret left for their honeymoon in a shower of rice to spend the first night of their married life in a quaint old cottage at Beaminster in Dorset. Ten years later, Margaret wrote, 'There still comes back to me the naturalness of our wedding night.'[20]

15. *My World*, p.177
16. *NL* HN to EN, 24 June 1889
17. McG I, p.8
18. *NL* EN to HN, 18 Aug. 1889
19. McG I, p.10
20. *NL* MEN to HN, 23 May 1908

That wedding night was in fact not the most natural imaginable. There was in effect a second woman in the bed: Ella. She was eagerly awaiting news in her London home. Newbolt had promised to include her in his marriage and he was true to his word. He wrote her a letter describing his sensations on waking beside Margaret on the first morning of the honeymoon, sensations Ella herself had so often experienced. 'She woke me with the light of a peculiarly bright eye just like a robin's before it pecks.[21]

21. HN to EC, Aug. 1889. Private Collection

CHAPTER 14

Celia

The Newbolts eventually moved into 14 Victoria Road on 7 November 1889 before it was ready, Margaret's passion for home-making being but luke-warm. They discovered that 'even a doll's house cannot be decorated and furnished in a few days'.[1] Margaret and Ella dreamed up colour schemes of the most tasteful kind: blue and green for the upper floor, terracotta for the ground and a yellow patterned paper for the drawing room, but there was no furniture. Finally, the couple moved into two small upstairs rooms, where they hung Newbolt's 'Praying Hands' by Dürer.

Entertaining was difficult in such conditions. Newbolt told his mother; 'We have only two tablespoons. Our soup is served out of a muffin dish.'[2] When the Duckworths invited themselves to lunch, the young homemakers panicked. 'I remember rushing out to

1. *My World*, p.177
2. *NL* HN to EN, Nov. 1889

Tottenham Court Road and coming back just in time with two wrought-iron fenders in a cab.[3]

Margaret objected to the role of lady of the house, with its endless chit-chat and cups of tea. 'We *yielded* to the conventionalities of tea,' she confessed to Ella on one occasion. And she could not escape being called upon. 'We've had a batch today. A couple of barristers' wives, then a cousin of Mrs Duckworth.' Worse still, these calls had to be returned. There was a Mrs O'Brien, who Margaret had hoped would be entertaining. 'Mary [Coleridge] had told me she was Sappho. She was not. It was furnishing again.'[4] Dining out could be penitential too, as Newbolt recalled. 'Margaret sat next to Mr Milman who looked like a frightened funeral horse and muttered dismally into her deaf ear.'

Household duties were beneath contempt, although on the first morning in the new house Margaret did go round to the Welsh dairy with a jug. This was recorded in the diary she kept for her sister, Helen. Beautiful and beloved Helen, who must not feel excluded from the marriage any more than Ella. Margaret scorned even to mend Newbolt's clothes. He confided to Ella 'She sewed on two buttons for me last night and mended a jaeger. Not a word to anyone!'[6] Normally he darned his own socks in front of an audience of Grecians, for they dropped in continually.

Ella was of course virtually a member of the household. Margaret spent every weekday at the Coltman mansion, where she could read poetry and study Greek without fear of interruption. Sometimes there were lover's tiffs between the two women. After one of these Margaret wrote of Ella. 'She would not allow that I had causes for deep discontent. I came crestfallen home for the first time under this roof, to unwrap my fiddle and tune him up.'[7] In spite of such interruptions, Ella spent most of her evenings with the Newbolts . On one occasion the two ladies endured a new board game called Hoppety. Margaret described Ella 'in that exquisite tea gown. I'm afraid she was dreadfully bored. She said it was the kind of game she hated but her arm round my neck was a support.'[8]

3. *My World*, p.171
4. MEN to EC, 27 Nov. 1889. Private Collection
5. HN to EC, Nov. 1891. Private Collection
6. ibid., 29 Aug. 1889
7. Margaret's Diary for Helen, 27 Nov. 1889
8. ibid., 26 Nov. 1889

Ella may have spent the evening entwined with Margaret on a sofa, but it was she who had to take a hansom cab home at the end of the evening. In spite of all Newbolt's efforts, she felt that she was the unwanted third party and told him so. He teasingly assured her that indeed she was. 'There is nothing worse than young married people pursued by the ghost of a pre-marital friendship. Didn't Canning write, "Save oh save us from a spinster friend"?'[9] In the end Newbolt found a simple solution to the problem: he made Ella his mistress. But the process took time. Two years after the marriage, Ella started to send letters of an intimate nature to Newbolt's chambers. The tone of these letters, in spite of the grey paper on which they were written, became increasingly warm. In reply to one, Newbolt wrote 'Oh my dearest Ella, it is so romantic to see your little grey envelope among the dusty briefs.'[10]

The exact moment at which Newbolt became Ella's lover is not known. It is certain that she began to spend nights at 14 Victoria Road about this time, and that Margaret knew of the arrangement. (Matters were simplified by the fact that she and Newbolt had separate bedrooms.) Neither woman appeared jealous of the other, perhaps because their lover was careful to divide his favours equally. Among Newbolt's papers there is an account sheet covered with neat columns of figures. They represent the number of times he slept with each of his women each month between 1904 and 1917, averaging as much as twelve per head per month.

Celia Newbolt was born exactly nine months after the marriage of her parents. 'An enormous child,' her proud father declared. He was delighted to see that she had not inherited his mouth, which he considered too small. He adored her from the first day of her life, and gladly endured the discomforts that a baby in the house involved, including Mrs Lee the midwife and Ada, the child's nurse, both in residence. Margaret was automatically confined to bed for three weeks. When she finally emerged, she was distracted by motherhood. 'We are *both* fully occupied with our professions,' she firmly declared.[11]

Celia quickly became a person for Newbolt, and, of the 300 letters he wrote to Emily over the next five years, only a few omitted a mention of her.

9. HN to EC, 23 July 1890. Private Collection
10. HN to EC, 2 Nov, 1891. Private Collection
11. *NL* MEN to HN, 7 June 1890

One Month: 'Succeeded in wriggling out of the arm chair, so fell with a flop and a bump on the floor.'

Two Months: 'Smiles when I whistle the overture to "Tannhäusser".

Six Months: 'Stood up yesterday holding on to a chair.' 'Stretched her arms to the (Christmas) tree to embrace all the lights and toys at once.'

Ten months: 'Fell into the tin bath in the dressing room. I rescued a little thing like a drowning Skye terrier in a Jaeger nightgown.'

One year: Shouted Dad-dad-dad.'

Eighteen months: 'Learnt to curtsey.'

Two years: 'Understands everything I say before I say it.'

Part of Celia's charm for Newbolt was that she was another Margaret, but a more approachable one. She was even named Margaret Cecilia. 'You cannot expect a father to be otherwise than pleased at the thought of seeing his wife's childhood reproduced before his eyes, and so make her acquaintance as it were, at an age when he never knew her.[12] In the mornings, before Newbolt went to work, Celia ran between her parents' bedrooms, saying, 'ta-ta!'[13] At night she brought him her box of bricks. 'I build castles and she knocks them down.'[14] When tired of that, she insisted on his drawing pictures for her. '"Draw Minou!" is so invariable that I've had to get M. to teach me how to draw a cat's head!'[15] His cup was full when Celia invented a name for him: 'Dear Old Man'.

Ella joined in the adoration of Celia. She had sacrificed her own hopes of motherhood, so she felt entitled to a share in Newbolt's child, and became the much-loved aunt who could be relied upon to read aloud a fairy-tale from one of the Andrew Lang coloured fairy books. The third member of the Grecians, Mary Coleridge, was equally devoted. She watched the wonder of life unfolding in the child of her Prince Otto (her name for Newbolt). Several of her poems were about Celia, 'the flower that sings.'[16] She was appalled when the flower was obliged to join a gymnastics class. 'Why,' she wailed, 'am I forced to behold 26 lovely children squatting like toads and swarming up ropes like cabin boys?'[17] Fortunately, Celia was also

12. *NL* HN to EN, 27 May 1890
13. *NL* HN to EN, 5 Nov. 1891
14. *NL* HN to EN, 5 July 1891
15. *NL* HN to EN, 17 Nov. 1891
16. *Collected Poems*, p.228
17. *Gathered Leaves*, p.258

attending dancing classes. 'She dances as she goes, all day long,' Newbolt wrote.[18] Margaret could not resist dressing her up, but not excessively. For a visit to Aunt Milly, she resembled 'a quaint little Dutch child', in charming contrast to overdressed Dido, who looked like 'a smart French ladykin.'[19]

There was another woman who felt she had a right to a share in Celia: Emily. She was not to have it. Celia was always taken to Orchardleigh for Christmas. Emily never went. Newbolt tried to include her, at least in spirit: 'You would like the old-fashioned Xmas feeling of it all: the piles of clothing for the poor, the entertainments in the school, the decorations in the churches.[20] It was to no avail; Emily felt that she had been ousted by Margaret. 'Divide me with Margaret,' Newbolt pleaded. 'The past is yours, the future is hers and the present you share between you.[21] Margaret attempted to placate 'Dear Little Mother' with letters, but hers tended to be short and lacking in enthusiasm. There were constant misunderstandings that Newbolt had to patch up. Celia became a cause of conflict. Margaret kept forgetting to thank Emily for presents for the child and then attempting to compensate with excessive gratitude. 'Baby admires her pink socks *immensely*.'[22] Emily would not even spend the night of Celia's baptism at Victoria Road.

18. *NL* HN to EN, Apr. 1893
19. *NL* HN to EN, 8 Feb. 1892
20. *NL* HN to EN, 23 Dec. 1890, letter (2)
21. *NL* HN to EN, 22 Dec. 1890
22. *NL* MEN to EN, 29 Oct. 1890

CHAPTER 15

The Settee

The Settee was a new name for the Grecians. The intention of its members, Margaret, Mary and Ella, was to indulge in 'book talk' on Thursday afternoons. Mary Coleridge's father gave it the name because it sat and sat, '*sedet eternumque sedebit*'.[1] Ladies were supposed to sit and *do* something in those days. These ladies just sat. Newbolt, being in chambers on Thursday afternoons, was not a regular attender. 'A love of literature was generally considered by the Profession to imply infidelity to the Law: but my scruples were removed by a lucky accident. I had allowed myself one dull afternoon to turn into a theatre in the Strand for a matinee and was dismayed on coming out to find myself close to a QC whose good opinion I wished to keep. I made as neat an excuse as I could but he quickly interrupted me and said that he was 'glad to see I could enjoy a good play as well as a dull case.' On the strength of this,

1. *My World*, p.179

Newbolt henceforth earmarked his Thursday afternoons for home entertainment.

The emphasis of the Settee changed from reading to writing when Newbolt read two of his poems aloud to Margaret, Mary and Ella. Then Mary read seven of hers that he admitted 'far excelled' his two. He at once consigned his own to 'a life of complete retirement' and settled down to writing a historical thriller with Mary. Each contributed a chapter in turn and read it aloud to Margaret and Ella. The novel, entitled *A Debt of Honour*, was not very good. It was eventually submitted to Cassell who offered to include it in their 'cheap department'.[2] The offer was proudly refused.

Newbolt now set about writing *Taken from the Enemy*, another historical thriller, this time alone. But there was another female assistant in the wings: Ella. Ella did not write. She read. She was developing her formidable powers as a literary critic as she approached her thirties. In April 1892, Newbolt handed her the complete manuscript. She demolished it. That is to say, she made a large number of suggestions. 'After 13 days' incessant writing,[3] the book had been revised. Newbolt sent it to Cassell once more. This time they turned it down flat. At 218 pages it was too short. Eventually, it was taken by Chatto for their Handy Books Series. (As cheap a department as ever there was.) By the end of 1892 Newbolt was a published author.

Taken from the Enemy was a tale about an attempt to rescue Napoleon from St Helena by submarine. Newbolt did not deny that he was strongly under the influence of Robert Louis Stevenson when he wrote it. 'Stevenson was then in the heyday of his reputation. The introspective novel was "out" and the story of adventure was "in".'[4] He posted the book to Stevenson, by now near to death in Samoa. Stevenson's letter gave complete satisfaction. 'I had taken up novel after novel and flung them away again with curses. Now, last night, being very tired and rather dull, I took up your story after dinner and finished it before I slept, with real amusement.' Stevenson made only one criticism: 'The note of ambiguity and deceit which broods over the whole story should have been more immediately and strongly struck.'[5] Perhaps just as

2. *NL* HN to EN, 10 Feb. 1892
3. *NL* HN to EN, 6 May 1892
4. *My World*, p.178
5. *Taken from the Enemy*, p.vii)

satisfactory to Newbolt was a letter from Mr Duckworth. He had been reading the 'handy novelette' late at night (and probably under the bedcovers). 'I took it up at 11.30 p.m. and could not put it down till I had finished it – I like both hero and heroine, and the death of Napoleon comes as a most opportune surprise. 29 pheasants, 18 hares, 112 rabbits today.'[6] The book was popular with the public too. 21,000 copies were sold in a year.

To complete Newbolt's happiness, Francis was born on 3 March 1893, the son that he had longed for. Rather surprisingly, it was agreed that he should be designated 'Ella's child'.[7] Margaret already had Celia, it was only fair that Ella should have Francis. At first, it looked as if Ella had the worst of the bargain. Everything went wrong with Francis. Cow's milk made him ill. Vaccination reduced him to a skeleton. He cried continually. Two years later, Newbolt was still hoping he would 'take a more reasonable view of life.'[8] At Orchardleigh, the three-year-old Celia was again the Christmas queen, and the 'Celian sayings' became even more amusing. Indeed, they formed the staple entertainment of the household on non-shooting days. To her mother, who had enquired, 'May I not enjoy myself occasionally?' Celia said, 'No. I want you to enjoy me!' She was a good mimic and could say, 'Oh nonsense!' just the way Papa said it. A few years later, at the age of six, she was the belle of the Orchardleigh Christmas children's party: 'Celia and Francis both appeared in white, but under very different aspects. Francis wore a white blouse and kilted skirt which made him look quite as solid as usual. He declined tea with the crowd downstairs and decided to have it with Lorimer [his nursemaid] in the nursery. Celia was in her Liberty silk dress and danced and floated about like a white butterfly: 'I was honoured with a dance with her, but she was so light that I could hardly keep her on the ground at all: she nearly floated me off once or twice,'[9] Newbolt's poem, 'Imogen: A Lady of Tender Age', perfectly describes a child dancing, although in this case the child was Imogen Booth, a friend of Celia's.

6. *NL* WAD to HN, 10 Nov. 1892
7. Interview with Theresa Whistler
8. *NL* HN to EN, 28 Oct.1895
9. 5 Jan.1896

Ladies, where were your bright eyes glancing,
    Where were they glancing yesternight?
Saw ye Imogen dancing, dancing,
    Imogen dancing all in white?
Laughed she not with pure delight,
    Laughed she not with a joy serene,
Stepped she not with a grace entrancing,
    Slenderly girt in silken sheen?'[10]

The Newbolts continued to spend their summers making a progress round their wealthier friends, but the children were rather an impediment. Even Mrs Chilton drew the line at babies in the house, 'tho' she lets dogs in the most advanced stages of decay live on the drawing room furniture'.[11] The solution was to leave the children with one or other of their grandmothers. Thus were the Newbolts able to be guests at nine houses in the summer of 1891. The greatest of these was Lorbottle Hall, Ella's home in Northumberland.

Newbolt was fascinated by the history of Lorbottle. It was in the domain of Callaly Castle, high in the Cheviots where every neighbouring hilltop bore a castle with a name resonant of border battles: Flodden, Otterburn, Chevy Chase. Rob Roy had fought here. 'The North came to be, for us, a place apart, just as the west had been ten years before, a country full of magic, with a mist of antiquity over moors and shores and towers.'[12] The character of the men of Northumberland was 'larger and bolder' than that of the men of the South.[13] One of the best was Ella's father, Frank Coltman. He quickly became one of Newbolt's father-substitutes. 'I have always felt that during the first half of his life a man needs the companionship with the paternal generation as naturally as he needs vitamins in his food. I am deeply grateful to those who supplied this need of mine.'[14] Coltman was a gentleman scholar, but happiest in 'the gay fellowship' of cricketers. He fielded his own eleven, who yearly did battle with the latest crop of Oxbridge undergraduates. Among them was Percival's son, Lancelot. Mr

10. S.P., p.68
11. NL HN to EN, 5 Nov. 1890
12. My World, p.226
13. My World, p.225
14. My World, p.225

Coltman himself occasionally played. His old-fashioned style of batting was admired for its 'stonewall determination' and his modest score was sure to be described in the local newspapers as a 'useful contribution at a critical point of the game'.[15]

A holiday abroad was achieved the following year, but for Newbolt only. It was financed by Tom Chitty who, at the age of forty, was showing alarming symptoms. His doctor had threatened him with an early death if he did not stop work and exert himself for a while on a Swiss mountain. The September holiday at Pontressina in the Engadine was a success, in spite of the fact that the hall porter steamed all the stamps off outgoing letters. Newbolt was tireless in exhorting Tom to exert himself. They never walked less than ten miles a day, and by the end of the holiday Tom looked 'like a prize fighter' and Newbolt's own muscles were 'as tight as whipcord. We kept ourselves warm in the evenings by playing hide-and-seek all over the hotel. On wet mornings "small" cricket was a great resort. We only broke one window'.[16] Relations between Newbolt and his brother-in-law were, for once, excellent. 'He's a wonderfully good-tempered and unselfish companion. He never thought twice about any bit of expenditure and was very tactful in keeping out of sight the fact that he was paying for both.'[17]

In the summer of 1894, Ella proposed to lead the Newbolts over the Alps into Italy. Italy was Ella's department. Her room at home was hung with black and white reproductions of Madonnas brought back from Florence, and she read Dante in the original. (Under her influence, Newbolt learned enough Italian to translate the stanza about dreams from the *Divina Commedia*.)[18] On the way to Lake Como the party stopped by chance at Soglio, a Swiss Alpine village with an Italian Renaissance palace in the middle. The Palace, built by the de Salis family, had been converted into a hotel (it still is one today) but for Newbolt it was the palazzo of the counts who built it centuries ago. The family coat of arms (a willow tree above a river) was carved over the entrance arch. There was a great panelled hall at the core of the building with galleries running round it. Armour hung from the walls and a fire burned

15. ibid.
16. *NL* HN to EN, 12 Sept. 1892
17. *NL* HN to EN, 18 Sept. 1892
18. SP, p.140

day and night, spreading a faint smell of woodsmoke. The finest bedroom on the first floor had been reserved for the English party; 'a beautiful double room in rich dark wood, looking into an old courtyard.'[19] A carved four-poster had been placed where its occupants could look across the courtyard. The occupants of this bed were to be Ella and Margaret. Newbolt had to make do with a valet's room not much larger than a wooden box on the floor above. He did not complain. He told Emily, 'There is a deep embrasure where you can sit and look into the garden of cut yew hedges.'[20] Two nights were all that he spent in this paradise, but Soglio was never forgotten. In *The Twymans*, he used it as the setting for his courtship of Margaret.

Newbolt was now putting the finishing touches to *Mordred*, a five-act play in blank verse about King Arthur's bastard son, and Newbolt's first published poetical work. It came out in a limited edition with Fisher Unwin in 1895. The number of people today who have read *Mordred* would probably not fill a room. The book is anyway almost unobtainable. In it, Newbolt returned once more to the world of Camelot. But his landscape was not that of Tennyson lit by 'a light that never was on sea or land' but the darker one of Malory, and his Arthur was not a 'blameless king' but an incestuous adulterer. A new edition of Malory's *Le Morte d'Arthur*, had just been brought out and Newbolt chose to base his play on the last four of Malory's 21 sections, the bloodiest and the bawdiest. They treat of the treachery of Sir Mordred, the child of Arthur's sister Morgan Le Fay. Mordred blackmails Arthur by threatening to reveal the secret of his birth and forces him to condone the adultery of his Queen Guinevere with Lancelot. At last Mordred takes up arms against his father. Arthur kills Mordred, while at the same moment Mordred inflicts on him a mortal wound. In his treatment of the subject, Newbolt was more successful with the carnage than with the adultery. The death of the Green Knight was graphically described:

> 'Cut off from rescue: like a lonely rock,
> Now bare, now hidden by the swinging seas
> We marked his crest awhile; then with a roar
> The full tide seathing above him.'[21]

19. *NL* HN to EN,14 Sept.1894
20. ibid.
21. *Mordred*, p.117

The critics were 'short and severe'.[22] Tennyson's admirers considered Newbolt's plot treason. Old Canon Dixon, the poet, was kinder. He wrote to Newbolt, praising him for the versification which he described as 'remarkably free and good', but commented that his phrases were not 'fresh and curious'. The well-known critic William Archer was also kind. In *Poets of the Younger Generation* (1902), he declared that the play had 'real dramatic feeling'. In the battle scene he detected echoes of Scott's *Marmion*. Newbolt himself never ceased to believe in *Mordred* and even approached Beerbohm Tree with a view to staging it at the Haymarket.

Meanwhile, Mary Coleridge had completed a second historical novel, *The King with Two Faces* (1897) based on the assassination of Gustavus III. As usual, Mary identified closely with the hero, a young aristocrat. Newbolt found her a publisher and revelled in the book's success. 'Her doddering Papa skips like a unicorn,' declared Arthur Coleridge.[23] and Newbolt himself 'ran round London bellowing.'[24] 'She is the new George Eliot,' he told Emily. 'And in fifty years' no-one will think that a compliment to Mary Coleridge.'

The Settee had now acted as midwife to four books, but it had one last task to perform. It set about securing Marconi's recognition as the inventor of the wireless. The young Guglielmo Marconi, a cousin of Mary's, had just arrived from Bologna with the oscillating aerial. 'At one of our Thursday meetings, early in 1896,' writes Newbolt, 'Mary presented to me the draft of an agreement by which he was to assign all his rights to a firm whose name I no longer remember. What struck me at once was the fact that he was to be remunerated only by a number of shares in the company. I had not spent ten years at the bar without learning that a company may be wound up.'[25] The Settee put Marconi in touch with Preece at the Post Office. The rest is history.

22. *My World*, p.189
23. *NL*, 7 Jan.1897
24. *NL* HN to EN, 1 Dec.1897
25. *My World*, p.181

PART V DRAKE'S DRUM 1896–1899

CHAPTER 16

Drake's Drum

An event that brought unknown reserves of salt water in Newbolt's veins to the boil occurred on 23 June 1893. Vice-Admiral Tryon went to the bottom on the bridge of his ship. There was no war on at the time. It happened during fleet manoeuvres in the Mediterranean. Tryon and his rival, Admiral Markham, were steaming parallel to each other off the coast of Syria, each admiral at the head of a column of 'ironclads', when Tryon gave the order for the leading ships of both columns to turn towards each other and return the way they had come. Unfortunately there was not space for this manoeuvre and Tryon took the full force of Markham on his starboard bow. His ship dived instantly to the bottom, her boilers exploded and hundreds were drowned. Why Tryon gave the order will never be known. Newbolt nevertheless eulogised the fat and balding admiral. He compared him to Nelson who would not cover up his admiral's stars, to Gordon who had faced the enemy alone at Khartoum, to Philip Sidney dying of thirst. None was so truly gigantic in simplicity of outline as Tryon on the bridge, giving the coxswain back his lifebelt and going down alone, an inch at a time.'

'Admiral's All' was the first of Newbolt's nautical ballads. It began:

> 'Effingham, Grenville, Raleigh, Drake,
> Here's to the bold and free!
> Benbow, Collingwood, Byron, Blake,
> Hail to the Kings of the Sea!'[1]

Each of the eight-line verses praised a different admiral, and the chorus invoked 'Nelson's famous name'. Newbolt sent it to Andrew Lang for his monthly column in *Longman's Magazine*. When the next month's number came out there was a typical note by Lang to the effect that he had received a poem about an admiral, but had lost it while fishing and forgotten the name of the author. Newbolt repaired these losses, and received in return a letter proposing to hand the verses to Charles Longman for 'the main body of the Magazine.' 'This introduction was a gift of real value to me; the Longman firm published in after years at least ten volumes of mine, and both Charles Longman and his nephew Robert became my intimate friends.'[2] Newbolt's relationship with Lang was to prove less happy. Lang is now remembered only for his collections of fairy stories. In fact the tireless Scot was active in many literary fields. Newbolt was to meet him at Corby Castle near Carlisle. 'A. L. is v. odd,' he confided to Emily. 'Margaret can't stand him for he never takes the trouble to speak to her.'[3]

Newbolt's admirals sailed into a sea of critical and popular acclaim. 'I hope Margaret told you about my song having been set to music by Dr Gray,' he wrote to Emily, 'and of his proposal to get Plunkett Greene to sing it.[4] (Plunkett Greene was of course an Old Cliftonian). Meanwhile, a live admiral, Sir Geoffrey Hornby, had sent the ballad to another songwriter, Michael Maybrick. Newbolt's

1. *S.P.*, p.31
2. *My World*, p.185
3. *NL* HN to EN, 19 Aug. 1895
4. *NL* HN to EN, 13 Aug. 1894

102

cup was full. 'This is the highest point I have ever reached.'[5] A second sea ballad, 'San Stefano', set in the Napoleonic period, appeared in *Longman's* three months later. It told of Sir Peter Parker of the *Menelaus* who destroyed a French brig moored off the Tuscan coast. The climax came in the fourth verse:

'When the summer moon was setting, into Orbetello Bay
    Came the *Menelaus* gliding like a ghost;
And her boats were manned in silence, and in silence pulled away,
    And in silence every gunner took his post.
With a volley from her broadside the citadel she woke,
    And they hammered back like heroes all the night;
But before the morning broke she had vanished through the smoke
    With her prize upon her quarter grappled tight.'[6]

The choice of the obscure Parker as a hero might seem a strange one. He was still very young and was to die in battle before he was thirty. But there was a better reason for Newbolt to pick on the *Menelaus*. His grandfather, Charles Newbolt, at the age of seventeen had served as assistant navigation lieutenant on board the ship. 'It must have been worth all the cricket in life to take a great frigate into that harbour in the dark and bring her out again successful.'[7] Once more, the poem was well-received. Virginia Woolf's father particularly admired it. 'Mr Leslie Stephen is so pleased with the 'Menelaus' that he has learned it by heart'.[8] Leslie Stephen, first editor of the *Dictionary of National Biography*, was in the habit of learning poems by heart and entertaining his family with his recitations. He used to practise in Kensington Gardens, where a nursemaid was once terrified by warlike rantings emerging from behind a privet hedge.

'Admirals All' was but a distant roll on the drum for what was to come. On the evening of 15 January 1896, Newbolt was walking home from Lincoln's Inn. Suddenly, on a news vendor's placard at the corner of the Strand, he saw two words only, in enormous capitals: the words were DRAKE'S DRUM. 'Drake's Drum' was the title of a poem he had just contributed anonymously to the *St James's*

5. *NL* HN to EN, 6 March 1895
6. S.P., p.33
7. *NL* HN to EN , 5 Dec,1894
8. *NL* HN to EN 6 Mar. 1895

Gazette, an evening paper. All the way home, at Holborn, Oxford Circus and Marble Arch, the newsboys were calling the name of his poem. As he emerged from the park into Kensington High Street, there it was again. Newbolt classified 'Drake's Drum' as a song, not a ballad, for it was based not on a historical incident but a legend, a legend of Newbolt's invention. The first two (of three) stanzas ran:

> 'Drake he's in his hammock an' a thousand miles away,
>   (Capten, art tha sleepin' there below?)
> Slung atween the round shot in Nombre Dios Bay,
>   An' dreamin' arl the time o' Plymouth Hoe.
> Yarnder lumes the Island, yarnder lie the ships,
>   Wi' sailor lads a-dancin' heel-an'-toe,
> An' the shore-lights flashin', an' the night-tide dashin',
>   He sees et arl so plainly as he saw et long ago.
>
> Drake he was a Devon man, an' rüled the Devon seas,
>   (Capten, art tha sleepin' there below?)
> Rovin' tho' his death fell, he went wi' heart at ease,
>   An' dreamin' arl the time o' Plymouth Hoe.
> 'Take my drum to England, hang et by the shore,
>   Strike et when your powder's running low;
> If the Dons sight Devon, I'll quit the port o'Heaven,
> An' drum them up the Channel as we drummed them long ago.'

There was a reason why a poem rallying the English against an invader should have had such popular appeal in 1896. The Kaiser had been adding to his fleet of battleships for some time and it had just been announced that the British were sending a Special Service Squadron to sea.[9] 'I had ready some verses suitable for the occasion and I packed them off to *St James's* who accepted them the same day.[10]

The success of 'Drake's Drum' with the public was overpowering. The critics liked it too. The *Gazette*'s editor wrote: 'We have had enquiries from Edmund Gosse and several others who have written to ask the author's name'.[11] Newbolt was pleased by a letter from Bernard Holland (not an easy man to please), who had just

9. *My World*, p.186
10. *NL* HN to EN, 17 Jan. 1896
11. *NL* HN to EN, 17 Jan. 1896

married Margaret's sister Helen. 'I did not know it was by you when I read it, but I meant to have cut out the lines to keep, only I left the paper in an underground carriage. I think the lines have a flavour of Kingsley at his best.'[12] There was now serious competition to set 'Drake's Drum' to music. Walter Hedgecock got there first. Margaret declared the tune 'unoriginal and hymnlike' but Newbolt thought it 'a jolly reminiscence of old sea songs.' Hedgecock's setting was supplanted in 1904 by that of Stanford, and it is Stanford's version that has remained a concert piece for baritones ever since.

Newbolt had meanwhile come to the attention of a famous poet. Robert Bridges was a hero after his heart. He had the dark good looks of a gipsy crossed with the presence (and the knowledge of Latin) of a Roman emperor *and* he had stroked the Corpus Eight. His poetic output consisted mainly of Elizabethan-style lyrics. 'He has a great gift of being poetical without ever verging towards the unmanly.'[13] Bridges had recently assisted Mary Coleridge. Violet Hodgkin, a relative of his wife, had brought Mary's poems to his attention. Overcoming Mary's objections to publication (she had considered it would be an insult to her famous great-uncle), Bridges had arranged for the printing of a slim volume, *Fancy's Following*. It was not perhaps entirely by chance that the Newbolts now proceeded to spend a holiday with Violet Hodgkin's relatives, the Waterhouses, who were the parents of Bridges' wife, Monica. Alfred Waterhouse lived at Yattendon Court near Newbury, and Bridges was his tenant at Yattendon Manor. Newbolt met Bridges for the first time at dinner with the Waterhouses, and was reminded at once of Wollaston. 'Here was the bearded voice and sudden temper and the same way of saying things in a rough indifferent way when he means more than usual'.[14] The conversation turned to statues in a local church. Should they be classed as idols? Bridges came suddenly out of his silence and argued decisively that not even the heathen *worshipped* wood or stone. According to Newbolt's autobiography the interchange continued roughly as follows:

Newbolt: Would that imply approval of all religious ornaments?

12. *NL*, 19 Jan 1896
13. *NL* HN to EN, 15 April 1896
14. *NL* HN to EN, 15 April 1896

Bridges: It would, if they were in good taste.

Newbolt: You wouldn't say that of ancient Greece?

Bridges: (*Eyes lighting up*) V-Very good! But then the Greeks were not idolaters! But we can't go on talking here – let us meet again tomorrow morning.

Meet again they did, and it was agreed that at Easter the Newbolts should rent Pargiters, a house in the village, which communicated with that of Bridges by a door in the wall.

Newbolt's apprehension was intense as Easter approached. He copied nine poems into a new notebook and pasted the printed version of 'Drake's Drum' onto a card, with the first two verses returned to their original order. (To his annoyance, the editor of the *St James's Gazette* had reversed them.) This he planned to hand to Bridges on arrival. He set off for 'the hole in the wall', feeling like Gulliver about to step on to the giant's palm.'I found Bridges lying in the sun on his own doormat, with his spaniel Ben beside him. He was dressed with the most elegant shabbiness in an old grey felt hat, an old lounge coat and lavender-grey trousers of nankeen, a material then so obsolete that I never saw it worn by any other man.'[15] Newbolt joined his hero on the mat and, as predicted, the poet eyed the notebook with alarm. 'You've got some verses for me,' he said. 'Is that fat book full of them?' Newbolt immediately handed him the card with 'Drake's Drum' on it. It worked. 'After some moments of absorbed silence he murmured, '"Awfully swell, awfully swell." Then he looked at me and said, "You'll never write anything better than that. It isn't given to man to write anything better than that. I wish I had ever written anything half so good."'

Newbolt was to become a frequent caller at the house that Bridges shared, not only with his wife and three children, but also with his deranged mother. The Bridges household was a musical place, with groups practising Byrd's madrigals behind every bush. Bridges was fascinated by early English music, and was also engaged in compiling the Yattendon hymnal, putting his own translations of Latin hymns to tunes by seventeenth-century composers. An unknown poet called William Butler Yeats came down one weekend. Newbolt had lent *Oisin*, Yeats's first volume of

15. *My World*, p.187

106

ballads, to Bridges, who admired it. 'We were sitting at table,' wrote Newbolt, 'when the sound of wheels was heard. Bridges sprang up and ran to the door returning to announce, "He is very good looking." The only trouble was that Yeats talked half the night about his visions. The following morning, Bridges declared, "I'm done up. Not with talking but with smoking pipes while he talked."' On Sunday afternoon, they put Yeats through ordeal by cricket. 'His costume was inappropriate. He wore throughout his visit a long frock-coat with gracefully flowing skirts, and round his neck an enormous tie of purple silk.' It was suggested Yeats should come again, but on one condition, no more visions.[16]

Illness always seemed to accompany success for Newbolt. Just as his digestion had collapsed on his wedding day, so, after 'Drake's Drum', he went down with a severe attack of 'flu. Emily sent a bottle of Limona. 'I have it every night when we are not dining out, which we always are.' He was so pulled down that Milly planned to send him to Australia.[17] Attacks of 'flu were to return and Newbolt already began to feel that he was no longer the man he had been. The poem 'Nel Mezzo del Cammin'[18] acknowledged that the best of life was over. The poet was nearly 35.

> 'Whisper it not that in late years
> Sorrow shall fade and the world be brighter,
> Life be freed of tremor and tears,
> Heads be wiser and hearts be lighter.
> Ah! but the dream that all endears,
> The dream we sell for your pottage of truth –
> Give us again the passion of youth,
> Sorrow shall fade and the world be brighter.'

Instead of going to Australia, Newbolt took Margaret to Venice. On the way they visited Mr Oakeley, the Clifton master, in his Swiss chalet above Lake Thun. Oakeley had not been idle in his retirement. Not only was he at work on the third enormously enlarged edition of the Clifton register, but he had fathered two children. Charlotte, aged seven, was 'bewitchingly pretty; M. is more in love with her than she has ever been with any child except

16. *My World*, p.192–3
17. *NL* EN to HN, 2 March 1896
18. *S.P.*, p.68

107

Celia. She played the child's little violin, sitting on the nursery floor.' When Margaret was not on the floor she was sketching the old Switzerland 'of the days before cockney tourists.'[19]

Venice was largely a maritime adventure for Newbolt. He hired a gondola and braved the open sea. He had, as gondolier, Giovanni, none other than the son of John Addington Symond's 'well-known and spoiled gondolier'. There were Italian men-o'-war in the lagoon. 'We were close to one of them when she fired her sunset gun and I was as childishly pleased as when we used to see the battery practising at Whitby. I am not sure but that this is one of the *most* exciting things I have seen here.'[20] The ships were being fitted out to join the British and the Turks in Crete against the Greeks. John Spender, of *The Times*, was particularly concerned. He was staying at one of the better hotels in Venice. 'If anything begins to happen in Constantinople he will have to take the next train for Fleet Street and write leading articles.'[21]

Sea bathing at the Lido was the other great occupation. 'The ladies sit on the balcony and the men walk about on the edge of the water in their hideous striped costumes and throw sand at one another. A very few swim.'[22] While Newbolt swam, Margaret trawled the antique shops with Helen Holland, who was also in Venice. She also composed 'scurrilous poems' about her husband (lost, alas). Bernard and Helen Holland had rooms at the Palazzo Foscolo. The palace was immensely romantic. 'Merely to land in their little dark canal and ring at the vast black door made one feel like a villain. The sole remnants of the great family of Foscolo live in the attics, two old countesses, with one little maid. For many years they have never been out of the house except to the Church round the corner.'[23] The Newbolts them moved to Florence, where it rained and the palaces of 'the murderous Medicis' looked like 'so many county gaols'. Margaret developed a 'st-m-ch ache' from sitting on a damp log, sketching. By the end of the summer they were glad to come home.

19. *NL* HN to EN, 1896
20. *NL* HN to EN, 23 Sept. 1896
21. ibid.
22. *NL* HN to EN, 28 Sept. 1896
23. ibid.

CHAPTER 17

Admiral's All

Newbolt's poems first appeared between covers (blue sugar-paper ones) in 1897. The volume was entitled *Admiral's All* (after the ballad) and was part of Elkin Mathews' Shilling Garland series. In appearance, it was scarcely more than a pamphlet, but it bore a stylised asphodel on the cover, typical of the elegance of Mathews' productions. The series was edited by the young Laurence Binyon, who was leading a revolt against *fin de siècle* decadence. He already numbered Canon Dixon, Mary Coleridge and Robert Bridges among his contributors. Newbolt was also approached by Mathews' great rival, John Lane, founder of Bodley Head and encourager of decadents like Aubrey Beardsley. 'It will be fun to tell him that I've just arranged to be published by his late partner Elkin Mathews who he cordially detests. I'll see him *somewhere* before I'll write for *The Yellow Book.*'[1] (In fact, John Lane speedily

1. *NL* HN to EN, Mar. 1897

109

acquired the copyright of all Newbolt's poems in the United States.) *Admiral's All* contained two of Newbolt's Big Four: 'Drake's Drum' and 'Vitaï Lampada' (the other two being 'He Fell Among Thieves' and 'Clifton Chapel'). 'Vitaï Lampada' (The Torch of Life), is more commonly referred to as 'Play up! play up! and play the game! – the words of its chorus. It was written as early as 1892. Newbolt had recently met a survivor of Omdurman, at a House reunion at Clifton. 'At 3 in the morning I was still sitting on his bed, reading extracts from his diary of the Soudan.'[2] These are the first two verses:

> There's a breathless hush in the Close to-night –
> Ten to make and the match to win –
> A bumping pitch and a blinding light,
> An hour to play and the last man in.
> And it's not for the sake of a ribboned coat,
> Or the selfish hope of a season's fame,
> But his Captain's hand on his shoulder smote –
> "Play up! play up! and play the game!"
>
> The sand of the desert is sodden red, –
> Red with the wreck of a square that broke; –
> The Gatling's jammed and the Colonel dead,
> And the regiment blind with dust and smoke.
> The river of death has brimmed his banks,
> And England's far, and Honour a name,
> But the voice of a schoolboy rallies the ranks:
> "Play up! play up! and play the game!"

The book of poems was published on 21 October (Trafalgar Day) 1897. A few days earlier Newbolt had written to Emily: 'No one has said anything yet.'[3] Then the first tentative words of praise were heard. The *Daily Mail* declared the naval songs 'uncommonly spirited. Unlike most of the poetry I receive which is rubbish unredeemed.'[4] After a pause, the book began to sell. 'One evening as I passed down the Strand I stood for a moment at the entrance of Dennys' shop in Holywell Street. One of the Dennys said, "Have

2. *My World,* p.205
3. *NL*, HN to EN, 16 Oct. 1897
4. *Daily Mail* 16 Oct. 1897

you come for your book, Sir? You are just in time, we've hardly a copy left tonight." "How many had you this morning?" I asked lightly. "I don't know, but we shall have five hundred tomorrow if we can get them! Perhaps you have not seen Archer's review.'" William Archer had written in the *Daily Chronicle* that Newbolt's songs 'will take an eminent and enduring place among our patriotic poetry. They are more spirit-stirring than anything that has appeared since Tennyson's "Ballad of the Revenge". If we should fall beneath our former selves when the great Armadas come, it will not be for want of a singer to pipe us to quarters.' The *St James's Gazette* added: 'Mr Newbolt's work has no tinge of the pessimism, cynicism or morbidity of the day.' The *Globe* declared him 'eminently virile'.[5] Then the weeklies and the monthlies came rolling in. *The Spectator*, in the person of its editor, St Loe Strachey, rejoiced in the return of the ballad and the rout of sonnets and elegies and all that 'humbugging literary rot'. Strachey picked out for special attention 'Admirals All' (as did many), but did not care for the dialect presentation of 'Drake's Drum'. Quiller-Couch added his praise in *The Speaker* but pointed out that William Cory had written patriotic verse ten years earlier 'in the very spirit which Newbolt has so admirably caught'. The book eventually ran to 21 editions.

There was, however, one dissentient voice: the critic who wrote for the *Athenaeum*, a periodical of such distinction that it was an honour, Newbolt declared, to be mauled by it. The effect of the review among Newbolt's supporters is suggested by a fairy tale written in French by Mrs Hugh Bell. *Cloudland: A Fable* ran roughly as follows: Once upon a time, a poet set off singing to the land of clouds. His public loved him, following him with cries of, 'Sing, poet!' On their way they met a herd of critics who said, 'Sing, poet!' and when they had heard, they too were ravished and they all set off once more. But then they came upon a solitary critic, and a solitary critic is more dangerous than one in a herd. He said, 'Poet, you sing of patriotism and heroes. These are not the subjects of poetry.' 'Ah!' said the poet, 'but they are. A hero has the soul of a poet and should be sung by a poet.' Everyone agreed and they cried, 'Sing, poet, sing' once more. The solitary critic was left to drum his heels by the wayside.

5. 4 Nov. 1897

With over 20,000 copies of *Admirals All* sold, it was natural that Newbolt's thoughts should turn to giving up the law. Robert Bridges had suggested it, saying, 'Ten years at the bar is quite enough.' Newbolt, however, was not so sure that he wanted to lead the life of artistic simplicity that Bridges led. Bridges had told him that he never made any money by his writing. And yet 'he has about ten volumes on the market. He is a very bad man of business I imagine, and has never gone out of the way to make even the little that can be fairly made out of poetry.'[6] Newbolt was not convinced that he could make even that little. His needs were more various than Bridges'. 'As long as red shoes and blue pinnies and legs of beef and air balls for small creatures, and railway tickets and lager beer' had to be provided, a certain amount of money was very desirable, he told Emily. In order to discover whether a decent living could be made out of poetry, he now set about writing it for money. Newbolt's chief source of inspiration in this endeavour was the *Dictionary of National Biography*. He even wrote a poem about it ('Minora Sidera').[7] He began to contribute ballads anonymously to periodicals at a rate of nearly one a fortnight. He described himself as a sausage machine. 'The machine turned out a fat one yesterday and today it is grinding out another', he told Emily[8] 'I am getting what seems to be large prices for them.' He was aware that some of his poetry was poor stuff. But he must take advantage of 'this little boom'. Publishers go on writing to me for verses for songs, and verses for magazines, and verses for volumes.'[9] Money, however, was never his sole aim. 'I want money, but not much, a little fame, but, above everything, sympathy and honour and friends.' He looked ahead to a time when he would have the leisure to write good poetry. 'When I'm a retired old bald pate I shall write quite decent verses for a year or two and then go out pop like the candles on last year's Christmas tree.'[10]

6. *NL* HN to EN, 15 Apr. 1896
7. *S.P.* p.45
8. *NL* HN to EN, 28 Jan. 1898
9. *NL* HN to EN, 1 Dec. 1897
10. *NL* HN to EN, 29 Dec.1896

CHAPTER 18

The Island Race

The Island Race, Newbolt's second collection of verse, came out a year later, in 1898. It was in fact an expanded version of *Admirals All*, with 28 poems added. They included 'Clifton Chapel' and 'He Fell Among Thieves'.[1]

"Ye have robbed" said he, "ye have slaughtered and made an end,
    Take your ill-got plunder, and bury the dead:
What will ye more of your guest and sometime friend?"
    "Blood for our blood", they said

He laughed: "If one may settle the score for five,
    I am ready; but let the reckoning stand till day:
I have loved the sunlight as dearly as any alive."
    "You shall die at dawn," said they.

1. *S.P.* p.61

He flung his empty revolver down the slope,
   He climbed alone to the Eastward edge of trees;
All night long in a dream untroubled of hope
   He brooded, clasping his knees.

He did not hear the monotonous roar that fills
   The ravine where the Yassin river sullenly flows;
He did not see the starlight on the Laspur hills,
   Or the far Afghan snows.

He saw the April noon on his books aglow,
   The wistaria trailing in at the window wide;
He heard his father's voice from the terrace below
   Calling him down to ride.

He saw the gray little church across the park,
   The mounds that hide the loved and honoured dead;
The Norman arch, the chancel softly dark,
   The brasses black and red.

He saw the School Close, sunny and green,
   The runner beside him, the stand by the parapet wall,
The distant tape, and the crowd roaring between
   His own name over all.

He saw the dark wainscot and timbered roof,
   The long tables, and the faces merry and keen;
The College Eight and their trainer dining aloof,
   The Dons on the daïs serene.

He watched the liner's stem ploughing the foam,
   He felt her trembling speed and the thrash of her screw;
He heard her passengers' voices talking of home,
   He saw the flag she flew.

And now it was dawn. He rose strong on his feet,
   And strode to his ruined camp below the wood;
He drank the breath of the morning cool and sweet;
   His murderers round him stood.

Light on the Laspur hills was broadening fast,
    The blood-red snow-peaks chilled to a dazzling white:
He turned, and saw the golden circle at last,
    Cut by the Eastern height.

"O glorious Life, Who dwellest in earth and sun,
    I have lived, I praise and adore Thee."
                                    A sword swept.
Over the pass the voices one by one
    Faded, and the hill slept.

The poem was based on the tragic death of a certain Lieutenant George Hayward near Chitral in 1870. Hayward was on a mission from the Royal Geographical Society to find a new route to the Pamirs. According to Lord Curzon, Newbolt improved on Lieutenant Hayward's end. As Curzon explained to Newbolt at a dinner twenty years later, Hayward did not spend the last night of his life as a prisoner reviewing the scenes of his life. He spent it as a free but very frightened man, keeping watch outside his tent. He was captured just before dawn, taken 3 miles up the river and executed. Curzon added, 'The story was afterwards spread – though it was doubted when I was on the frontier – that before being executed, Hayward asked to take a last look at the rising sun, and was permitted to do so.' Most of Newbolt's Indian ballads were inspired by Frank Younghusband, his fellow Old Cliftonian. Later, Younghusband was to open Tibet to the west.

'Clifton Chapel' is not a ballad, but a hymn to chivalry inspired by 'one who rests in a frontier grave'. A father shows his son round the school. 'This is the Chapel: here, my son, your father thought the thoughts of youth.' He points out the brass memorials of heroic old boys, and sets out the creed for which they died:

To set the cause above renown,
    To love the game beyond the prize,
To honour, while you strike him down,
    The foe that comes with fearless eyes;
To count the life of battle good,
    And dear the land that gave you birth,
And dearer yet the brotherhood
    That binds the brave of all the earth –

Another new poem, 'Fidele's Grassy Tomb', was on a lighter theme. It told the story of Fidele, a hound of the Danish breed, who had dragged his master from the sea at Elsinore. By way of reward he was buried at his master's feet in the island church of Orchardleigh. But the Bishop of Bath and Wells demanded that the dog be moved to a tomb outside the church:

> 'The grave was dug; the mason came
> And carved on stone Fidele's name;
> But the dog that the Sexton laid inside
> Was a dog that never had lived or died.'

A century later, when the church floor was relaid, the bones of an enormous dog were found safe in the tomb of the squire. Newbolt wrote the poem four days after Christmas Day 1897, while on holiday at Orchardleigh. 'I shot rabbits in the morning, hunted 3 teal on the lake in the afternoon, played several games of billiards, and made a ballad on a staghound.'[2] The ballad first appeared anonymously in *The Spectator* for February 1898. It finally blew the gaff on Newbolt's anonymity as a contributor to periodicals. 'The mention in it of O.L. [Orchardleigh] has been the final intimation of my identity.[3] Mr Duckworth declared that he had never heard of the legend of Fidele, and Newbolt wrote hastily to assure him that he would find it in the proceedings of the Somerset Archaeological Society. 'Sir Gilbert Scott, investigating the state of the foundations, broke into the grave under the chapel and found the skeleton of a large dog buried with one of the Champneys.'[4] The truth of the tale of Fidele has been confirmed by Michael McGarvie, in *Sir Henry Newbolt and Orchardleigh*. McGarvie recently discovered that Fidele's tombstone, a vast stone urn, had been moved up to the terrace at Orchardleigh. It was returned to the island and an appropriate service was held in the island church in 1991. The occasion was a sad one, for the Duckworths sold Orchardleigh for conversion into a golf course shortly afterwards.

1899 should have been an *Annus Mirabilis* in Newbolt's life. At Commem, John Percival recited 'Clifton Chapel' to a vast audience. 'It was very wonderful to sit and hear him in his old voice and accent

2. *NL* HN to EN, 29 Dec. 1897
3. ibid.
4. *NL* HN to WAD, 25 Feb. 1898

116

reminding us of dead heroes and quoting, "Let who will, make the *lars* (laws) of a nation, if I may make the ballads.'"[5] Elated, Newbolt wrote to his mother: 'There is no doubt I have done what he would have had me do, to an inch or so. I am wondering what to do next.'

What came next was death. First, Aunt Selina Harrison went. Newbolt had to leave the concert at Clifton to visit her as she lay dying just down the road. Dr Alfred Harrison had moved to Clifton after he retired, but Selina quickly became ill and did not long survive an operation. 'The dear remains are lying upstairs,' wrote Uncle Alfred. 'I hope the angelic smile will keep.'[6]

Uncle Charles Newbolt died about the same time. He was the Revd Henry Francis's seafaring brother. 'I never saw the man,', wrote Newbolt.[7] 'It so often seems a toss-up if one is born to be a goat and one a sheep. Weakness in face of liquor seems such a small thing to swing for.'[8] A source of more immediate pain had been the death of Bernard and Helen Holland's first baby, Christopher. The child had become severely ill during the summer of 1898 at Orchardleigh, with 'gastric catarrh'.[9] Margaret had been there alone with Helen when it happened, the Duckworths being away, 'opening a Church or about some other pious work.'[10] The baby's death cast a shadow over Orchardleigh. When 'some fool' selected the hymn, 'There is a place of peace, good angels know it well', Helen broke down completely in Orchardleigh chapel. Newbolt agreed that there was no comfort to be found in these words. 'They sounded unutterable twaddle (as they truly are) in the presence of real grief and real faith.'[11] Newbolt wrote a poem about about it, entitled 'In July'.

> He knew not Autumn's chillness,
>   Nor Winter's wind nor Spring's;
> He lived with Summer's stillness
>   And sun and sunlit things:
> But when the dusk was falling
>   He went the shadowy way,

5. *NL* HN to EN, July 1899
6. *NL*, 1 Jan. 1890
7. *NL* HN to EN, 5 Dec. 1899
8. ibid.
9. *NL* HN to EN, 25 Sept. 1898
10. *NL* HN to EN, 29 Sept. 1898
11. *NL* HN to EN, 2 Oct. 1898

And one more heart is calling,
Crying and calling
For the love that would not stay.

Now disaster threatened even closer to home. Milly was suffering from severe depression. She had been having psychological problems for three years, but had now been sent away to a clinic. She was unable to take decisions for herself and refused to communicate with her family. Newbolt blamed Tom's meanness. 'He must see that she has regular holidays from nursery maiding. If Margaret had as much of her children as Milly I shouldn't wonder at *her* breaking down.'[12] 'Tom refuses to pull his nose out of his law books or open his purse. The experts advise him to move into the country but he persists in staying at Leinster Gardens and chancing it'.[13] The *Annus Mirabilis* had turned out an *Annus Horribilis*. Meanwhile, the time to part with the Law had come. 'The Law for me.' Newbolt admitted, 'has been an unmistakable failure'. [14] Work in chambers was 'dull as ditchwater'.[15] The Courts were 'stuffy', the streets round them 'hot and malodorous' in summer and choked with fog and mud in winter. Newbolt complained constantly to Emily of minor ailments: of lethargy, of a cold in the head, a pain in the left eye, a pain in the right eye. There had been a brief lightening when he became assistant to Sir Ralph Neville, QC. Neville was a distinguished pleader and offered Newbolt the profitable task of pre-digesting his cases. Neville swiftly became 'one of the most intimate and delightful friends I ever had.'[16] Newbolt often visited his country seat, Banstead Place. But no sooner had Neville started to bring in work for Newbolt, than Neville fell seriously ill with tuberculosis.

Tom Chitty's *Law Digest* had also come to an end. It had supported Newbolt almost from the beginning. His contribution to this massive work had been 12,000 pages of decisions on wills. Yet he had never been able to hide his jealousy of his prosperous brother-in-law. It had been galling to see Milly magnificently gowned and riding in her own carriage. (He swore that on one

12. *NL* HN to EN, 8 Oct. 1896
13. *NL* HN to EN, 8 Oct. 1899
14. *NL* HN to EN 1 Dec, 1897
15. *NL* HN to EN, 17 Nov. 1891
16. *My World*, p.151

occasion she cut him in the park.) When the *Law Digest* finally went to press in 1896, Newbolt vacated his chambers. In a letter to Emily, he wrote: 'I am not proposing to leave the Bar formally. On the contrary I shall let people go on thinking me to be still at it. I say this because I think some of Margaret's blessed relations would hardly be pleased.[17]

Froissart's *Chronicle* now took the place of the *Law Digest.* Dalton, the publisher, had asked Newbolt to make selections from the tales of the fourteenth-century Frenchman who had spent years at the court of Edward III. Froissart was a man after Newbolt's heart. Not only was his account of the wars between France and England vivid, but he had the right attitude. Froissart was as imbued with the rules of courtly etiquette as Malory. 'I hope my Froissart may do something for Chivalry which would be more useful than all the Peace Societies in the world, for men must always fight, the only difference being how they do it.'[18] Newbolt chose to work from the fifteenth century translation of Lord Berners, not a more recent one. The work involved many visits to the rotunda reading room at the British Museum. Berners was only available in a rare reprint of 1812, and Newbolt needed to refer to other even more obscure texts. He was fortunate in having Laurence Binyon (an employee of the museum) as a friend, for he allowed him to enter the stacks to select for himself books 'which ordinarily would have taken half an hour to reach me'.[19] Another facility a modern reader might envy Newbolt was the Vienna Café in New Oxford Street, which came to take the place, for him, of the Common Room at Lincoln's Inn. There he met members of the Bloomsbury Group like Roger Fry and Edward Garnett, as well as Samuel Butler, John Masefield and Baron Corvo. Among the painters, there were Sickert, William Rothenstein and William Strang. The group came to be known as the Anglo-Austrians. 'We talked faster and more irresponsibly than any group in my memory. The confusion in which we gave a dozen orders to Joseph, our Italian waiter, and the recklessness with which we divided portions with one another in shares impossible to disentangle, was extraordinary. An onlooker might

17. *NL* HN to EN, 1 Dec. 1897
18. *NL* HN to EN, 29 June, 1898
19. *My World,* p.218

have taken us for a Bohemian society of students.'[20] One of the most valued friends that Newbolt made at the Vienna Café was George Calderon, the playwright, 'by nature happier than all the rest of us.'[21] Calderon was the grandson of a Spanish protestant and a writer of fashionable plays. 'I can at any moment recall his clear brown features, his active grace upon the cricket field, his voice in tones of persuasive affection or combative oratory. His plays were Bernard Shawish, but chaotic.[22] After the first night of *The Fountain* there was a dinner at the Gaiety Restaurant, and 'lovely visions, with stage names inextricably muddled up with their real names, were introduced.'[23]

Newbolt completed Froissart two months ahead of Dalton's deadline. The last part was written in the summer house of a house called the Chough's Nest, at Lynton. He was working at fever pitch. After his work session on Sundays, he habitually answered up to twenty letters, and by the end of the day he was often 'quite unable to hold a pen'.[24] The book did well financially. A.P. Watt, Newbolt's agent, sold it to Macmillan in the United States on very good terms. It looked like becoming the standard edition on both sides of the Atlantic. To his mother he wrote, 'My pen may prove your best coalmine'.[25] (Emily had an interest in a coalmine, which was proving an unmitigated disaster.) Encouraged, Newbolt immediately set about a second collection of Froissart stories.

The move to 23 Earl's Terrace, a few streets from No. 14, was not because of Newbolt's success, as he implies in his autobiography. In fact, he and Margaret were catapulted out of 'poor dear little fourteen' with only 48 hours' notice[26] for reasons unknown. For a time they were homeless, Newbolt staying with Tom Chitty, Margaret with 'Good Mrs Over-the-way' (her aunt, Loo White). It was painful for her to look out of the window at night and see the old bedroom window, which had been left open 'like an open wound through which the soul had escaped.'[27]

23 Earl's Terrace was a handsome stone terrace house. It stood

20. *My World*, p.209
21. *LLL*, p.29
22. *NL* HN to EN, 30 March 1909
23. ibid.
24. *NL* HN to EN, 13 Nov. 1898
25. *NL* HN to EN, 6 Nov. 1898
26. *NL* HN to EN, 5 Oct. 1897
27. *NL* HN to EN, 1 Nov. 1897

on the south side of Kensington High Street protected from the traffic by a belt of trees and a service road. Newbolt was delighted by its size and elegance. It was not only more dignified 'than little fourteen, with its Adam cornices and basket fireplaces' but it had two well-proportioned drawing-rooms upstairs and a large dining-room downstairs. Everything about the house was large, Newbolt claimed, even the bath, in which 'one could boil an ox'.[28] Only his own study was, as usual, small, although there was room for the chair in which Emily liked to sit and lecture him on her increasingly rare visits. Newbolt was also pleased with the garden, 'not a large one, but it gave access to a really fine one of some acres, where one could sit in a deck chair and see the wild geese fly northwards over London.'[29] (Newbolt referred to leafy Edwardes Square.)

Margaret was determined to preserve the simplicity of her family life in spite of the grand new surroundings. She refused to buy new furniture, although the old stuff would have to be spread very thinly. Newbolt agreed. 'We look forward to sailing under very bare poles.'[30] Margaret turned down offers of new carpets from the competing mothers, preferring her own 'dear dinginess'. But eventually she succumbed to a pale green carpet with a darker border, woven specially for the sitting room. When no one was around the children skated on this carpet. She always knew from the skid marks in the pile. A portion of it can still be seen on the floor of Theresa Whistler's cottage in North Devon.

The move proved the usual nightmare to Margaret. Emily complained that she was absurdly slow and Newbolt rushed to his wife's defence. Margaret, he insisted, had 'a turn' for domestic affairs. 'I'm sure no one could possibly have managed agent, builder, workmen and servants with as much tact and success'. In fact, Margaret's tact in the matter of servants was not outstanding. Lorimer, the children's nurse, had left, to loud laments from Celia. Her replacement, a French governess, was already planning to return home 'She will have to go to the cool reposeful tomb before she finds an easier place',[31] was Newbolt's comment. A pair

28. *NL* HN to EN, 1 Dec, 1897
29. *My World*, p.215
30. *NL* HN to EN, 1897
31. *NL* HN to EN, 12 Dec. 1898

of untrained Cornish maids was an unknown and untrained quantity. They didn't last.

At last, the Newbolts had space for everybody. There was not only a room each for the children, but Ella now had her own room under Newbolt's roof for the first time. She was completely accepted as part of the family by Celia and Francis. They called her T'Ella (an abbreviation of Aunt Ella). A letter from Margaret to Francis (after he went away to school) gives a vivid picture of the home life of the three of them: 'Father, T'Ella and I all dined at different places today, so we had a great deal to tell each other when we returned home.'[32] In another letter, she wrote 'Father, Aunt Ella and I sat round the fire after dinner and read our friend Countess von Arnim's latest story.'

But the three were not alone often. The chief joy of Number 23 was the dining room. At last, the Newbolts had space to entertain properly and many were the evenings of prolonged conversation round the long dining room table downstairs. Newbolt rejoiced in picking his 'most congenial companions and arranging them in new combinations. As on a stage we saw all our own company act their parts.'[33] On one occasion, Robert Bridges was so carried away on the subject of hymns over the port that the ladies upstairs all but gave up hope of being joined.

There were, of course, invitations to other convivial dining rooms, none more memorable than that of Holman Hunt at Draycott Lodge, in the wilds of Fulham. So eager was Newbolt to meet the famed pre-Raphaelite that, in spite of a blizzard, he managed to bribe a hansom to take him there one evening. Nobody else went. The Newbolts dined alone with the bearded and venerable painter of 'The Scapegoat' and his 'distinctively dressed' wife, who sat at opposite ends of a long table. When Margaret had retired with Mrs Hunt, Holman spilled the beans about Ruskin's failure to consummate his marriage with Effie, which 'made a very strong and painful impression on me, and diminished my faith in the trustworthiness of human motives.'[34]

32. NL, 19 Mar. 1903
33. *My World*, p.216
34. *My World*, p.223

PART VI THE MONTHLY REVIEW
1900–1904

CHAPTER 19

The First Issue

The new century brought Newbolt a new project. John Murray, the publisher, invited him to edit a magazine. At first he demurred; he felt he had more poems left in him, and besides, he was halfway through the second Froissart volume. Also there were already too many periodicals. But John Murray was insistent. He invited Newbolt in strictest confidence to his magnificent offices at 50 Albermarle Street, within a stone's throw of the Ritz. 'It was good fun,' Newbolt confessed, 'to talk to John Murray IV in the very room in which Scott and Byron used to talk to John Murray II.' John Murray persuaded Newbolt that 'although there are far more

---

1. *NL* HN to EN, Mar. 1900

magazines and reviews now in existence than were really wanted, *the* review has yet to come.'[2] He followed up with a letter declaring that 'to no one would we entrust the editorship more readily than to yourself, because of the position you have won in the world of letters, coupled with your own personality (if you will allow me to say so)'.[3] The new magazine was to deal primarily with the Arts, surveying Politics 'from the library window rather than from the drill ground.' Gradually Newbolt began to fancy himself as an editor, 'talking easily to the town on a wide range of topics' in the manner of Addison.[4] A salary of £1500 was offered, and it was agreed that Newbolt and Margaret should each buy a thousand shares in the project. Newbolt was provided with an office in the basement of 50A Albermarle Street. Seated at his desk, he had a good view of people's legs as they passed along the pavement.

The *Monthly Review* did not have a staff. It had Ella. She sorted out the unsolicited contributions, ensuring that only the best reached Newbolt's desk. She also edited copy and coped with the ever-rising tide of correspondence. When she was on holiday, things would get out of control. 'My pockets are bulging with unanswered correspondence,' Newbolt wrote the following summer.[5] Even when he installed pigeonholes in the back dining room at Earl's Terrace, things did not improve noticeably. More than this, Ella also wrote most of the ten-page book review section at the beginning of the magazine.

Ella and Newbolt did not plan the first issue in a London basement. It was June and the time for the summer migration had come. Margaret and the children were already at Lynton, and once more Newbolt worked all day in the summer house, this time side by side with Ella. 'My mails astonish the post office' By the time the two reached Ormidale in the Highlands, only the magazine's cover remained to be chosen. There still exists in John Murray's archive a telegram from Ormidale saying: 'I vote for all black.' But when he received the black cover he hated it.[6] He complained from Aberdeenshire, which he had now reached: 'The gilding is tawdry.' Ella suggested a grey-blue cover with a medallion of Pallas Athene

2. *My World*, p.239
3. *My World*, p.240
4. *My World*, p.240
5. *NL* HN to EN, 21 May 1901
6. John Murray Letters, 4 Aug. 1900

'like one of the Wedgwood plaques.'[7] She had her way but not before the 'tide of letters' had driven them both back to Albemarle Street.

Newbolt had still not given up hope of completing his customary three-month summer holiday. Ella's parents had rented a grand house in Bedfordshire, large enough for all their maiden daughters. Although 'rows of cabbages' were a poor substitute for grouse moors, it was closer to London than Aberdeenshire. From there, Newbolt and Ella saw the magazine through the press. One day in mid-September, he travelled down to Bedfordshire, carrying with him a grey-blue paper-covered volume nearly an inch thick. It was the first issue of the *Monthly Review*. The list of contributors read like a seating plan for one of Margaret's dinner parties; Laurence Binyon, Mary Coleridge, Mrs Hugh Bell, Alice Meynell, Ralph Neville, Rowland Whitehead, Robert Bridges, Edith Sichel and Bernard Holland were all there. Cliftonians were not forgotten. Quiller-Couch reviewed T. E. Brown's letters, and 'even lank yellow-headed Geoffrey Cookson from Worcester Crescent' turned out to be a poet.

7. ibid. 30 Aug. 1900

CHAPTER 20

The Arts

All the arts were covered in the *Monthly Review*. The first issue included a 25-page lecture on Giotto by Roger Fry. 'I had the pleasure of publishing his earliest lectures, tho' he has long outgrown and disowned them.'[1] There was the unavoidable serialised novel. (Newbolt himself could not abide novels in this form, declaring that he found 'the milestones' distracting.) Anthony Hope contributed one about a disputed will in Mayfair, entitled *Tristram of Blent*, and Mary Coleridge followed it with *The Fiery Dawn*, a swashbuckling tale of young blood set aboil by the Vendée rising. Arthur Coleridge, now widowed, was pathetically grateful on behalf of his daughter for its publication. 'Claret jugs and silver inkstands would inadequately express my gratitude to you for your chivalrous and fraternal care of the Ostrich's interest,' he wrote.[2] The Ostrich herself 'observes a colossal silence and blows her nose. (She has a

1. *My World*, p.241
2. *NL*, 16 Aug. 1901

126

cold.)' Poetry, however, was to have pride of place in the magazine. 'When I agreed to founding the *Monthly Review*, one of my conscious motives was a desire to bring about a change in the estimate of Poetry.' In 1900 it was vain to look for poetry in the 'serious' reviews. Newbolt did not merely publish poems, he published very long ones. Binyon's 'Death of Adam' ran to twenty pages and Bridges' 'Epistle to a Socialist' to fifteen.

Newbolt now began to make the acquaintance of many celebrities in the world of the arts. Thomas Hardy was one of these. Newbolt gained the gratitude of the Grand Old Man by writing one of the few favourable reviews of *The Dynasts*.[3] The subject of the Napoleonic War was of course attractive to Newbolt, particularly now that the Boer War was under way. The two men proceeded to correspond about God (in whom Hardy, of course, did not believe) for many years. Finally, in Newbolt's honour, an After-Scene was added to *The Dynasts*, conceding that the Inadvertent Mind might one day gain cognition.

Among painters Newbolt got to know Charles Furse, creator of 'Diana of the Uplands'. He was one of a family of talented brothers, which included Henry the sculptor, Michael the don and Bill the soldier. But for sheer brilliance of conversation, Charles outstripped them all.[4] He was married to Katharine, daughter of John Addington Symonds, and the Newbolts were often invited to stay with them at Yockley in Surrey. The artist would spend the mornings doing massive equestrian portraits 'butt end on', and the afternoons driving his guests around in a stylish dogcart. Charles died of tuberculosis at the age of 36. Had he lived, there were those who thought he would have rivalled Sargent. The death of Charles brought the Furse clan and the Newbolts closer together. Katharine wrote to Newbolt, acknowledging his letter of condolence: 'Do you remember, we made plans? Charles and Mrs Newbolt were going to Paris and you and I to the Alps?'[5] It is doubtful whether Newbolt would have been in danger of compromising himself with Dame Katharine, as she became. She had been reared under the impression she was a boy, and was in turn to bring up her own two sons more as a father than a mother.

3. *Monthly Review*, Mar. 1904
4. *LLL*, p.81
5. *NL*, 2 Nov. 1904

CHAPTER 21

Ella and Bamburgh

The *Monthly Review* altered Newbolt's relationship with Ella. She was now a working partner, and had taken a room in Kensington where she could be away from her family. Newbolt wrote to Murray about it in strictest confidence. 'There is a lady of great ability who has read and reported on a thousand things this year. I made no arrangement with her, but she had to take a room away from home to work undisturbed'.[1] Newbolt suggested that Murray should contribute £30 towards the rent. But the room had more than one purpose. It was a place where Ella could meet her lover without Margaret being present.

Ella was neither well nor happy. A mistress does not have the privileges of a wife. Only a few people in London included her in invitations. One of these was William Rothenstein, who on one occasion wrote to Newbolt, 'Perhaps you and Mrs Newbolt and her

1. John Murray Letters, 27 Sept. 1901

128

friend will come and have tea one afternoon?' And of course she could not have Newbolt's children. She made lengthy expeditions to the continent on her own every summer, and while she was away she often became ill. On her way home from a cure at Krenznach, she collapsed at Cologne; Margaret almost had to go out and rescue her.[2] Eighteen months later she had a major operation and spent weeks convalescing, deeply depressed, 'beside the bracing sea'. Her thoughts were all of death and the release it brings, she told de la Mare, who put them into the mouth of Grisel. 'Don't I know that awful Land's End after illness; and that longing for Ultima Thule.'

Saddest for Ella was the loss of Lorbottle, the Coltman's house in Northumberland, the scene of her girlhood romance with Margaret. 'Dear old Frank Coltman' had given up the lease in 1895 on orders from his wife, 'the Duchess'. Bamburgh Castle, rented by Violet Hodgkin's father, now became the Northumberland retreat of both Ella and the Newbolts for a month in the summer. The Norman castle at Bamburgh near Alnmouth was a northern version of St Michael's Mount, rising from a rock surrounded by the sea at high tide. It had been transformed into what Newbolt described as 'a most picturesque and comfortable home.'[3] 'The Library was like a ship in mid-ocean. When night came we felt ourselves slipping back into the mists of pure romance.'[4] The bedrooms were in turrets and lit by skylights. (Unfortunately, tourists on the battlements could see you through the windows of these while you were changing for dinner!) Dr Thomas Hodgkin was a Quaker historian. When he gave finally gave up the lease, he organised a midnight picnic on the beach below the castle. 'It was as if we had landed from a Danish ship of the ninth century except that there were servants in uniform handing out grog.'[5]

On one occasion, the party made an expedition to Lorbottle Hall. It was a sad sight. The new tenants had neglected both the house and grounds, and rabbits were devouring the formal gardens. Ella, now over forty, surveyed the ruin and saw in it her own lost youth.

2. *NL* HN to EN, 14 Sept. 1902
3. *NL* HN to EN, 28 Aug.1895
4. *My World*, p.233
5. *My World*, p.233

CHAPTER 22

Walter de la Mare

Ella made one major contribution to the world of literature. She discovered Walter de la Mare. When a batch of poems entitled 'Characters from Shakespeare' came through the office letter-box in February 1902, she immediately brought them to Newbolt's attention. They were signed only W.R., but both he and Ella felt sure they were by someone well-known. Eager to discover the author, they searched *Who's Who* for men with these initials and came up with only Walter Raleigh and, far less probably, Sir William Richmond. Finally, Newbolt discovered that W. R. stood for Walter Ramal, the second word a partial reversal of 'de la Mare'. This news was swiftly followed by de la Mare himself, who 'walked in upon me at Albemarle Street and took my hand with a grip which has never once loosened in the thirty years that have followed.'[1] De la Mare has left a vivid portrait of Newbolt: 'Aquiline

1. *My World,* p.281

in face, with a finely moulded head, a small mouth, and a dominant nose, alert and ready in speech and laughter, he surveyed the world, friend, foe or stranger, from grey-blue eyes at once intent, penetrating and contemplative.'[2]

De la Mare was invited to dinner at Earl's Terrace. Years later, Margaret still recalled that first evening. He was agonisingly shy at first. He stood by the mantelpiece that had an eagle-crested mirror above it, 'unable to talk at all'. 'He knew nobody' declared Newbolt. His origins were humble. His father had been a City clerk living in Woolwich and he had won a scholarship to St Paul's Cathedral School. Since the age of seventeen he had been a clerk at the offices of the Standard Oil Company.

However, as they sat round the dinner table he began to talk. His conversation moved in a series of intuitive flashes. Newbolt compared him to the dabchick in *Alice*. You can ask him an intelligent question, but instead of answering it, the dabchick goes down bob, and comes up again forty yards away.'[3] De la Mare, in turn, admired the logic and learning of Newbolt's conversation. 'Owing to his training in the law, he seldom failed to master anything on which he set his mind. He was a full, ready and lucid speaker, a vivifying conversationalist.'[4] When de la Mare went home that night he wrote: 'Every subject has so keen a scent, one goes breathlessly on, and runs nothing down. That is the fun of it.'[5]

Ella, with her deep-set, observant eyes, was also present at that dinner and she fell in love with de la Mare. (He was a handsome young man.) She began to give him help with his work, pruning his poems and preparing them for publication. Much of de la Mare's subsequent success as a poet was due to her. She also took an interest in his home life. He had a difficult wife, Elfie, and three children, and there were continual problems about where to live and how to pay the rent. Ella frequently house-hunted for the family, even giving them small sums of money from her own not very adequate allowance. Once she handed over the whole of a legacy she had just received from an aunt.

Newbolt loved de la Mare's poetry because of its dreamlike

2. *Dictionary of National Biography*
3. *AHL*, 13 May 1933
4. *Dictionary of National Biography*
5. De la Mare to HN, 14 Nov. 1902; Theresa Whistler, *Imagination of the Heart, A Life of Walter de la Mare* (1993), p.107

quality. De la Mare believed in the promptings of the Unconscious. Characters came into his head complete. 'We are dreaming all day,' he declared, 'as well as all night.' Like de la Mare, Newbolt also believed in fairyland. He was excited by de la Mare's first book of poems, *Songs of Childhood*, and he asked Mary Coleridge to review it for the March 1902 issue of the magazine. Mary was also a lover of Faerie, and believed that there was a time 'betwixt the mirk and the morning' when every dock leaf hides its elf. Strangely, Newbolt failed to appreciate de la Mare's first collections of poems for grown-ups. In August 1902, de la Mare sent them to him with a view to publication by John Murray. Newbolt sat on them for four months while de la Mare tried to support his family on £2 6s.11d. a week. In December came Newbolt's verdict: he refused to show the poems to Murray, but agreed to print a selection in the *Monthly Review*. On Newbolt's advice, de la Mare now turned to prose, producing *The Return*, which Newbolt was wildly enthusiastic about. 'It seems impossible that a book so original can fail to capture the whole position at once, from the citadel to the suburbs.'[6] In the event, the book, to use de la Mare's words, proved 'a dismal failure'. Newbolt was chiefly useful to de la Mare as a champion. Unlike de la Mare, Newbolt loved a fight and when his mouth tightened with disapproval or temper those who disagreed with him knew there was trouble ahead. 'Awkward fences were cleared, in the manner of the born steeple-chaser, by not noticing they were there.'[7] In 1905 Newbolt decided that de la Mare must be rescued from the Dickensian offices of Standard Oil whether he liked it or not. He succeeded in securing a Royal Bounty for him of £200 but it was for one year only. It was Newbolt's task to disburse this sum. Within ten days of the first payment, de la Mare was begging for a further £25 to clear off debts. To help out, Newbolt secured him a job as a reader at Heinemann, which he hated.

It was Newbolt also who, with the aid of the Settee, finally made the selection for de la Mare's book of adult poems, *Poems 1906*. But de la Mare's reputation was not finally established until he wrote 'The Listeners' in 1910. 'You might safely print it beside the 'Lady of Shalott' or 'St Agnes Eve'', Newbolt told him.[8] A pleasant post-

6. *Whistler*, p.165
7. Ralph Furse, *Henry Newbolt, A Perpetual Memory* (1939)
8. *Whistler*, p.167

script to the relationship is preserved in the BBC archives. In 1952, long after Newbolt's death, de la Mare read some of his poems in a programme entitled, The Speaking of Poetry. Recordings of Newbolt were also used. Newbolt's accent was clipped and upper class; he spoke quietly in measured phrases, almost as if he were thinking aloud. De la Mare's style was markedly similar, and this was not surprising, for Newbolt had spent many hours coaching him in the art of recitation.[9]

9. *Whistler*, p.249

CHAPTER 23

Conrad

Newbolt now became involved with Joseph Conrad. William Rothenstein had requested his assistance for the Polish author, who was in financial difficulties. Rothenstein suggested that Newbolt should see Edmund Gosse, who should see Balfour about a grant from the Royal Bounty Fund. Newbolt was anxious to be of help to 'a genius of whom we cannot know too much'.[1] He had admired *Lord Jim* and had met Conrad at the Savile Club. There, after lunch on Saturday afternoons, a small symposium of writers was in the habit of chatting round the fire. Conrad had been the guest on one of these Saturdays. His 'oriental face produced the effect of intellectual calm' but this was belied by his manner. 'The more he talked, the more quickly he consumed his cigarettes.' He rolled them so fast that 'the fingers of both hands were stained a deep yellow almost as far as the palms.'[2] Conrad told Newbolt that

1. *My World*, p.300
2. *My World*, p.301

he 'was the only son of Apollo Korseniowski, head of an ancient and wealthy landed family'.[3] (Conrad did not confine his fiction to hard covers.) It was this aristocratic background that caused Newbolt to hesitate in the matter of the bounty. Would Conrad regard it as charity? Rothenstein assured Newbolt that Conrad had already accepted money from the Royal Society of Literature and would have no objection. Eventually, a sum of £500 was granted to be disbursed in small amounts by Newbolt and Rothenstein, who would act as trustees.

When the news reached Conrad, who was wintering in Capri with his wife and child, he wired for money to be sent immediately to pay his fare home. This was refused and he demanded an interview with Rothenstein as soon as he landed. The interview went on until late at night, leaving Rothenstein exhausted. Conrad then turned on Newbolt, who spent a long and painful afternoon with him. Conrad wanted to draw upon the pension at will, as if it were a bank account, and demanded £250 right away to pay 'certain very pressing debts', which he had run up in Capri, a place he claimed he had visited for his wife's heart condition. (In fact, Jessie, whom Virginia Woolf had described as 'that great lump of a woman', was suffering from knees damaged by a fall in the street. She had embarked for Capri carried in a chair.) Then there were debtors nearer home – doctors and tradesmen in Hythe. Above all there was 'Mr Hogben my friendly farmer landlord'.[4] Conrad was at this time living at Pent Farm, near Ashford in Kent, which he had taken over from Ford Madox Ford. After listing his debts he proceeded to a heart-rending description of his own condition, claiming that he often wrote 'from ten to twelve hours on end till consciousness is lost.'[5]

Newbolt and Rothenstein had a long discussion about Conrad's request, and finally they reached a compromise. The debts must be paid, but to make sure that Conrad spent the money only on settling them, a lawyer would write out the cheques for him. Conrad was outraged. His honour had been called in question. Above all, he would be humiliated in the eyes of Farmer Hogben. He declared that he was so upset that, as he wrote, he could feel 'a

3. *My World*, p.301
4. *NL* Conrad to HN, 1905
5 ibid.

horrible fit of gout coming on.'[6] In the end, it was Conrad who suggested a new compromise: 'You will give me the various sums in cheques made out to me which I shall endorse in your presence and put into envelopes already addressed to my creditors.'[7] Newbolt was satisfied. Rothenstein commented: 'Our duty is now done, and his affairs are as bad as ever.'[8] He little knew how bad. Jessie was pregnant with her second child and the couple were soon afterwards to embark on the disastrous trip to France, during which Conrad threw all the baby's clothes out of the window of the train.

6. *NL* Conrad to HN, 1 June 1905
7. *NL* Conrad to HN, 5 June 1905
8. *NL* Rothenstein to HN, 5 April 1906

CHAPTER 24

H.G. Wells

Newbolt's intimate (if brief) friendship with H.G. Wells was one of the most surprising results of his stint as an editor. Wells had burst upon the world with *The Time Machine* in 1895, and seven years later Newbolt reviewed with enthusiasm his strange novel, *The Sea Lady*. In it, a mermaid called Doris Thalassa became friendly with a mortal called Chatteris, on holiday at Lummidge's Family Hotel. Doris is totally amoral. Sexual fulfilment comes before everything for her, and she takes Chatteris down into deep tangled places. The book expressed Wells's own desire at that time, not only for sex outside marriage, but for sex without love. Encouraged by Newbolt's praise, Wells invited him to join the Co-efficients, a dining club founded by Beatrice and Sydney Webb 'for politicians to meet thinkers'. Balfour, R.B. Haldane and Lord Grey of Falloden were members, while a young man called Bertrand Russell spoke for free-thinking Radical Whigs. Newbolt was the only poet, and he took part in several of the lively debates for which the club was famous.

Shabby little Herbert George, son of a housekeeper, with what Gissing called 'the wild face and the naïve manner', was hardly Newbolt's type. But Wells was a charmer. The two men started to have walks and talks together and they even 'went on a bust'[1] at the Earl's Court Exhibition. (Wells was quite ill afterwards.) Wells was extraordinarily open to Newbolt about his physical ailments, even confessing to a boil on his bottom. 'To be perfectly frank I have some malignant growth inside my rectal sphincter.'[2] But their most intimate interchanges were held at the *Monthly Review* office when subjects too deep to mention on paper were discussed. 'Come up here' Newbolt would say, 'where the postman can't hear us.'[3] Newbolt was aware that he had fallen precipitately into the friendship. 'I've not had time to know you yet. My affections always work quicker than my brains.' Certainly, there was much to divide the two men. Wells accused Newbolt of 'streetwalking' public school ideals. 'You believe in the "Great Age" in rare moments, but your heart is with Clifton and the accidents of your own life. You come near the spirit of the thing at times, in "Commemoration" for instance, and then you're away again.'[4] Newbolt defended himself: 'There is no such thing as "petty loyalty" since loyalty is a quality, not a quantity, and cannot be petty: nor is the obligation to practise it any less binding in smaller affairs than in greater.'[5]

Newbolt wrote a long piece on Wells in the *Monthly Review* of June 1903. He started by pointing out that of course he did not agree with everything Wells said, but at least Wells was someone he could argue with, unlike George Bernard Shaw. 'Arguing with Shaw is like arguing with a jack-in-a-box.' Newbolt declared that he himself would be glad to see much of the Victorian claptrap swept away. But Wells swept the past away too completely in his desire to create a new world. 'Must the monarchy and the peerage give way entirely to government by hustings-bawling, newspaper clamour and rich business? Must a new aristocracy be born with such titles as Knight of the Order of Urban District Sanitary Authority? I too am sick of most of the old formulas, but I don't believe the truth

1. *HGW Hofstra*, Letter from HN, 30 July 1904
2. ibid, 1 June, 1904
3. *HGW Illinois*, Letter, 11 July 1904
4. *HGW Hofstra*, Letter, 9 May 1904
5. *My World*, p.95

they expressed no longer exists.'[6] 'Of course I don't know what *reality* is but I intend to die looking for it, and if you want me to agree to abandon personal immortality, Christianity etc., I am quite ready but you must show me that they have nothing to do with reality. I guess you are one who doesn't feel that beauty is very near to *reality*, and therefore the desire of it one of the strongest possible motives for human action. The beauty I see in the past is all important.'[7]

Wells hotly objected to the suggestion that he did not care for beauty. 'Do you fancy I have never walked with God in beautiful places? I am a poet whose medium is lean prose.'[8] Perhaps not surprisingly, considering his relationship with his assistant editor, Newbolt did not quarrel with Wells's theory of Free Love, expressed in *A Modern Utopia* 1905. There, Wells declared that what went on between consenting adults was no business of the authorities. Wells wrote to Newbolt: 'Very many thanks for your appreciation. My impression is that the unregenerate man wants to have any woman he fancies and all the others to stand about ready if he calls.'[9] So, he added, did the unregenerate woman, only less so. Newbolt was well aware that Wells put these principles into practice, for had he not just very publicly seduced Amber Reeves, the daughter of a fellow Co-efficient?

In 1905, Wells invited Newbolt to a debate at the Whitefriars Club. The subject was to be 'Public School Training', and the speakers for the public schools were Arthur Pearson (owner of the *Evening Standard*) and Welldon, the Socialist Bishop of Manchester. Newbolt well-nigh exploded. 'Do you propose,' he wrote, 'that I should listen to prolonged slobbering over the Public School Spirit by these unctuous, bulging-bellied, flag-wagging BOUNDERS to the cheering of the Swells, and the sneering and the jeering of the Wells? Ask Harrow and Winchester what they think of these two beauties. And ask me another time.'[10] But it was a piece of the social ineptitude which brought their friendship to an abrupt end in 1906. Wells's final *faux pas* was probably connected with the death of Lord Grey of Falloden's wife. Wells wrote to

6. *HGW Illinois*, Letter, 7 May 1904
7. *HGW Illinois*, Letter, 30 June 1905
8. *My World*, p.95
9. *HGW Hofstra*, Letter, n.d.
10. *HGW Illinois*, Letter, 5 Mar. 1905

Newbolt: 'I forgot, confound it, about Lady Grey. But you know I shall never be a gentleman, so one more sin hardly matters.'[11] Newbolt thought it did.

11. *HGW, Hofstra*, Letter, n.d., 1906

Emily Newbolt, 1871
'I had such a wonderful dream last night - I saw your father quite clearly,
and he spoke as if he had never gone away.'

Henry John Newbolt,
aged twelve

Henry Francis Newbolt, b.1824, d.1866
'In some ways he was swallowed up and lost
in the heart of the Black Country.'

Newbolt (right) with his brother
Francis (centre) and a friend

Lt. Col. George Newbolt
'He and two other retired officers
were known as the three holy colonels,
chiefly remarkable for having married
between them eight wives and having
thirty three children.'

G.H. Wollaston, Newbolt's
housemaster in North Town.
'I had only one mother,
and one Wollaston.'

Addlestone, Wegbridge. 12th August 1887
Engagement of Francis Newbolt and Alice Bright
Standing on porch: Alice, Frank, Henry
Seated: Emily, Milly
(Just over two weeks later, Henry first met Margaret Duckworth)

Lynton, 1888
Emily, Milly, Tom Chitty
Henry, Margaret, Evelyn Duckworth (Margaret's sister)

Margaret Duckworth, 1889
'She seems to be sitting in the centre of a circle and we around her at some little distance. She's lovely but doesn't want to be.'

Ella Coltman, 1902
'A still listening face [and] eyes that seemed to recall some far off desolate longing for home and childhood.'

Netherhampton House

Lady Alice Hylton

Celia and Francis Newbolt, 1900

Henry Newbolt, 1910

Henry Newbolt, 1908

CHAPTER 25

The Boer War

The Boer War was hardly a subject that could be ignored by the poet of patriotism. Newbolt's first real war almost doubled his output of poetry without increasing its quality. A poem, 'The Sailing of the Long-Ships'[1] celebrated the embarkation of 50,000 men for South Africa. The six verses, which commenced: 'They saw the cables loosened, they saw the gangways cleared' had appeared in *The Spectator* in November 1899. They were published in a book of the same name in 1902. 'For patriotic verses I am top dog among the present lot,' Newbolt declared. But for him it was Clifton that was at war, not England – just as H.G Wells had said. Almost at once *The Old Cliftonian* reported 29 O.Cs at the front. True, only three had been hit and none killed, but a death seemed near.'A very young lieutenant called Gunning has pleurisy as well

1. *S.P.*, p.74

as a bad wound and must be in danger,' wrote Newbolt to Emily [2]
A spate of school-at-war poems followed.

Surprisingly a sense of the sadness of war began to prevail in Newbolt's verse. There was 'Commemoration', the poem H.G. Wells had liked, in which the poet peopled the school chapel with the dead, and 'A Sower',[3] which owed much to *A Shropshire Lad.* The fourth verse ran:

> But the dumb fields
> Desire his tread,
> And no earth yields
> A wheat more red.

Meanwhile new editions of *The Island Race* were selling well. It was carried as the sole extra baggage in countless knapsacks, and songs from it were sung round many a camp fire.

Newbolt naturally commented on the war in the *Monthly Review.* The first year had proved disastrous, leaving Mafeking and Kimberley under siege. General Buller had been continually unsuccessful. Yet Newbolt remained optimistic. He entitled an editorial 'Have We Been Humiliated?' and concluded, 'No, we have not.'[4] The second year of the war, 1900, was the year of British victories. Ladysmith as well as Mafeking had been relieved, and Newbolt noted with satisfaction that '73 waggons of chops and tomato sauce had been taken in to supplement mule soup and meal'.[5] Yet even Newbolt could not deny that the third year of the war, the year of mopping up, was long and depressing. He wrote an editorial entitled 'National Fog', complaining of 'a cloud of darkness and bewilderment'.[6] On top of all this, there was Kipling to contend with. Kipling, was not only universally popular, but he had returned from South Africa and attacked the public schools in a poem in *The Times,* entitled 'The Islanders'. It argued that public school boys like Buller had been responsible for the disasters of the first year of the war. The 'flannelled fools' had proved no match for the Boers. It was Kitchener who had saved the day and he was not from Eton. Newbolt replied in a poem entitled 'An Essay on

2. *NL* HN to EN, 13 Nov. 1899
3. S.P. p.91
4. *MR*, Nov 1901
5. *NL* HN to EN 2 Mar. 1900
6. *MR*, Dec. 1901

Criticism'.[7] He advised Kipling to stick to subjects he knew:

> O Rudyard, Rudyard, in our hours of ease
> (Before the war) you were not hard to please:
> You loved a regiment whether fore or aft,
> You loved a subaltern, however daft,
> You loved the very dregs of barrack life,
> The amorous Colonel and the sergeant's wife.

Newbolt followed the poem up with an editorial defending chivalry. 'War,' he declared, 'is either a game or else a brutality worse than bestial. The Islander, the child of all ages upon our playing fields, will "play the game": he will win if he can do it within the rules but not at the cost of that which is more than any game.'[8] He quoted Wordsworth's 'Character of the Happy Warrior': 'he who plays in the games of life, that one where what he most doth value must be won.' War, Newbolt declared, is beastly unless it is conducted under the rules of Chivalry. And had we stood by them in South Africa? Yes. 'They have been in the pocket-book of our army in South Africa, a rule of conduct prescribed neither by field-marshal nor chaplain but founded in the blood and memory of the race itself.' Newbolt had written this at a time when Dutch farms were being burnt down and women and children were dying in concentration camps. Bernard Holland was not so sure that this was 'keeping the rules'. He was now on the Transvaal Concessions Commission. 'It does not seem to me that life is a "game" at all,' he wrote, 'but a serious work and business, and so possibly it may seem to Dutch Republican farmers who have not been bred on football and cricket.[9]

Even Newbolt could not claim that the Boer War ended in a glorious victory. He admitted that many of the generals had failed, though not because they were from public schools, but because they were old. 'Their training had been obliterated by thirty years' exposure to the influence of luxurious, idle and frivolous society.'[10] Out of the cleansing furnaces of South Africa, he said, must grow a New Army, and particularly, according to Frank Younghusband,

7. *S.P.*, p.109
8. *MR*, Apr. 1904
9. *NL*, Feb. 1901
10. *MR*, Sept. 1902

a new and lighter cavalry armed with rifles, like the Boers. The signing of the treaty at Vereeniging came in May 1902, and the Newbolts at Earl's Terrace celebrated appropriately. 'The good ship "23" flies the biggest flag of all,' Newbolt proudly announced.

Newbolt now joined the Clifton war memorial committee. Forty-three Clifton volunteers would not return. Soon there was disagreement about the form the memorial should take. Percival wanted to expand the chapel 'into a kind of young cathedral.'[11] In the end, a statue was agreed upon, a figure in bronze representing patriotism. Some wanted a soldier in contemporary uniform; Newbolt wanted St George in fourteenth-century armour. Newbolt won, and set out for the studio of G.F. Watts to commission the work. He found him 'a courteous and humourous old gentleman', but Watts refused to take on the statue. He was too old and tired and was engaged on his statue of 'Physical Energy'.[12] (He was eighty-six years old and the famous colossus destined for Hyde Park in fact finished him off.) Ultimately, the Clifton statue was executed by Alfred Drury and unveiled in 1904 by a battered veteran of the recent war, Lord Methuen. The young warrior in bronze stands bare-headed, his peerless face turned towards the Close from which, as Lord Methuen predicted, so many more would offer themselves. Perhaps it is for these that he weeps green copper-oxide upon his stone pedestal. Or perhaps his tears are for the death of chivalry that had already begun. Beneath the statue there is a bronze tablet on which is engraved Newbolt's tribute:

> Clifton, remember these thy sons who fell
> Fighting far over sea;
> For they in a dark hour remembered well
> their warfare learned of thee.

Newbolt for some reason was not present at the unveiling. 'It was a great day for me really,' he exclaimed to Emily, 'though I wasn't there.'[13]

After the war, Newbolt felt a sense of anticlimax summed up in his four-line poem, 'Peace'.[14]

11. *NL* HN to EN, 21 May 1901
12. *NL*, HN to EN, 5 Feb. 1903
13. *NL*, HN to EN, 2 July 1904
14. *S.P.* p.80

No more to watch by Night's eternal shore,
    With England's chivalry at dawn to ride;
No more defeat, faith, victory – O! no more
    A cause on earth for which we might have died.

He sent this poem to Virginia Stephen, who replied: 'Your little postcard with a little poem on it gives me great pleasure – and pride. I have spent Sunday at a house where the only book is your *Admirals All*, and now I come back to find this.'[15]

The *Monthly Review* was not only concerned with army reform but also with naval. In 1902 Newbolt commissioned three articles from his friend Julian Corbett, criticising the education of naval officers. The younger men were 'clamouring to be taught what they were expected to know, and sighing for some such system as countries like Chile and Portugal had.'[16] The subject of naval education had been under review since 1870, but so far all that had been achieved was the laying of the foundation stone of the Dartmouth Royal Naval College. Newbolt was alarmed when, after the first of the articles appeared, he received a letter from Admiral Fisher, the First Sea Lord. '[It] was abrupt but not apparently hostile – he merely shouted, as it were, that I was expected next day at the Admiralty.' Newbolt knew that Fisher was capable of 'warm feelings and unhesitating language.' As he entered the office, he expected grapeshot, but Fisher appeared to have forgotten why he was there. He 'rattled on' about Dreadnoughts, and suggested that Newbolt return at 8 o'clock the next morning 'to see the finest thing in the service, the line of three hundred charwomen leaving the Admiralty.' Then suddenly he came to the point, putting his hand on Newbolt's knee. 'You must give me that man Corbett! He finds things out!'[17] After that Newbolt had many conversations with Fisher. 'He was the possessor of an almost mesmeric power of attraction. Walking me up and down the Admiralty corridor he kept me alive by the flow of his own extraordinary vitality, pouring into me from the big nervous hand upon my shoulder.[18]

Sir Julian Corbett (as he later became) was to develop into the

15. *My World*, p.250
16. *My World*, p.225
17. *My World*, p.25
18. *My World*, p.257

most important writer on naval matters in the first half of the twentieth century. Churchill declared that Corbett, although a civilian, was the only man capable of writing adequate 'accounts of sea-fighting and naval strategy.'[19] Corbett was a lawyer and a scholar of private means. His fame as a naval historian was achieved only after he became a lecturer at the new Royal Naval College at Greenwich. Before that he had written novels about the Spanish Main based on papers in the newly-founded Naval Records Society. It was the *Monthly Review* articles that set him on a new course.

As a result of Corbett's three articles, Fisher declared that Lord Selborne's New Scheme of Naval Education should have top priority, and indeed staked his career upon it. Two years later, Fisher became First Lord of the Admiralty and he carried out many of the suggested reforms with the maximum of brutality. He said of officers who opposed him: 'their wives shall be widows, their children fatherless.' During this period Corbett was constantly at his side. Corbett kept Newbolt informed of the movements of 'the Jack-fish' in a series of letters.[20] Fisher himself wrote to Newbolt to say that the *Monthly Review* had been a powerful influence in shifting the dead weight of naval lethargy.[21]

19. Winston Churchill, *The World Crisis* 1911–1914
20. *Corbett Papers*, Ed. Tunstall 1958
21. Donald M. Schurman, *Julian S. Corbett*, 1981

CHAPTER 26

Chillingham

Long breathing spaces in Northumberland were now more necessary than ever. At Chillingham Castle near Belford the welcome wind howled continually over the Cheviots. It was one of the homes of Sir Andrew Noble, and was big and inconvenient, being built, like an Oxford College, round a quadrangle. To reach the suite of apartments reserved for favoured guests, it was necessary to pass through successive state rooms. 'In a house where many kept late hours there would always be talk going on in the drawing-room after I had gone to my own room. There, as I soon found, I was a prisoner from the moment of taking off my evening dress. I might wish to retrieve a book or railway timetable but I could not go down without passing through the drawing-room, and that was not possible without resuming full dress.'[1] It was now understood by Newbolt's friends that Ella should be

1. *My World,* p.263

147

included in any invitation and the three of them preferred the Prince of Wales wing, which contained 'the Bower of Beauty'. This was a thirteenth-century stone-vaulted room with a window that looked across the formal garden (once a tilting ground) and beyond to 'the green sunlit hills'. Mary Coleridge wrote a poem about it:

> Let music whisper from a casement set
>   By them of old,
> Where the light smell of lavender may yet
>   Rise from the soft loose mould.

All this peace and beauty was founded on guns. Sir Andrew Noble was an arms manufacturer. He was chairman of the Armstrong Ordnance Company of Elswick, Newcastle and it was he who introduced the rifled breech-loading field gun. When Newbolt knew Noble he was developing a new gunpowder and experimenting with explosions in closed steel vessels. Some of his experiments were done late at night in his laboratory at Chillingham, and it was there also that he wrote much of his famous book *Artillery and Explosives* (1906). Newbolt saw the self-made Scot as one of Froissart's earls, 'a wise knight of high enterprise and of good counsel'. At his court 'all manner of tidings of every realm and country might be heard'.[2] And then there were Noble's four fine sons and two daughters. One of the daughters had a performing dachshund. Further entertainment was supplied by rows between Sir Andrew and his Canadian wife, Margery. 'Whether Lady Noble or her husband was the more dominating figure we could never decide.' He would call her "woman" and she would call him "a very foolish old man".[3] The famous Chillingham herd of wild white cattle was another source of entertainment: Celia and Francis were taken on expeditions to see them. 'The hill on which they lived was not far off, but passed through tracts of enormously high bracken. My children took great delight in getting lost in it. When we reached the open ground above, it was not easy to know how to approach the cattle. They had made, at various times, very sudden and dangerous attacks on visitors.'[4]

2. *My World,* p.260
3. *My World,* p.261
4. *My World,* p.262

CHAPTER 27

The Liberals

As the Boer War ended, another, Newbolt's war against John Murray, began. There had been mild disagreements between editor and proprietor from the beginning. Newbolt, for instance, encouraged all shades of Christianity in his religious contributors, but Murray objected to a certain Father Shepherd's views, which included open avowal of peas in the shoes and the rejection of any drink but tea. 'I daresay he is a true enough picture of those contemptible hybrids, the Extreme Romanising Anglicans,' wrote Murray, 'but the reader will be at a loss to understand him. Roman Catholicism,' he added, was 'opposed to my most rooted convictions. I have been a good deal mixed up with friends and relations who have joined the Roman Catholic Church.'[1] Murray was also upset by Alfred Ollivant's serialised novel, *Danny*. Ollivant had made his name with *Owd Bob*, a blameless tale of a sheepdog,

1. Letters, 11 Oct 1902 and April 16 1903, John Murray Papers

but now he ventured into the world of sex. Murray wrote to Newbolt, declaring the final chapter of the serial was altogether too crude, indeed 'nauseatingly vulgar'. Newbolt (on holiday in Northumberland as luck would have it) conceded that there was 'occasional coarseness' and that Ella, 'who has very good judgement', agreed. Feeling unable, out of respect for the artist, to make alterations on the manuscript, he forwarded Murray's letter to Ollivant. Ollivant's response, ill-written in red ink, ran: 'I am most thankful to the *nauseated* one for his rude remarks. He was absolutely right and if the *nauseating* bits had been published nobody would have been more *nauseated* than their author.'[2]

However, it was in the matter of politics that Newbolt and Murray most seriously disagreed. Newbolt had been aware, when he took on the editorship, that Murray was a Conservative, but at the time had made light of the problem. 'The Murrays are, or believe themselves to be, Conservatives: but they have become more liberal of late years,' he wrote.[3] He did not think Murray would see his Liberalism as a serious threat; after all, the Liberals had been out of office since the fall of Lord Rosebery in 1895, and Newbolt considered himself only a moderate Liberal. 'I am not a party politician, and I do not wish to pretend to greater sympathy with the present Liberal Party than I really feel, but I may say that the principles in which I believe are liberal principles,' he wrote to Lord Grey of Falloden in May 1900.[4] Parliament, however, was dissolved while Newbolt was planning the first issue of the *Monthly Review*, and his good resolutions flew out of the window. Here was a chance to get Lord Salisbury's coalition government out. After the magazine appeared on the bookstalls, certain newspaper cuttings 'broke in upon the peace of St Andrew's', where Murray was playing golf. He was particularly concerned about one from *The Huddersfield Examiner*, asking for the support of every Liberal for the *Review*, declaring that 'the magazine's Liberalism may be described as philosophically Imperialistic,'[5] Newbolt wrote to Murray contritely: 'I am sorry that some friend of yours was moved to wrath by the wildness of our Liberalism. I assure you I am

2. ibid. Letter, July 1903
3. *My World*, p.270
4. *My World*, p.271
5. *My World*, p.242

continuously watching, like an old spider at the centre of a web feeling various twitches.'[6]

It was the treacherous pro-Boer Liberals, led by Campbell Bannerman, that threw Newbolt into the arms of their opponents, the Liberal Imperialists, led by Lord Rosebery. Newbolt naturally opposed anyone who opposed the war in South Africa. When he heard in 1902 that 'the pro-Boer crew' were planning to launch 'a half-crown Liberal review', he wrote to Murray: 'This will give us the leverage to get Rosebery, Asquith, Grey, etc, to write for the *Monthly Review.* Lord Grey of Falloden, a future foreign secretary, was his first big catch. Grey was a man after Newbolt's heart. A true country gentleman with his roots in Falloden, his estate in Northumberland, he was laterally descended from Lord Grey of the 1832 Reform Bill. Newbolt had wanted Grey to contribute since the foundation of the magazine, but so far had only achieved a snatched interview after cricket at Lords, a year earlier.[7] Only now did Grey agree to write for the *Review* on politics, while protesting he would much rather write about fly fishing.

Newbolt also decided to seek an interview with the eccentric Lord Rosebery, while at the same time remarking, 'I hope he will be too busy trying on his coronation robes to see me.'[8] (The Great Queen had gone at last and Edward Vll was about to be crowned.) Rosebery was a man of immense wealth. He owned three Derby winners, and his London mansion was hung with magnificent pictures, mostly portraits, including 'the famous one of Pitt'.[9] Newbolt was received in the study, where the talk turned to Shakespeare and Rosebery made the remark: 'I would happily die this minute if Shakespeare were to walk into this room.' But there was never the feeling of intimacy that Newbolt had with Grey. 'His face is a mask. You continually think you see through, but you don't.[10] Eventually, Newbolt was invited to one of Rosebery's famous all-male dinners. Twenty-four men, no two of the same profession, sat round the vast oval table. This was Rosebery's stage, where he was at his ease. Newbolt was not. It was Rosebery's idea of fun to set his guests at each other. 'He asked me suddenly across

6. Letter, 28 Nov. 1900; John Murray Papers
7. *My World,* p.273
8. *NL* HN to EN, 22 June 1902
9. *NL* HN to EN, 29 Mar. 1903
10. *NL* HN to EN, 29 Mar. 1903

the table whether I thought Swift was ever guilty of snobbery. I replied that in his place-hunting days he looked like a snob on a colossal scale. "Ah!" said my host, "then you don't agree with Sir Henry Craik, who has just painted him as an archangel of humility?" There, only two places from me, was Craik himself, roaring like a lion with a thorn in its paw!'[11] On another occasion, Newbolt went to one of Rosebery's small dinners, but found himself no more at ease. 'I had slipped that morning and cut my face deeply, so that my left cheek – the one towards my host – was conspicuously bound up in black plaster. All through dinner I was aware of Rosebery's wide and curious eye fixed upon my patch and of his still more curious mind silently conjecturing in what sort of an affair I came by it.'[12] There was an air of dissatisfaction about Rosebery. He had treasures without number but not enough to enable him to lead what he called 'the true ducal life', which should have included a palace in each of the ten greatest cities of Europe, each with a dinner prepared nightly in case he should drop in. Once he showed Newbolt a drawing of himself as a young man, 'a brilliant mind looking out from a beautiful and almost eager face. He stood close to it and stared at it with an expression of great sadness.' Suddenly, Newbolt knew that this was not the man to be the next Liberal Prime Minister.[13]

Despite early skirmishes, there was comparative peace on the *Monthly Review* in the matter of politics until the issue of Free Trade emerged in 1903. Balfour (Salisbury's nephew) was now the Conservative Prime Minister in control of a coalition. It was his Secretary for the Colonies, Joseph Chamberlain, who aroused widespread anger by proposing to introduce a tariff on all imported goods in order to protect home industries. Free Trade, that great Victorian principle, was to be abandoned (although Imperial Preference would remain). The Roseberyites rose under the Free Trade banner and the *Monthly Review* became their mouthpiece. Newbolt had never been so busy or so happy. 'I rejoiced to find myself fighting in a real battle and in the sight of both armies. I was entirely possessed by the Free Trade doctrine, which I felt to be supported by an irresistible logic.' Between July

11. *My World*, p.276
12. *My World*, p.276
13. *My World*, p.278

and November 1903, he pursued great men relentlessly, commissioning articles, and secured contributions from a host of economists.

One of the hardest of the big fish to land was Sir Michael Hicks - Beach, known as Black Michael because of his fearful frown. The first problem was that Hicks-Beach admitted to no address. Somebody hinted that he might be found at Londonderry House and Newbolt hurried thither. 'I stood at the foot of the staircase and saw the great man coming down upon me like Olympian Zeus about to thunder. On the last step he stood growling, "How did you know I was here?"' At this point the amiable Lady Londonderry appeared indicating firmly that the two men could talk in the library. Accepting defeat, the old boy went in meekly, having 'left his thunderbolt outside.'[14] An article was commissioned.

The young Winston Churchill proved quicker to hook, but harder to land. The Conservative member for Oldham was known to have Liberal leanings and had promised an article for the November 1903 issue. On 12 October he declared that he couldn't do it. Newbolt would not have this. 'I called [at Mount Street] next morning at an hour when a busy member of the House would not be likely to be out of bed. The servant informed me that Mr Churchill was about to dress for his ride in the park. I was admitted and found him sitting up among his pillows reading with approval a copy of *Punch* which contained a caricature of himself.' After some discussion, Churchill capitulated: 'You'll let me have my ride first: and then I'll do the blessed thing.'[15] His article makes lively reading. It draws an apocalyptic picture of a Protectionist England where Mr Balfour rules like a dictator, 'a sturdy beggar with a red robe flung about his shoulders.' Meanwhile Murray surveyed the pages of his magazine with increasing dismay. He also surveyed its sales figures which were decreasing, particularly among older and more staid sections of his readers. Newbolt countered briefly, 'our contemporaries read it and the rest are dying off anyway.'[16] The truth was the *Monthly* lacked the steady financial backing the Conservatives gave to their *Quarterly*. Sometimes an issue,

14. *My World*, p.246
15. *My World*, p.248
16. John Murray Papers, 27 Sep. 1901

containing, say, three articles by men of rank on burning questions of the day, would sell out. At other times copies would be left on the shelf. At the end of the second year the fees to contributors had to be cut. Nobody moaned about that except the Expressionist poet Arthur Symons who made a tremendous scene.

Newbolt now set about drumming up support for the magazine. This involved attending a great number of dinners. Replying at the Shakespeare dinner at Birminghan on 23 April 1903 was rapidly followed by speaking at the Authors Club and a Whitefriars dinner. 'I also propose to dine at the House of Commons two or three times, to spread the light.'[17] And dining out in Edwardian times was no light undertaking. Hostesses competed with each other in elaborate ritual. At a dinner given by Lady Burghclere, the latest fad had been adopted for placing the guests at table. 'Cards are offered on a silver salver to each gent in the hall before entering, and he picks out the one addressed to him and opens it. It is like a Christmas game or a Bazaar lottery! I sat between Lady Nicholson, wife of the Petersburg ambassador and Lady Vantage.[18] The many courses that followed this ceremony put no small strain upon the digestion.

Newbolt resigned from the *Monthly Review* in the summer of 1904. At this time there was talk of yet another general election, and he wanted to be free to express his opinions. He hoped to leave the magazine at the end of July 1904 and start a prolonged summer holiday, but Murray was having difficulty in discovering a replacement. In a letter to H.G. Wells, Newbolt explained: 'I may be kept a little longer by the arrangements for the funeral. They haven't yet found the Phoenix who is to rise from my ashes.'[19] In the end, Newbolt agreed to produce the November issue in collaboration with the new editor, Hanbury Williams, but the task proved beyond him. In a letter to Murray dated 8 Oct. 1904, he wrote, 'I find it impossible to put together enough material for you. The copy should have gone to Bliss [the printer] on October 1st. It would not have been a book of any mark. I must therefore postpone the pleasure of appearing under your auspices again. Hanbury Williams seems to have picked up the reins with perfect ease.'[20] It was the only sharp letter he ever wrote to Murray.

17. ibid. 20 Apr. 1903
18. *NL* HN to MN, 25 June 1912
19. HGW, Hofstra
20. John Murray Papers

There is a postscript to the story of the *Monthly Review*. It provided Newbolt with space in which to air some of his more personal foibles. In one editorial, for instance, he confessed to detesting 'the twin scourges of our century, the game of Bridge and the motor car'. He knew of people who began to play Bridge after breakfast and played for ten hours, barely stopping to eat. Politicians lost their interest in work, wine connoisseurs lost their palate and, worst of all, young men lost their interest in girls. He personally knew of two girls on the verge of 'coming out' who had been obliged to spend an evening talking to each other while the men played.[21] As for cars! An incident with one of these led him to write an editorial entitled 'Motors and Manslaughter'.[22] Ralph Neville had told him how a cyclist had been killed on the bridge at Banstead Down by a driver 'doing at least 30 mph.' The national accident rate was up to two a week! By 1924 it might be as high as twenty. It would be the end of civilised existence, and the only hope was 'to build separate tracks for the cars, as we have for the locomotives, so that they would cease trying to steer among the pigs, poultry [and] paralytics.' Along with a dislike of the new went a continuing nostalgia for the old. Newbolt drew a picture of his type of old gentleman, who detested 'poachers, Bank Holidays, Dissenters, pro-Boers, barbed wire, and the hunting of captive foxes.'[23] In another article he spoke up for rabbits 'captured alive, kept in confinement, carried to execution and huddled and stifled in misery, turned out in strange surroundings half paralysed with terror and worried to death without even the possibility of escape.'[24] (Pigeons also suffered this fate before the invention of the clay pigeon.) During the last three years of the *Monthly Review*, Hanbury Williams was to give it a more frivolous tone. Emily was pleased with the extra serials, because she liked serials (as long as they were not historical). Milly had liked all the serials, but Milly was dead.

21. *MR*, Oct. 1901
22. *MR*, Aug. 1904
23. *MR*, April 1902
24. *MR*, Apr. 1902

CHAPTER 28

Milly

Milly had died suddenly on 17 August 1903. She had been ill for four years, and Newbolt had continued to be convinced that she must move to the country. Tom Chitty was equally determined that she should not. In the end, Newbolt prevailed. 'Don't be afraid of Tom,' he told Emily. 'He is very weak, and he means well in a feeble way. I think I have some influence with him, which I have never weakened by any sign of hostility.'[1] The Chittys moved to Caterham and, sure enough, Milly was once more her cheerful self, perhaps too cheerful. Newbolt described a visit to Ralph Neville's when she walked over to tea. 'She never stopped talking and laughing.'[2] She was still talking and laughing four and a half hours later when she drove her brother to Sutton station in Tom's car. Within two years the Chittys were back at Leinster Gardens, but Milly still appeared

1. *NL* HN to EN, 10 Jan, 1900
2. *NL* HN to EN, 19 July 1900

cheerful. In the autumn of 1902 she wrote Newbolt two sprightly letters, about her son Michael, now at prep school. These letters were among the few of hers that Newbolt preserved. In the second she described her visit to the 'dear blessed lamb' at school. 'No indecorous rush to his Mother's arms but a careful shutting of the door, and a placid advancing smile after it was duly latched!'[3] She compared him favourably with Frank's girls, 'two poor white mice' who had taken so long to settle at their school. 'I hope Alice won't dig them up to see if the roots are growing.' At the end of her letter, Milly admitted quite casually to a new symptom: 'The muscles of my legs refuse to act when I am at all played out and I cockle up on the floor.' Tom reported that she had become increasingly irritable, and Newbolt declared, 'She writes me affectionate letters but would probably scalp *me* too if I were nearer at hand'.[4]

There may have been another reason for Milly's increased irritability with her husband – she was seeing more of him! Tom, at the age of 47, had suddenly resigned from the bar and decided to give up his vast common-law practice. Having been 'earmarked for the Bench' all his career, he suddenly turned his back on the prospect of becoming a judge, and instead accepted the comparatively obscure post of Master of the Supreme Court, but planned to devote the greater part of his time to tabulating court decisions. The change was said to have been made for his health, but perhaps it was for Milly's. In fact, incessant hours of work at the courts were merely replaced by incessant hours of work at his desk (with a little time off for cabinet making in the basement). In the next 25 years he was to edit (among much else) all 31 volumes of Lord Halsbury's *Laws of England*. This task took him ten years. The change of occupation led to a considerable loss of income. 'A practice of £7000 p.a. will be thrown among the dogs,' Newbolt declared.' Tom will now be able to play at being rich on £1,500 after so long playing at being poor on thousands.'[5]

Some alarming physical changes began to take place in Milly. She was putting on weight in an extraordinary manner. In December 1902, she was diagnosed as suffering from Myxodoema

3. *NL* 13 Oct. 1902
4. *NL* HN to EN 10 Jan. 1901
5. *NL* HN to EN, 30 May 1901

by the brain specialist, Sir Victor Horsley. Myxodoema is caused by a thyroid deficiency, resulting in an accumulation of a mucinoid or glue-like substance in the tissues. For Milly, a beautiful and witty woman, it was a cruel affliction. Not only did her features coarsen, but the disease is known to produce a slowing down of the brain and loss of memory. (In older medical dictionaries it is even referred to as 'cretinism'). Sir Victor prescribed eating the thyroid of a sheep, administered (by 1902) in tablet form. Its effect on Milly was instantaneous. Within two months, Newbolt declared 'she looks as she did before she was ill and weighs only 9½ stone.'[6] Six months later she was dead. She collapsed suddenly while on holiday at Park Lane Cottage, Southwold, on the Suffolk coast.On her death certificate the cause of death was given as 'brain haemorrhage', but it seems more likely that it was a heart attack. It is known that excessive doses of thyroid can have adverse effects upon the heart.

Milly's death was too painful a subject for Newbolt to mention in his autobiography. All he wrote was: 'in August my brother and I suffered a very severe loss'.[7] A month afterwards he suddenly took off for Venice with Frank. 'We felt that nothing would lighten our load so much as an escape from England, for however short a time.' He returned after ten days, just in time to get the November 1903 *Monthly Review* to the printers.

Milly continued to haunt him for the rest of his life. Three years after her death, during a visit to Winchester, he went with Celia, then aged sixteen, to pick anemones in Hursley Copse. 'It was [there] that my youth came back to me for a moment, and I called to my own young daughter, who had strayed from us in the underwood, by the name of my sister, more irrevocably lost. This was the first of several such momentary illusions when I no longer feel that the generations of the past are gone so far from the realities of our own life.'[8] He wrote a poem on the subject, 'Ave Soror.'[9] The last verse ran:

> As through the copse she went and came
>   My senses lost their truth;
> I called her by the dear dead name
>   That sweetened all my youth.

6. *NL* to HN to EN, 9 Feb. 1903
7. *My World*, p.247
8. *LLL*, p.57
9. *S.P.*, p.104

For Emily the tragedy was as great as the death of Henry Francis had been. She chronicled it in *My World*, 'By the open grave she had a kind of vision. She suddenly knew that her youngest darling child had been given back to her in spirit, and she gave thanks for the new and happy life of her child in Paradise. Hers was so sweet and gentle a nature, so unselfish and good. Only her mother knew of the want of strength she often felt in carrying out her duties as a wife and mother. With Milly there now passed away much of Emily's old life, when she had comforted and advised and helped her daughter.'

Emily now became an increasing burden to Newbolt. She was a prey to endless imaginary complaints, 'putting Dr Viney through verbal gymnastics daily. He looks arch and resorts to fibs.'[10] In exasperation, Newbolt wrote his mother 'Put the kettle on the fire and fill it with carbolic and all the other "antis" and sit over it all day.'[11] Yet Emily continued to exhaust herself with charitable works. 'When the weather is 85 degrees the bus horses go half speed, but you go double.'[12] Eventually, it was decided that she must have a companion. Immediately her complaints shifted to the companion. These unfortunate ladies followed each other in quick succession. There was a certain Miss Searle, whom even Newbolt couldn't abide. She rewrote his poems for him in the style of Browning. In the end his tolerance snapped, and he declared he would not visit his mother until Miss Searle had gone. Next, Emily became obsessed with moving house; Addlestone was damp and she must move to Sidmouth, to Farnham, to a spa. Winchester was finally agreed upon, and Emily rented a house on St Giles's Mount, not far from the college. Soon she was busy with wall-papering and deeply interesting callers (mostly the wives of clergy). The family gathered at the Mount for the Christmas after Milly's death, taking a few days off from Orchardleigh. Six months later there was a fresh shock: Tom Chitty remarried. 'My breath was taken away,' declared Newbolt. Tom's second wife was the children's governess, Beatrice Margaret Hale. As a governess who could impose discipline, she had been welcomed. 'She has made quite a new crew of Tom and the chicks,' declared Newbolt.[13] But as a wife she was out of the question. Her style of letter-writing

10. *NL* MEN to HN, 16 Sept.1902
11. *NL*, HN to HEN, 4 Jan. 1902
12. *NL*, 18 July 1903
13. *NL* HN to EN, 2 July, 1904

alone, said Newbolt, proved she was from the wrong class. (In fact she was the daughter of the Revd. Edward Hale of Eton.) Newbolt had always declared there was something not quite right about the upbringing of his brother-in-law either. Tom Chitty had gone straight into the courts after he left Winchester because of his father's early death, he lacked the finish that Oxbridge would have given him. After the marriage, the Chittys moved to 47 Queen's Gate Gardens, only a short walk from Earl's Terrace, but Newbolt ceased to see them.

Henry Chitty, Newbolt's godson, was now the only link between the two households. He was twelve when his mother died and he detested the second Mrs Chitty, refusing to call her Mama. (They all called her Steppy.) He never forgave her for throwing away his toy soldiers when he was away at school. Newbolt became a sort of substitute parent to Henry, visiting him at Winchester. Tea at the Mount and games of hide-and-seek in the overgrown shrubbery became one of Henry's memories of school. There is a touching letter in my husband's possession that Newbolt wrote to his father on the occasion of his confirmation in December 1906. It consists of three sheets of stiff, high quality paper, covered with Newbolt's small, forceful handwriting. As young Henry opened it he must have seen a sermon coming a mile off, but the sermon proved palatable enough to be preserved for half a century. Newbolt compared life to a long-distance run. 'Take a five-minute halt in the middle of the run and ask yourself who are the men I really admire? Then fix your eye on someone ahead of you.' There remained the problem of which great man, and the answer was Christ. 'Christianity is not a set of rules made by clergymen but simply the only rule of life.' Then Newbolt moved to more personal matters. 'Sometimes your father may be, for some reason, unable to help you. He might disagree with you about something you have done, or wished to do. Well, be sure to remember that you have me to fall back upon. Not to support you against your father, of course, but to consult with. The letter ended, 'Goodnight dear boy, I'm afraid this is much the longest letter you have ever had in your life: but you can answer it on a postcard.'

Newbolt's own son, Francis, had yet to enter public school. At the age of nine he had been sent to Horris Hill, near Newbury, a preparatory school which specialised in getting boys into

Winchester. It was chosen perhaps because Quiller-Couch was sending his boy Bevil there, and because Mr Evans, the founding headmaster, was a 'prodigious cricketer'.[14] The Newbolts and the Quiller-Couches travelled down together on the first day of term, and were entertained to lunch by Mr and Mrs Evans before the other parents arrived. After lunch, Evans asked the boys questions on cricket, and Francis gave ready and observant answers. 'The "Q" chap is *not* a cricketer.'[15] Francis's class work, particularly his maths, was below standard, but by the end of his first year he was coming second in his form 'with perfect regularity'[16] and had gained a place in the football team (although not the cricket). 'Evans says he is a beautiful mover'.[17] Newbolt would drop work on the *Review* and hurry down to Newbury for school matches, suitably attired in tweed. (He was unaware that this costume, combined with his somewhat aquiline profile, earned him the nickname of 'Sherlock Holmes' among the boys.[18] Francis eventually gained a place in the exclusive top form which ensured that he would pass into Winchester without difficulty. There remains a curious epitaph to him at Horris Hill. Jimmy Stow, a later headmaster, has pointed out that all the seats round the cricket field at Horris Hill had 'Play up! play up! and play the game!' officially carved on them in gothic letters.

14. *NL* HN to EN,22 June 1902
15. *NL* HN to EN, 25 Oct,1902
16. *NL* HN to EN, 2 Dec. 1903
17. *NL* HN to EN, 12 Oct. 1902
18. *AHL*, n.d. 1914

PART VII NETHERHAMPTON HOUSE
1905–1913

CHAPTER 29

Trafalgar

No longer an editor, Newbolt felt 'a free man with a clear sky above',[1] And across that sky he saw the mizzen-topmast and riddled sails of the *Victory* sway. What more suitable subject for the centenary of 1805 than a book upsetting accepted views of Trafalgar? Dakyns of Clifton had, in fact, suggested the idea to Frank a year earlier. 'Why does that Poet brother of yours not write a book about Nelson?'[2] In fact, it was February 1905 before Newbolt started the book and, to get ahead of the competition, it had to be out by mid-June.[3] Newbolt wrote the book in under six

1. *My World,* p.296
2. *FN II,* p.167
3. *NL* HN to EN, 25 June 1905

months. He claimed that during that time he had never been happier. 'My imagination had long been stimulated by the letters of my grandfather, Charles Newbolt, who went into the Navy at the age of twelve and reached the Trafalgar fleet on October 15th. His ship was a frigate and took no part in the action, but his letters were long and ardent.' Like many before and since, Newbolt quickly became fascinated by the tactics of Trafalgar, 'the great game' that was played with ships for pieces. It had always been assumed that Nelson had approached the enemy (whose ships were arranged in a concave semi-circle ahead of him) in two columns (one ship behind the other). Nelson commanded the left column and Collingwood the right. But in 1898, Admiral Colomb had put forward the line-abreast theory. Newbolt insisted on a return to the column theory, but with a variation. He deduced that the ships in Collingwood's column individually took a turn to the right so that they approached the enemy in a line of bearing, not in succession. Newbolt's case rested upon the time at which each of Collingwood's ships engaged its opposite number. He combed the seven published volumes of Nelson's *Letters and Despatches* and spent hours at the Public Record Office, reading captain's journals and master's logs, paying special attention to chronometer readings.

There was a correspondence in *The Times*. Admiral Bridge jumped to the defence of Admiral Colomb. Newbolt immediately replied at length. In his autobiography, however, he omitted to mention that Bridge's letter had been provoked not by his book, but by a book by his old friend Corbett that had been published earlier.[4] *Fighting Instructions* was a collection of documents concerning Trafalgar edited by Corbett, who believed in the column theory, but without the addition of Collingwood's starboard turn. It was Corbett's description of 'Nelson's mad perpendicular attack' that had provoked Bridge. It should be emphasised that there were never any hard feelings between Newbolt and Corbett over this slight deviation in theory.

On 21 October 1905, Newbolt 'mafficked' round the decorated column in Trafalgar Square with the best of them. 'One amusing result of *The Times* correspondence has been that Admiral Sir

4. Schurman, Donald, M., *Julian S Corbett* 1981 p.123

Reginald Custance has invited Corbett and me to dine on the 26th to meet our opponent Admiral Sir Cyprian Bridge! Sir George Clarke, who agrees with us, is also coming, so we shall be in the majority when it comes to throwing the decanters! I am very much attracted by Custance, whose acquaintance I made early this year, and who said after meeting me, to our host: "I like that fellow. He's got something of the sea about him."[5] Seven years after Newbolt's book was published, the Admiralty appointed a committee to examine and consider the evidence relating to the tactics employed by Nelson at the Battle of Trafalgar. Again, Newbolt implied that his book had brought this committee into being: 'The Report of this Committee was presented in 1913 and gave me the most complete and unhoped-for shock of good fortune that I ever received in my working life. My estimate of the evidence, my marshalling of it, my conclusion on the principal of issue and even my amateur plan of the action, were all unequivocally confirmed.'[6] But, once again, it was in fact a book by Corbett that had stirred up the admirals. In 1910, Corbett published his *Campaign of Trafalgar*. In it he developed the column theory, while practically ignoring Newbolt's book, (in spite of Newbolt's protests to the contrary). Undismayed, Newbolt went on to claim that it was *his* plan of the battle that was exhibited on the *Victory* at Portsmouth. It is there to this day. However, the ships on the plan, though in two columns, show no sign of a deviation to the right. It was Corbett's plan.[7]

Newbolt added five of his ballads at the end of the book. The latest of these, 'The Old Superb'[8] was about a ship 'green as grass below' that came limping up just in time for Trafalgar. This and four older favourites, including 'Drake's Drum', all set to music by Stanford, were included in Sir Henry Wood's Promenade Programme for the Nelson celebrations in 1905, and remained part of the programme until 1924.

5. *NL* HN to EN, 12 Oct. 1905
6. *My World*, p.298
7. Peter Newbolt does not entirely agree with my interpretation of Newbolt's theory.
8. S.P., p.95

CHAPTER 30

The Old Country

By now Newbolt, like Hardy, had realised that novels paid better than poetry, and embarked on one. In *The Old Country*, Stephen Bulmer, a twentieth-century man visiting Orchardleigh (Garden-leigh) falls in love with Aubrey. While wandering among ruins in the grounds he drifts into the past, becoming involved with the family of Sir Henry Marland. He meets Marland's niece, Aubrey, and with her enters the old house down by the lake, with its suits of armour and log fires. There they have rather few adventures and listen to rather a lot of long theological disputes. Newbolt declared the book 'a complete success'[1] when it came out in October 1906. Only the 'poor hacks working for low-grade newspapers' failed to appreciate it.[2]

H.G. Wells liked it. He wrote from Spade House, Sandgate, to

1. *LLL*, p. 38
2. *NL* HN to EN, 9 Nov. 1906

166

congratulate Newbolt on transporting his time-traveller into the past without mechanical aid. 'You've thrown just the right veil of indefiniteness over all that, a veil of moonshine and summer mists and sunlit distance.'[3] Newbolt confessed that he had in fact considered using a time-machine, 'but your book of course put that out of the question.' Calderon was equally congratulatory, but then the book had been his idea. At his house on Hampstead Heath, during the summer, Newbolt had confessed that he would like to do something about the connection between patriotism and 'a passion for the soil itself. People were not then troubled about the Preservation of Rural England and I was at times looked upon as a kind of faddist or lunatic. I conceived that there was an active principle at work upon those who live closely with the land. They enriched it by their lives, and perhaps haunted it in spirit when freed from bodily encumbrance.'[4] There remained the question of what form such a work should take. '"Good bard," said Calderon, "you must write a play". But I knew that however I began I should soon be writing *my* play in verse, an unpopular method for the stage. "Then you must make it a historical novel, with plenty of conversations."'[5] Henry James flattered *The Old Country* in the sincerest way. He imitated it. After his death Newbolt discovered that James had left a half-finished book, *A Sense of the Past*, which closely echoed his own, although it was set in the eighteenth century. The Duckworths, of course, had opinions about any book based on Orchardleigh. Mr Duckworth wrote to Margaret:

'My dearest Maggie,

I hope the book will be a *financial* success – but I think it is too literary to be popular – and those persons who take it up expecting a *light* novel will throw it aside. The description of Gardenleigh has been recognised in this neighbourhood and our bookseller in Frome is out of copies. Aubrey has a little spice of Helen in her, but I never met the hero in real life.

with love to Hal
your loving
Father'

3. *LLL*, p. 39
4. *LLL*, p. 32
5. *LLL*, p.331

Margaret's godmother, Mrs Smith, wrote less dryly, but she too declared that Stephen was a mere lay-figure, 'an idea in trousers'.[6] She was convinced that Lady Marland was Mrs Duckworth (in spite of Newbolt's denials.) Where else, she enquired, 'had Harry got the ideas of Mothers' Meetings in the fourteenth century? And the sweeping away of Aubrey by her mother whenever the conversation took an objectionable turn was pure Mrs Duckworth.' Gertrude Bell, the famous Middle Eastern traveller, step-daughter of Mrs Hugh Bell) wrote emotionally, 'You have touched the strings of my heart. They are still vibrating, and I cannot be certain whether I am sending you the kind of letter I ought to send.'

The Newbolts were now frequent summer visitors at the Bell's house, Rounton Grange, near Northallerton in Yorkshire. Hugh Bell was now Sir Hugh, the famous iron-founder. Eventually, Mount Grace Priory, the Bell's guest house, became the Newbolts' permanent holiday home. 'On the morning after our arrival Gertrude Bell took us across the fields to inspect Mount Grace. The long facade of the building gives you all the charm of the fourteenth century, but the poetry of the place seizes you when you pass to the Great Cloister behind, with its roofless church and the remains of the fifteen cells. In this house, summer after summer, we welcomed our friends and saw our children and grandchildren grow up.'[7] The Newbolts virtually camped out, above the magnificent view. Margaret did the cooking and supplies were sent up from London by train. Newbolt considered it was particularly good for Francis to be there 'roughing it'. Celia had inherited her father's love of birds and could whistle the owls down from the woods. In his journal for 1906, Newbolt noted that Celia (now sixteen) had captured and reared a young barn-owl in the ruins of the church. But best of all were the ghosts. 'The place is so full of ghosts that it is impossible to forget them even for a moment'.[8] And if the ghosts failed to appear, Newbolt kept a white Carthusian habit in an oak chest in the hall. When he donned it his face was completely hidden by the cowl, and he became the fifteenth-century Nicholas Love, first prior of Mount Grace.

Newbolt's next historical novel, *The New June* (1909), was partly set

6. *NL*, 21 Nov. 1906
7. *LLL*, p.124
8. *NL* HN to EN, 30 Sept. 1910

in Mount Grace. It was a sequel to *The Old Country*, but bloodier. (He advised Emily not to read it.) The hero was young John, grandson of Sir Henry Marland, and the story was of the conflict in his life between fighting for the cause of Richard II and becoming a monk at Mount Grace. He opted for 'playing the game of life'[9] which included suing for the hand of Margaret Ingleby, declaring 'a man's cloister is his lady's heart'.[10] Newbolt used Dick Peile, now a clergyman, as a model for Nicholas Love, confessor to young John Marland.[11] The still celibate Peile often stayed at Mount Grace. 'A dear fellow, but he once told me life terrified him. He wants to escape from living altogether.' When the book came out it was criticised for its use of modern speech. *The Times Literary Supplement* complained that Newbolt's knights and squires were more like modern undergraduates. Newbolt wrote a letter to *The Times*, pointing out that, although the young men of Chaucer's day jousted and rode rather than playing cricket and travelling by train, they 'behaved otherwise very much as modern young men do.'[12] *The Madras Mail*, on the other hand, thanked Newbolt for sparing them the 'belikes', 'meseems' and 'withals' of Sir Walter Scott.

9. *New June*, p.75
10. *New June* p.385
11. *LLL*, p.127
12. *LLL*, p.131

CHAPTER 31

Netherhampton House

While Newbolt was pursuing Aubrey and other mediaeval dames through the land of romance, his real-life Aubrey had departed in pursuit of other game. Margaret had fallen in love with another man. He was Henry Furse, the sculptor, older brother of Charles Furse, the painter. Henry, like Charles, was that attractive combination, a country gentleman turned artist and in need of a wife. He had a fine yard of horses down at Netherhampton House, near Salisbury and was a superb rider, When he was on horseback you could forget his crippled legs. It was Charles, so recently dead, who had first admired Margaret's chiselled profile. She had noticed him staring at her in a railway carriage and when she enquired what was the matter, he merely replied, 'You'll do!' By this he meant that he wished to paint her portrait. He never did. Now Henry wanted to immortalise the flawless profile with the bronze head now in the possession of Patrick Furse.

When Margaret moved into Netherhampton House for a month in the spring of 1907, it was ostensibly for the purpose of having her head sculpted in Henry's studio. Also he had no one to run his house for him. (His wife had died recently and his sister had left to get married.) In effect, this was a trial separation from Newbolt. She wrote him affectionate daily letters, but they were about Henry. She was an artist herself and she described in detail the process of building up the maquette of the head in clay, a pinch at a time. Henry Furse encouraged her to draw. But, much more important, he took her on the longest, fastest rides of her life. She wrote to Newbolt of wild gallops on the downs. 'The air was simply lovely, the kestrels circling against a blue sky and the larks singing. On the way home in the dark there was no track and we seemed to be cantering into space. It required care not to ride into invisible harrows left at the corners of fields.'[1]

Gradually, however, the tone of Margaret's letters changed. She began to plead with Newbolt to come down at weekends. 'I am the only woman here and I feel so alone at dinner parties.' Also a new side of Henry's character was appearing. He was not just a lonely widower, he was a manic-depressive and was now sliding into one of those periods of depression when he refused to go out and needed someone to distract him constantly. Margaret realised it was Netherhampton she was in love with, not its tenant. Nonetheless the thought of returning to London was intolerable. The family must move down to Netherhampton.

At first Newbolt hesitated. He had now lived in London for twenty years and was a devoted clubman. On the other hand, he loved shooting and fancied himself as a squire. Finally, he was won over by a series of letters from Margaret describing the summer foliage in the lanes and the roses in the walled garden. He decided to try the experiment for a year, giving up the lease at Earl's Terrace and putting the furniture into store. It was a painful business. 'We feel as if we were dying ourselves.' Earl's Terrace had seen the children grow into young people. It had witnessed the rise and fall of the *Monthly Review* and hosted many gatherings of famous men. The family moved into Netherhampton on 30 September. Henry Furse did not move out. Not only did Newbolt have two wives, Margaret now had two husbands.

1. *NL* MEN to HN, 23 Mar. 1907

Netherhampton House is now considered one of the finest small mansions in England. Newbolt described it in *The Twymans*.[2] It was 'built in the days when a manor house was not bound to be a palace. [It was] a house of three storeys placed end-on to the road, and separated from it by a forecourt with a pair of wrought-iron gates.' In *The Twymans* version, the coat of arms above these gates was that of Percy's family. In reality, it was that of Edward Gauntlett, a maker of clay pipes, who had built the house in 1560. On his first visit, Percy did not enter at once. He was led through a gate in the wall to the left and found himself on a lawn flanked by the whole length of the original brick-built building. A white Corinthian porch opened out of the drawing-room on to the lawn, and the far end of the lawn merged into a wilderness garden with meadows beyond. On the other side of the house there was a quadrangle and a walled garden with a sundial in it.

The Newbolts arrived at Netherhampton in pouring rain. Newbolt scribbled a note to Emily: 'Useless to write letters. The ink would run. Useless to go out, it is too murky to see the country. Useless to breathe the fresh air, it is half mixed with water. Thank God for Aquascutum.'[3] Then the wind began to blow. 'I woke half a dozen times and thought every elm in the village must be down. Coming home from Salisbury it blew me off my bicycle and put my lamp out, a most ludicrous spectacle if it had not been in the dark!'[4] But then the signs of spring began to appear in the garden. 'A thrush has been heard talking loudly of taking a house here,' Newbolt told Emily[5] and on Shrove Tuesday 'the Reticulata Iris sprang into flower.' Suddenly Newbolt was converted to country life. 'I had not realised how complete the change would be. To wake invariably to an open skyline, to realise that the house was not one in a crowd, that to go out was to be merged in the life of the garden or the downs.[6] Magical summer days were to follow. Margaret told Newbolt of descending from the downs on horseback with Henry Furse 'into the village [which] was a dream of beauty in its deep green trees'.[7] Autumn was almost as good. 'You have missed the

2. *The Twymans*, p.125
3. *NL* HN to EN, 19 Oct 1907
4. *NL* HN to EN Feb. 1911
5. *NL*, 24 Nov. 1913
6. *LLL*, p. 85
7. *NL* MEN to HN, 24 May 1908

finest day of the year,' wrote Newbolt to Margaret, 'a still blue sky with the golden elms clouds down the village street, and this evening a moon and a deep orange glow in the west.'[8]

Newbolt's study at Netherhampton was a long attic known as the Ark, looking south towards the downs. Because the facade of the house had been added at a later date,the exposed roof timbers of the old house sloped across the room, causing a considerable hazard. Here Newbolt could enjoy 'hours of work, uncompelled and uninterrupted; my own books all in sight, wholly my own. It was a new pleasure to know that in the wing across the courtyard was the refuge of another artist, intent on setting forth his thought not in words but in bronze.[9] Newbolt also slept in an attic, not from choice, but because the large next room next to Margaret's must be set aside for Ella's visits. 'Do you think I might go back to Ella's room instead of that little garret?' he once asked Margaret. 'Then I can try to go to bed early and not work last thing.'[10]

Newbolt now set about playing the part of the country squire. He ran his household with the solemn regularity of a *pater familias*, rising early to say prayers before breakfast, (although often nobody came). Margaret usually kept him waiting for breakfast as well. (A letter of sincere remorse for this shortcoming exists.) He also took an active part in the life of the little church across the road. 'I had a busy week over my Churchwarden's Accounts,' he told Emily. 'You would laugh to see me examining the churchyard railings and collecting the Voluntary Church Rate.'[11] He was not as keen on horses and hounds as was Henry Furse, although he encouraged hunting, and got on well with the hunt servants. Even his forays into dog-owning were not successful. He bought a puppy for Celia, which was always getting lost. First it followed his bicycle into Salisbury and temporarily disappeared. Then it disappeared permanently. An attempt at cat-owning was not much more successful. The mice were eating the tulip bulbs and Margaret procured a kitten – 'but it only hunts its own tail.'[12]

But the lure of London was strong, and within weeks of arriving at Netherhampton, Margaret was there on a visit: 'Such a

8. *NL*, 3 Nov. 1908
9. *LLL*, p86
10. *NL*, 11 Feb. 1913
11. *NL*, 26 Mar. 1913
12. *NL*, 29 Nov. 1909

rapturous 1½ hours with the Mozart Quartet in D major. The cello, viola and violin were so friendly and jolly. The mud-coloured atmosphere outside all added to my happiness. But oh *how* queer not to turn into 23 afterwards – not to find you sitting with your feet on the drawing-room fender stool, with the tea-tray by your side and a manuscript on your knees and the beloved green carpet glowing under the tall lamp near the door – Ella's key turning in the latch.'[13] Newbolt was in London even more often, staying with a selection of friends and, when they failed, at the Savile. At times, he seemed to all intents and purposes, to be a commuter. The platform of Salisbury railway station became a familiar place. Margaret once walked into Robert Bridges there 'in such an exquisite rose coloured tie and grey suit [that] he lit up the station! He refused to shake hands with me because I had on white gloves, so we shook the book he was carrying!'[14]

13. *NL* MEN to HN, 2 Dec. 1907
14. *NL* MEN to HN, 24 May 1908

CHAPTER 32

Friends and Neighbours

Mary Coleridge had died suddenly of appendicitis just before the move to Netherhampton. She was barely forty. Margaret, on holiday at Mount Grace, had seen her only a few days earlier, lost in eager conversation as she escorted Arthur along the promenade at Harrogate. The Newbolts attended the service at Lawnswood cemetery near Leeds. Mary's fellow Grecians were there; Violet Hodgkin and Edith Sichel. Before setting out for the funeral Newbolt dashed off an obituary for *The Times* at Northallerton post office on ten telegram forms. 'A noble soul,' he declared, 'had entered very deep shadows, always returning towards the gates of Light.' Now at last Mary's poems could be printed in full, and Newbolt, as her literary executor, collected 237 of them in one volume to be published in 1908. In his twenty-page introduction he spoke of the lyrics that gave, in frank words, 'the bitterness of a moment's agony.' Two years later, Edith Sichel published *Gathered*

Leaves, a selection from Mary's prose works. It included a memoir which Newbolt did not care for.[1] Perhaps he found the description of Mary as three-quarters poet and one-quarter saint a little excessive.

Meanwhile Newbolt had 'fallen in friendship' with another poet who was also a novelist, Maurice Hewlett. The two men already knew each other, Newbolt had invited Hewlett to read a poem at the Omar Khayam Club in 1903. But they met much more frequently after the move to Wiltshire. Hewlett lived at Broad Chalke, only a few miles over the hill. He had bought an interest in a fine old rectory in the Ebbe valley. Newbolt used to bicycle over in full evening dress. Dinner, however, was often a scratch affair. Hewlett and his wife had separated. 'I only have one servant [and] a daughter to pack off to school, but you will guess how much I feel the need for speech with the likes of you.'[2] Hewlett, like Newbolt, had made his name with a sudden literary success. It was a novel of chivalry, *The Forest Lovers* (1898). Also like Newbolt, he had then abandoned the Law for literature. He claimed to be one-quarter Huguenot. Newbolt was attracted by his appearance, in spite of his peculiarities of dress. 'His face had the distinction that was not of the English type. In its keen, world-worn intellectuality it was French, yet it had something young and wild in it too, a touch of the faun who has not left his native forest.'[3] Hewlett admired 'Drake's Drum'. 'It is sure of immortality' he wrote.[4] He also felt a genuine affection for 'dear Harry'. In a letter to Ella, he wrote: 'He has a very sweet nature. I like his mind and I share a great many of his ideals. He has far more culture than I have.'[5] (Hewlett had only done a year of Greek at the Palace School, Enfield)

Newbolt also sought the society of his more aristocratic neighbours. Salisbury was dominated by Lord Pembroke of Wilton House, who was also his landlord. (Netherhampton House stands almost under the park walls of Wilton House.) Lord Pembroke used to invite Newbolt to shoot. However, Newbolt's pleasure was greater in another neighbour, Lady Glenconner, who had her seat at Wilsford, ten miles away. Pamela Glenconner (Lady Tennant

1. *NL* HN to MEN,2 May 1910
2. *LLL,* p.155
3. *LLL,* p.153
4. *The Letters of Maurice Hewlett,* 7 June 1911
5. ibid.

when Newbolt first met her) was a Wyndham by birth. She was as different from the stolid, industrial, Glaswegian Tennants as it was possible to be. Lord Alfred Douglas was her cousin. She was an acknowledged and pampered beauty, still in her thirties, with a liking for poets and artists. Wilsford, her house in the Arts and Crafts style, had only just been completed. It stood in the Avon Valley and was built of stone with gables and mullioned windows. Within was silvered-oak panelling and Morris wall-hangings. The bedrooms had names like Lily and Jessamine. Pamela Glenconner was a passionate woman, and it was an open secret that she had affairs. One of her lovers was her architect, Detmar Blow, who confessed that he would sometimes put out the candle and pretend to be asleep when he heard her approaching Celandine (his room).[6] Another lover was Lord Grey of Falloden, whom she later married. Pamela's heartily detested sister-in-law was Asquith's wife, Margot, who said of her, 'I can't stand women who are always draped with children.' Lady Glenconner certainly loved her children. She used to play at gipsies with Bim (Christopher), David and Clare, using a real horse and caravan. At other times, she would stroll in the water-meadows with John Drinkwater and, of course, Newbolt.[7] Margaret gave an amusing description of one of Lady Glenconner's visits to Netherhampton House when Newbolt was away. 'I walked her up and down the grass paths which were very wet. Pamela walked modestly inside a very narrow and short skirt and piped sweet things in her coolest voice. It made me feel hopelessly vulgar and loud.'[8] Lady Glenconner and Margaret, however, were not without an interest in common. They were both active *against* the Suffragettes. Although in sympathy with Margaret in this matter, Newbolt refused to be drawn in. 'No, I can't go about on suffragettes and suffragitis,' he said.[9] He did, however, organise a debate at the Co-efficients, where the ladies were successfully clobbered.[10]

6. Stephen Blow, *Broken Blood: The Rise and Fall of the Tennant Family* 1987
7. ibid. p.130
8. *NL* MEN to HN, 9 June 1912
9. *NL*, 8 Dec. 1908
10. *NL* HN to MEN, 26 Feb. 1909

CHAPTER 33

The Channel Fleet

In 1908, Newbolt was summoned to the Channel Fleet or, to be more precise, on board Admiral Custance's flagship, H.M.S. *Hibernia*, through the offices of his friend, Arthur Pollen, the gunnery expert. The Channel Fleet was organising a nine-day manoeuvre under Admiral Sir Charles Beresford, which would culminate in the ceremonial welcoming of the French president at Dover. Newbolt was to report at Portland at the end of May. He obeyed, taking with him Frank's camera, and promising Margaret he would sent her 'a letter diary'. He was immediately enchanted by the ritual of life on board a fighting ship. Eighteen sat down to dinner that first night, and admirals from other ships were piped on board with the bosun's whistle. At 9 p.m., in the middle of dinner, there was a routine disturbance. 'A midshipman enters and glides round to the Captain's chair. "It is nine o'clock," he says. The Captain's portly bulk rises slowly and bends towards the Admiral.

"It is nine o'clock, Sir." "Thank you;" says the Admiral. The Captain sinks into his seat again, remarking to the midshipman, "Very good; make it," and BANG goes the (nine o'clock) gun, driving your dinner home like a hydraulic rammer.'[1]

Life at sea, Newbolt found equally congenial. He was not even displeased by his little metal box of a cabin above the engine room. 'I slept like a top, in a very snug cot, and was woken by every kind of noise at once, engines pumping, men rushing, huge weights bumping and chains rattling.[2] Nor was he bothered when water came in at his porthole at 5.00 a.m. 'The blue-jackets were swabbing the decks very vigorously.' He saw the battleship as a marvellous machine in which each human cog played its part. 'Every man knew his job and did it. Officers who had made themselves so friendly to me at the table ten minutes ago, now walked not only past, but almost *through* me, to speak to a blue-jacket by his name. I felt then that I was but the invisible ghost of my grandfather.'[3] Best of all was Admiral Custance himself. On the bridge, 'he is quite transformed, his expression one of eager, keen thoughtfulness. There is an odd Nelsonian touch about the little man.'[4]

The weather was perfect until they reached Dover, and even there it stayed calm long enough for the officers to play a cricket match against the young gentlemen of Dover College (and lose). Then a fearful sea blew up and Admiral Sir Charles Beresford, who had been visiting *Hibernia*, only just managed to return to his own ship to take charge, 'dropping off the stern gallery and getting his gold-laced dress trousers soaked.' To make matters worse, this was the moment when the fleet was supposed to welcome the president of France, the whole fleet saluting him with salvos. Newbolt tried to take photographs but there was too much gun smoke. He had to satisfy himself with three snaps of Custance's dog for Celia. Despite the storm, he showed few signs of seasickness, although he confessed that he did once go down to his cabin with a headache. That was after a particularly large lunch (they seemed to seldom stop eating on *Hibernia*), but he was up on deck again a couple of hours later in a dry cardigan and socks. All too soon, it was time to return to dry land. He told Margaret: 'I

1. *LLL*, p.119
2. *LLL*, p.109
3. *LLL*, p.117
4. *NL* HN to MEN, 24 May 1908

have now seen what I suppose no one outside the Navy, not even Arthur Pollen, has ever seen, the whole fire-control of an English battleship.'[5] He had also observed a few *faux pas* which he only mentioned privately. There was the occasion when the French president's ship almost ran down some sailors in a picket boat. The sailors 'thought they were sinking. So they all began throwing off their clothes. The flag lieutenant called them "disgusting brutes" for undressing, but their boat was filling up with water.'[6]

Six poems resulted from Newbolt's visit to the Channel Fleet, five of them later set to music by Stanford as *Songs of the Fleet*. The best loved of these was 'The Middle Watch', describing the seemingly motionless movement of a body of ships by night.

> In a blue dusk the ship astern
> Uplifts her slender spars,
> With golden lights that seem to burn
> Among the silver stars.
> Like fleets along a cloudy shore
> The constellations creep,
> Like planets on the ocean floor
> Our silent course we keep.
>
> From a dim West to a dark East
> Our lines unwavering head,
> As if their motion long had ceased
> And time itself were dead.
> Vainly we watch the deep below,
> Vainly the void above,
> They died a thousand years ago –
> Life and the land we love.[7]

The cycle was performed at the Leeds Festival in October 1910, and should not be confused with the earlier, more popular song cycle, *Songs of the Sea*. According to Newbolt, the concert was somewhat spoiled when Harry Plunkett Greene suffered a bronchial attack which caused him to be drowned by the chorus. Newbolt at this time was also planning a song cycle for children,

5. *LLL*, p.114
6. *NL* HN to MEN, 26 May 1908
7. Chorus omitted. *SP*, p.119

with the composer Walford Davies. Davies was choir master and organist at the Temple Church, and one winter afternoon laid on a private recital for Newbolt. 'A boy sang "The Wings of a Dove", the choir departed, the lights were turned out and the organ played an overture by Handel and a fugue by Bach.[8] Newbolt was deeply moved.

8. *NL* HN to EN, 9 Nov. 1908

CHAPTER 34

Celia and Francis

Celia's 18th birthday was a quiet affair, shared only with Robert Bridges' daughter Margaret. 'Our Celia looks so delicious in her blue cotton. She and Margaret B. sit each side of the garden table under the portico painting blue speedwells in their botany books.'[1] Celia was seriously interested in botany, but her general education was virtually over. She had never been to school, unlike her Chitty cousins who had gone to Cheltenham Ladies' College. Nor was there any suggestion that she should go to University. (Frank's daughter Molly had gone to Lady Margaret Hall). For all his love of intellectual women, Newbolt does not appear to have approved of classroom education for women. Celia had been educated at home by a series of governesses, along with her friend Winifred Evans (known as Fred) and at sixteen had gone to stay with Nora, daughter of Horace Darwin of Cambridge, one of *the* Darwins.

1. *NL* MEN to HN, 27 May 1908

Celia gave Darwin secretarial assistance.

As her eighteenth birthday approached there were important changes in Celia's appearance. Her hair went up and her skirts came down. Ella took her to Paris and Henry Furse sculpted her head. But at seventeen she had still been capable of behaving like a child. The summer holidays at Mount Grace had found her coated in mud. 'Celia and Francis are very busy building a raft, intending to navigate the Prior's fish pond. They go up into the woods with a saw and the donkey and bring down as much as the patient beast can carry of logs (left by Sir Hugh Bell's woodmen for very different purposes). What the raft will be like I don't know, or whether it will float, but the joke is that the farmer has just run off all the water to turn his wheel and the pond is an empty space full of mud on which moorhens run about, joyfully devouring the insects'.[2] However, at eighteen, life had to be taken seriously. In the spring of 1908, Celia took part in a masque at Wilton House written by her father and 'looked charming (though they darkened her eyebrows too much).'[3] Masques were all the rage in the Edwardian era. They provided an opportunity for showing off eligible daughters uncorsetted and semi-draped. Pageants were also popular, usually marking some historical event. Newbolt wrote an Armada scene for Frank Benson's Winchester Pageant in 1908. He was tempted into it because a Newbolt had been Mayor of Winchester at the time. In it he openly compared the Kaiser to King Philip II:

> Think twice of it: our men are sea-begotten
> And they dread nought: twill cost you longer breath
> Than King or *Kaiser* ever yet have drawn.

Presentation at court for Celia would have been too expensive[4] but a series of balls (both given and attended) could not be avoided. There were coming-out balls in Cambridge and London in the summer, and at Christmas Celia was presented to the (somewhat clerical) Wiltshire county circle. At the Salisbury ball Pamela Glenconner was her sponsor. 'I was a chaperone for the first time in my life,' wrote Newbolt, 'and Celia was the sole *young*

2. *NL* HN to EN, 14 Aug. 1907
3. *NL* HN to EN, 2 Feb. 1908
4. *NL* HN to EN, 28 Mar. 1909

lady in the room, except for Miss Cavendish, who was debutting under Lady Pembroke's wing.' There were also sojourns at grand country homes. Newbolt accompanied her on a visit to High Hall, the home of Canon Barnard of Salisbury Cathedral. When Celia got home, 'she poured scorn on all houses where there are butlers and footmen. She prefers Maurice Hewlett's house to High Hall! Happily there's no young man at High Hall to tempt her!' (Hewlett had a son known as Cecco.) All this expensive effort in the end proved unnecessary. At the age of nineteen, Celia fell in love with the boy next door, or rather the boy in the same house. Ralph Furse, son of Henry Furse, was an Oxford undergraduate, a lively youth of remarkable looks who, when in a festive mood, liked to swish off the heads of poppies with his sword.[5] He was being prepared for the Colonial Service. Celia was already committed to Ralph by the start of her second season. He invited her to an Oxford Commem and Margaret went along as chaperone. 'The other chaperones [were] frightful, but most of them danced now and again and so did I (Ralph gallantly offered). Otherwise I should have been a corpse by now without exercise – chaperoning *deadly*.'[6] The 'two giddies' of course, enjoyed it. 'They could have gone on gaily for another week of dancing till morning.'[7] Luckily they also enjoyed escaping to the river, and so did Margaret. One evening they rowed after dark. 'Both Ralph and Celia were struck by the style of my sculling! We went up the narrow stream beyond Ferry Hinksey. It was all quiet and lost, not a bit like Commem.'[8] A year or two later, Celia had a brief flirtation with Percy Lubbock, literary critic and a Furse relation, but she came back to Ralph.

Newbolt's 45th birthday had just preceded Celia's 18th. Mrs Duckworth (now rising eighty) wrote: 'I do not like the word Mother-in-Law, for I hope I am a *love* Mother to you my very dear Harry'[9] and appended a substantial contribution to the children's 'holidays-abroad fund'. De la Mare sent a cake. (He was a noted maker of these.) At tea the cake was wreathed with fresh herbs by Celia, 'with my age and initials (on top) in gold leaf.'[10] Life,

5. *NL* HN to EN, 22 Aug. 1910
6. *NL* MEN to HN, 22 June 1909
7. ibid.
8. ibid.
9. *NL*, 6 June 1907
10. *NL* HN to EN, 6 June 1910

Newbolt told Emily, that had once appeared endless, now seemed to pass as quickly as a train journey. Yet at times he declared he felt no older than Francis or at most an Oxford undergraduate.

Francis also was reaching an expensive age. He was now at Winchester, not Clifton. Various reasons were given, but the true one was that he could not be got into Eton. Francis entered Winchester in 1906 at the age of thirteen. His father, mother and sister travelled there with him and witnessed the ceremony of 'Hills', in the course of which Dr Burge (the head), stood on top of St Catherine's Hill and called the roll. Each boy in turn had to answer 'Sum' (except that Francis was too shy to speak). 'There he was, the little tadpole, very smart in a new hat-ribbon of his House Colours.' Francis was in 'B' House in Kingsgate Street, and thither the party made their way afterwards for a breakfast presided over by Mr Fort, the housemaster.

At first, all seemed to go well with Francis at Winchester. He wrote home to say that Bevil and the other Horris Hill chaps were excellent to him and the big fellows were not beneath entering his 'toys' (study stall) and asking him who his 'gov'nor' was. He first made his mark as a treble in the choir, and also sang 'Cherry Ripe' solo in a school concert. (He was nicknamed 'Cherry' ever after.) He continued to be keen on sport and made a foray into running when he was fourteen. Newbolt exhorted him to exert himself: 'You must learn to have no pity on yourself, to get the last ounce out of that soft fellow Newbolt. I used to hurt the other Newbolt like anything and the end of it was a lot of silver pots and a good deal more pluck than I was born with.'[11] Francis appears to have followed this advice only too well when applying it to football. He came home at Christmas very 'done up'. Emily, in Winchester, was instructed to see that he did not strain himself again. In his fourth year, all problems were forgotten – Francis had won his house football colours. 'The breakfast table of guests at Netherhampton was told of my boy's elevation to the shirtage.'[12] Surprisingly, Francis showed no great enthusiasm for having his parents watch a big House match. 'He was lukewarm about our coming and he failed to catch us at the station. Nevertheless, it was a glorious victory and a splendid match to watch.' Francis specialised in

11. *NL*, 18 March 1909
12. *NL* HN to EN, 10 Mar. 1910

Maths, German and Chemistry in the Fifth Book. Later he dropped Chemistry. He was accepted by New College, the college favoured by Wykehamists. Longer-term plans were already being made for him. 'We are securing as far as possible his entry into the Foreign Office. Unless he is keeping his eye on it all through Oxford he won't do it,' wrote Newbolt to Emily.[13]

Francis's relationship with his father seems to have been generally good. He was not afraid of criticising Newbolt when he failed to measure up to other parents sartorially. Margaret wrote: 'he suggests that you might soon hand over the direction of your wardrobe to him! This I warmly applauded!! Your billycock hat and soft collar in conjunction hurt *my* sensitive feelings too. You might come in for some of the cast-off coats and shirts of the Winchester men!'[14] Father and son got on best on the rugged holidays at Mount Grace. 'We went up to the Black Tarn and Francis insisted on unchaining the old boat. He used pieces of board for paddles and took me out for a delicious quarter of an hour. On the way back (over the moor) we tried a short cut and fell into holes among the deep bracken, and altogether behaved just as Francis loves to behave.'[15] The boy was suitably grateful for holidays. 'After a month shooting at Orchardleigh, as I was driving to the station, Francis came up alongside on his bike and caught hold of the waggonette. "Father, thank you awfully for the shooting" he said. Just as he had about the fishing and the lunch at Harrods!'[16]

Yet Francis was more at ease with his mother. Margaret described a day with him at home. He had become editor of *The Wykehamist* and they were collaborating on a leader to be entitled 'Unconventionality' (a subject dear to Margaret). She added, 'We also had quite a talk about the difference between St Francis and Lady Glenconner.' (Their conclusions were considered too indiscreet to commit to paper.)[17] In the spring of 1912 the Newbolts took their young adults to Rome (Celia was by now 22). This was to be a last family holiday before they fled the nest. 'They grow up like mushrooms,' Newbolt declared.

By now Francis had been up at Oxford for a year. He quickly

13. *NL*, n.d. 1910
14. *NL* 10 Jan. 1907
15. *NL* HN to EN, 2 Aug. 1908
16. *NL* HN to EN, 17 Sept. 1908
17. *NL* MEN to HN, 17 Jan. 1911

achieved the college football team. On the academic side, he came top in 'divvers' and was assigned to H.A.L. Fisher as history and moral tutor, 'the best in the college.'[18] Celia was his guest at the New College Commem that year, and divided her dance card between him and Ralph. Francis behaved with perfect decorum, 'so happy and good-looking,' declared his mother. 'He gave me two heavenly dances'.[19]

18. *NL* HN to EN, Dec.1912
19. *NL* MEN to HN, 25 June 1912

CHAPTER 35

Ella and Margaret

Meanwhile, all was not well with Ella. Her black moods were more frequent. She had family problems. Her father had died suddenly, mourned almost as much by Newbolt as by Ella. Frank Coltman had been the best of substitute fathers. 'No one of that generation was so thoroughly devoted to my interests.'[1] Ella now was in charge of Atherton Terrace, a household composed of her aged mother, 'the Duchess' and her ageing siblings, all childless. Hew, Hilda and Anna were not easy company. Maurice Hewlett became speechless in their presence. 'Your household,' he wrote tactfully, 'wants some handling'.[2] Added to this was the problem of their constant ill-health. Ella gave herself to them selflessly. 'She is a generous creature,' wrote Hewlett to Newbolt. 'But she's a woman so it's of course'[3] Hew, the only boy, was the worst. 'The Hew troubles are

1. *NL* HN to EN,11 Jan. 1908
2. *The Letters of Maurice Hewlett*, 21 July 1911
3. ibid., 28 Oct. 1912

provoking,' wrote Margaret.[4] When he was not losing his money at the gaming tables he was being ill. Ella was nursing Hew through one of his illnesses when Newbolt called in unexpectedly. She turned on him angrily, '"Didn't you get my note? Hew has influenza."'[5] Hilda, Ella's favourite sister, was 'an extraordinary triumph for Ella and her doctors.'[6] She and Ella, like the Schlegel sisters, went to many concerts together. One year, Ella invited Hew and Anna down to Netherhampton. 'Anna was sticky and Hew rather down, so poor Ella made more and more effort and looked older and blacker every half hour,' reported Newbolt.[7]

However, the real problems were between Ella and Newbolt. Occasionally they were happy alone together at Netherhampton, when she replaced Margaret as housekeeper, and there was one weekend when everything went right. Although it was February, the sun shone. 'We walked along the Lark Way. The plough was covered with a mixed throng of red and green linnets.' Before the fire that night, 'Ella was buried in the works of Chateaubriand, carrying on an incessant subterranean gurgling of amusement and quotations. It appears that Chateaubriand says many things which will do for digs at me!'[8] But there were too many visits to Netherhampton when it was otherwise, such as the one when Ella hosted a dinner for Pamela Glenconner and Maurice Hewlett and everything went wrong.[9] At least she and Newbolt parted amicably at Salisbury station. 'I think that was the very nicest parting you ever made,' he wrote to her. 'I went homeward feeling warmed all through and hopeful and comforted about the future.' He added a verse.

> "Old walls," thou sayest, "beaten with many tears,
>   Wait but the final shock."
> Yet love a mortar lays that with the years
>   Sets into living rock.

Emotionally Ella was starved. When a 'particular friend', Mrs Galton, announced that she was coming to England, she was almost ecstatic with joy. 'So seldom anything comes to give her that

4. *NL* MEN to HN, 5 Nov. 1908
5. *NL* HN to MEN, Apr. 1910
6. *NL* HN to MEN, 9 Mar. 1910
7. *NL* HN to MEN, 25 May 1910
8. *NL* HN to MEN, 22 Feb. 1909
9. *NL* HN to MEN, 23 June 1909

soft and grateful kind of happiness,' Newbolt commented to Margaret.[10] On the advice of her doctor, Ella continued to pass a large part of every summer on the continent, and spent at least one winter in Rome. Her most affectionate letters were often written during these holidays. One, Newbolt reported to Margaret, was 'the most intimate and dear I ever had.'[11] However, Ella started to become seriously ill in the autumn of 1910. Newbolt saw the warning signs: 'Had hoped to see Ella and Hilda before they went to their Japanese lecture, but Ella was tired and upset, taking burnt brandy.'[12] A few months later she had an operation, and it was eighteen months before she was truly herself again. Massage was prescribed but it seemed to do her more harm than good. 'She comes back quite done from her horrid "rubber" and I don't believe it's good for her to have so much of it.'[13] She found Newbolt more satisfactory as a masseur.

Ella now turned to religion. Newbolt, oddly, went some of the way with her. One Sunday morning, in Sloane Street, he 'saw the Holy Grail come down out of heaven on a shaft of sunlight and I trembled and wept.'[14] They took to attending Matins at Dick Peile's Kensington church. Even here there was a misunderstanding. 'While I was swallowing tears through Dick's sermon poor Ella thought I was bored. She says I sighed! Poor human life, how imprisoned it is.'[15] Peile's rise in the Church had not proved as meteoric as Newbolt had expected. He had been ill the year before and had considered giving up his parish and his house at 34 Rutland Gate. He was still 'thin and older-looking'.[16] Now he was trying for a bishopric. 'I am glad they didn't make him Archbishop of Capetown,' Newbolt confided to Emily, 'I think Winchester would suit him better.' Meanwhile, he was writing books on theology with a modern slant. 'Have you seen his new volume *Ecclesia Discens?*' Two years later Peile married a woman half his age, Daisy Drummond, 'not our sort'. The fashionable wedding filled Newbolt with gloom. 'The Church was crowded with a much-

10. *NL*, 24 May 1910
11. *NL*, 28 Aug. 1910
12. *NL* HN to MEN, 9 Nov. 1910
13. *NL* HN to MEN, 11 Feb. 1913]
14. *NL* HN to MEN, 17 Jan. 1909
15. *NL* HN to MEN, 18 Jan. 1909
16. *NL* HN to EN, 22 Mar. 1909

befurred assembly. He looked silver about the top, she looked about 35 instead of 22'. She had a 'tough woman-of-the-world' manner and Newbolt preferred her mother. He could not imagine Daisy at Netherhampton.

It was at this time that Newbolt's religious poem, 'Il Santo'[17] appeared in *The Cornhill Magazine*. It referred to the expulsion of Father Tyrrell, the Continental Modernist, from the Jesuit Order. Father Tyrrell asked leave to publish it in an Italian newspaper. He died shortly after it appeared. Newbolt's sympathy with Tyrrell was understandable. Like him, he had a strong religious sense, but could not accept all points of orthodox doctrine. In his heretical book, *Christianity at the Cross-Roads* (1909), Tyrrell envisaged a universal religion of which Christianity was only the germ.

Eventually, Newbolt decided that the only true cure for Ella's problems would be to get her away from her family and into a home of her own. It happened that this solution suited him too. Since the move to Netherhampton he had had no London base and was tired of begging a bed from friends. It was his task to do battle with Ella's mother, the formidable 'Duchess', to get permission for Ella, now well into her forties, to leave home. Finally, it was granted and Ella set about house-hunting. She settled upon 29 Campden Hill Road, a little terrace house, standing in a tree-shaded street just north of High Street Kensington. The front door opened into a corridor, flanked on the left by two small sitting rooms. The first floor front was set aside for Newbolt, and his go-to-London top hat reposed proprietorially in the hall (The house now bears a plaque to Newbolt, erected by English Heritage in 1994.) Gradually he began to spend more days each week at Ella's house. Margaret felt she was losing him; she was becoming the country wife and Ella the town wife. Once she met him by chance in London and he seemed almost a stranger: 'It was delicious to see you but it *was* so queer and seemed to remind me of our old meetings before we were married!! Each of us disappearing into a separate world 'till the next meeting'.[18]

The next morning Margaret sat at Newbolt's desk in the Ark, 'looking at the landscape and reading poetry and wishing I had

17. *Poems New and Old* (1909) not in *SP*
18. *NL*, Nov. 1908

nothing else to do.' Perhaps she read the erotic 'Viking Song', written after their marriage:

> When I thy lover first
>   Shook out my canvas free
> And like a pirate burst
>   Into that dreaming sea,
> The land knew no such thirst
>   As then tormented me.
>
> Now when at eve returned
>   I near that shore divine,
> Where once but watch-fires burned
>   I see thy beacon shine,
> And know the land hath learned
>   Desire that welcomes mine.[19]

It was as well Margaret did not see the letter Newbolt was to write on the occasion of their silver wedding anniversary: 'I have been married twenty-five years today: and the "occasion has been marked" by the arrival of sundry objects in silver, some quite hideous. I had hoped that we might escape any general kind of festivity.'[20]

Margaret, like Ella, was beginning to suffer from ill health. She had migraines and sought relief in long sojourns away from home. With Bernard and Helen Holland in their large house at Harble-down near Canterbury she seemed able to enjoy life again. She lay all day under an apple tree and ate meals at the unconventional hours they favoured. Best of all, was the company of Bernard himself. He was writing a biography of Lord Hartington, Gladstone's war-secretary. 'He took me into his study after the midday *déjeuner* and sitting side by side on the floor we read letters from the Queen.'[21] Newbolt knew she was unwell. He wrote: 'Dearest Wife, I have been sadly minded about you lately. If only this holiday might put your headaches away! It is quite an amusement for Ella keeping house. I think you might try it in alternating weeks even when you are at home!' But he soon

19. *S.P.*, p.89
20. AHL, 15 Aug. 1914
21. *NL* MEN to HN, 24 May 1910

discovered Ella was no substitute for Margaret. 'Netherhampton is dead without you'.[22]

Matters were not made easier by Furse's breakdown. His severe depressions were deeply distressing to Margaret, and Newbolt did his best to entertain Furse during her absence. Many a boring evening was spent with him before the fire in the front hall. 'You can imagine us two old gentlemen playing piquet.'[23] Like many depressives, Furse also suffered from anxiety. The loss of an overcoat precipitated a crisis: 'My best friend has lost an old coat and must have a new one or he'll collapse and leave me to live on Bovril for the remainder of my life.'[24] In 1912 there was a more serious crisis and Furse went down to Halsdon (the ancestral home in North Devon that he had abandoned because it depressed him). Margaret visited him there in May. It was her second visit to the extraordinarily beautiful place that was to be Celia's future home. She had explored the steeply wooded valleys with Furse the year before: 'He riding a rough pony and I walking ahead of him along the narrow paths, the river in its curving valley seen through the bare oak stems as through a veil.'[25]

Margaret was away in all for five periods in 1912, the first being a holiday in Switzerland in February. She went to Wengen with her brother and sister, Campbell and Evie, and learned to ski with a Swiss mountaineer called Fuchs (she preferred to call him Fox). The sparkling air soon blew her headaches away. She was once more Margaret of the Uplands. On the way down the mountain one day Fuchs offered her a ride on his toboggan and she was sorely tempted, but she felt it would be immodest to sit between his knees. Life was not such fun down on the level. The lake at Wengen hardly differed from a London drawing room, except that the guests wore skates and 'mad, beatific expressions. You kept bumping into people you knew.'

As a matter of fact, Margaret was quite glad to bump into Violet Hodgkin's brother, 'now solid and fortyish', as she needed a partner for waltzing on ice and Campbell was 'such a weed'. Campbell Duckworth was a poor companion. His middle age had

22. *NL*, n.d. 1909
23., *NL* HN to MEN, 23 Nov. 1908
24. *NL* HN to MEN, 2 Mar. 1909
25. *NL* MEN to HN, 5 May 1912

brought him no 'portly dignity. Though I go into his bedroom and practise skating figures on his parquet floor in my dressing gown, I do not really get any *talk* with him. Evie and he *chat* very fluently at meals. I generally read a book.' Evie wanted to 'fizz-up in the evenings and watch the dancing'. Margaret often did not even go down to dinner, but preferred to eat off a tray in her room. Indeed, her increasing deafness made her feel like a ghost on most social occasions, but she was sleeping better. 'I don't dream painfully as I did the first week.' When the weather broke she came home. She had had enough of 'the land of chocolate, cheap watches and telegraph posts. It was funny of me to come here, wasn't it?' No doubt she had been persuaded by that great winter sports pioneer, Kathleen Furse. Now she wanted only to see 'the exciting new parlour maid' whose arrival Ella had reported. When Margaret returned, Newbolt reported her 'better mentally', but she soon felt the need for a fourth escape, this time with Ella to Paris.

CHAPTER 36

Alice Hylton

There was a reason for both Margaret and Ella's unease: Newbolt had fallen in love with a third woman, Lady Hylton. Alice Hylton was beautiful and intelligent, the wife of the third Baron Hylton and mother of his four children. She was also, with the aid of Lutyens, creator of the garden at Ammerdown Park, near Radstock in Somerset. Lady Hylton was a Hervey (related to Lord Hervey of the memoirs) and the daughter of Lord Bristol. She was described by those who knew her as having 'a pretty wit and quick repartee'.[1] The Italophile, Walburga, Lady Paget, also declared herself favourably impressed when she entertained her at her tower above Florence. 'Lady Alice certainly is unusually cultivated, for she knows something of Italian history and literature.'[2] She had also studied art under Sickert.

1. Jane Brown, *Gardens for a Golden Afternoon*, 1982 p.199 n17
2. Walburga Lady Paget, *In My Tower*, 1924 p.209

Ammerdown Park was an eighteenth-century house set in a Capability Brown-style park. When Alice Hylton came to it there was no flower garden, the deer could be fed from the ground-floor windows. In 1902 she set about designing an Italian formal garden, based on that of the Villa Bernardini near Lucca. Jane Brown, in her book on Lutyens' gardens, included it among her '24 saveable gardens, for its tribute to the eighteenth century. It was Alice Hylton's gift to posterity.'[3] Alice's garden appeared to be carved out of a thicket of solid yew. There was a circular centre with elaborate box-edged beds of scarlet flowers and a fountain. Statues stood round in niches scooped out of the yew, and six paths opened into other gardens. The most secret of these was the rose garden with an astrolabe.

Ammerdown was within a carriage drive of Orchardleigh, and it was at Orchardleigh that Newbolt met Alice in 1908. Then they started to have brief meetings in London. On one occasion they could manage only an hour at the Tate to see William Strang's drawing of Newbolt. 'We laughed heartily.'[4] On 20 April 1909 they met at the New Gallery and became so entranced by a fisherboy embracing a mermaid that they had to be turned out at 6.00. 'Such a thing has never happened to me before!' Newbolt told Margaret. (He was completely open with her about Alice.) The next day he showed her the Froissart manuscripts in a private room at the British Museum. Then, on an impulse, they fled to Kew, 'where we roamed the gardens until the 7.10 train took us home.'[5] 'The sense of fellowship is grown a radiant mystery,'[6] he told Margaret.

Meetings with Alice in her garden were the most delightful. Newbolt first saw Ammerdown in 1909. By then the yew hedges had been planted seven years. They had not reached their present height of twelve feet, but they were growing taller. Newbolt's relationship with Alice released a spate of love poems such as 'Love and Grief', written after he came upon her weeping in the garden:

> One day, when Love and Summer both were young,
>   Love in a garden found my lady weeping;
> Where at, when he to kiss her would have sprung,
>   I stayed his childish leaping.

3. Jane Brown, *Gardens of a Golden Afternoon*, 1982 p.79
4. *NL* HN to MEN, 23 Nov. 1909
5. *NL* HN to MEN, 21 Apr. 1909
6. *NL* HN to MEN, 29 Apr. 1909

"Forbear" said I, "she is not thine to-day;
　　Subdue thy silence to await her;
If thou dare call her from Death's side away
　　Thou art no Love, but traitor."

Yet did he run, and she his kiss received,
　　"She is twice mine," he cried, "since she is troubled:
I knew but half, and now I see her grieved
　　My part in her is doubled."[7]

The cause of Alice's grief on that occasion was the misfortune of her cousin, a very special friend, 'a sort of Ella' who had been recently widowed in Florence and whose child had just died.[8]
Margaret and Ella were united in their well concealed dislike of Alice. They referred to her as Lydia Languish. 'She will be a wreck after Gotterdämmerung,' Margaret said to Ella. 'It starts at 4.30!'[9] Newbolt worried about Alice's health almost as much as did Alice herself. 'I shall not be out of the wood 'till I know my dear lady is *not* ill with 'flu.'[10] He even showed concern about Alice's son Billy's short sight. He now began to write *The Twymans*. He claimed he wrote it for Emily, but it is more likely he wrote it for Alice, to display himself as the gallant young man he had been, full of hopes and ideals. He denied that the characters were based on himself and his family, but admitted that no one can create characters without 'drawing on his own experiences'.[11] When the public took the busy, well-meaning Amelia to their hearts, he admitted that Amelia was Emily and even took to calling his mother 'Amelia'. Before *The Twymans* came out, Alice and Newbolt brought out an anthology entitled *The Book of Cupid* (1909). It consisted of a hundred love poems, none later than the seventeenth century. Alice contributed childishly sentimental illustrations. 'It is a very pretty book,' Newbolt told Emily. 'But it is not likely to interest you very much. I only sent it so that you can give it away for Christmas.'[12]
Newbolt now had enough poems to fill a fourth volume of verse, *Songs of Memory and Hope*, published in 1909. It did not sell as well

7. *SP*, p.106
8. *NL* HN to MEN, 26 May 1909
9. *NL*, 24 May 1910
10. *NL* HN to MEN, 21 May 1909
11. *NL* HN to MEN, 6 Dec. 1910
12. *NL* hN to EN, 23 Nov. 1909

as *The Long-Ships*. On the other hand, it was the first of his books to go into a cheap edition. 'Me at one shilling! And they hope that 30,000 bobs may be produced.'[13] A book of his verse for children, *Goodchild's Garland*, under the pseudonym 'Henry Nemo', was privately printed by Elkin Mathews in the same year. It was subtitled 'Diversions and Perversions'. Newbolt described it as 'all kinds of old rubbish which may amuse folk.'[14] 'The Frugal Aunt' was included, and also 'Vice Versa', in which Newbolt imagined changing places with Celia as she had been at the age of eight.

> Then I could daily give your doll
>   Her early evening tub,
> While you in easy-chairs could loll
>   At some or other Club.[15]

'Rilloby-Rill', the most delightful of Newbolt's ballads for children, was written too late to be included. It appeared in the Christmas issue of *Country Life* for 1909. The first and last verses went as follows:

> Grasshoppers four a-fiddling went,
>   Heigh-ho! never be still!
> They earned but little towards their rent,
> But all day long with their elbows bent
>   They fiddled a tune called Rilloby-rilloby,
>   Fiddled a tune called Rilloby-rill.

> Ah! but nobody now replied,
>   Heigh-ho! never be still!
> When day went down the music died,
> Grasshoppers four lay side by side,
>   And there was an end of their Rilloby-rilloby,
>   There was an end of their Rilloby-rill.[16]

Three years later, in 1912, Newbolt published *Poems New and Old*. It is as near as a collected edition as he came in his lifetime, and went into many editions. John Murray was the publisher and Newbolt was proud to announce to Emily, 'at last you can see me decently dressed.'[17]

13. *NL* HN to EN, 14 June 1910
14. *NL* NM to EN, 17 Aug. 1909
15. Not in *SP*
16. *SP*, p.123
17. NL HN to EN, 1 Nov. 1912

CHAPTER 37

Politics

The death of Dorothy, wife of Lord Grey, had deprived Newbolt of the friendship of a fine, open-hearted woman. She had died in a carriage driving accident at Falloden. But at least Newbolt's sympathy for Lord Grey renewed *their* friendship. Now Grey started to invite Newbolt frequently to his home off Birdcage Walk. Here they would talk for hours over the fire in the little dark smoking room. Grey was never fully to recover from Dorothy's death. 'He lives in a world that is not this world,' wrote Newbolt.[1] Eager to record Grey's political opinion, Newbolt started another of his letter diaries to Margaret. (He would bring it up to date in Grey's dressing room while Grey changed for dinner.) At first he was disappointed. The great man (who had just become foreign secretary) would talk only of birds and of Wordsworth, 'by the yard'. On 6 November 1908, however, before the maids had left

1. *NL* HN to MEN, 10 July 1907

the room, Grey plunged into comments about an interview with the Kaiser. 'I didn't know whether the screen hid a pair of listeners, but I soon saw that we were alone by the extraordinary frankness with which Grey talked.' He confirmed that the stories of the Kaiser's violent tirades against England when he was with Americans were true. Newbolt enquired whether the man was a fool. 'No,' replied Grey, very seriously, 'he is mad. It is a fearful nuisance. Germany has the most powerful army in the world and it is at the command of a madman.' Grey seemed confident, however, that danger could be averted by balancing one Balkan state against another. Newbolt was rather shocked by Grey's attitude to Serbia: 'He doesn't sympathise over much with the Serbians. He says they are barbarous, unreasonable and not nearly so fine a people as the Bulgarians. I urged their courage in recklessly hurling themselves into a hopeless war, to which he replied that his admiration of that was diminished by their fanatical language: "We demand to be led to death", "meet me on the *crimson* field", etc.'

At the end of 1910 there was a general election. In the course of the campaign Lloyd George seriously affronted Newbolt: he made a speech in Mile End that appeared to be a direct attack on the upper classes. 'A speech which seemed to inaugurate a new era in English politics, one which could not be thought of without feelings of repulsion and dismay.'[3] Newbolt declared himself no longer a Liberal; he would refrain from casting his vote. Then he wrote a letter to *The Times* dissociating Grey, with his 'lofty simplicity of character' from Lloyd George and the advanced Liberals 'with their destruction of sympathy between rich and poor.' Grey was understandably furious. He wrote: 'I will tell you exactly what I feel. I think it very unfair to my colleagues to put me on a separate pinnacle. Asquith, Morley, Haldane – to mention only a few – are just as entitled to your praise as I am. What you have said about me, ignoring them, cannot but tend to separate me from them. Some of them are not only my colleagues, but my intimate friends.[4]

The friendship with Grey never completely died. Grey did confide in Newbolt at least a couple of times in the next two years.

2. *NL* HN to MEN, 6 Nov. 1908
3. *LLL*, p.46
4. *LLL*, p.151

Once Newbolt cornered him in a train leaving Waterloo. 'I hunted through the corridor and found an Eminent Statesman in a solitary compartment entirely strewn with F.O. papers. He gave me some harmless ones to read, and then took "an interval" which lasted for the remainder of the journey.'[5] They discussed the miners' strike. On the second occasion (in 1912), Grey asked Newbolt to a big lunch at his house and after coffee pulled him back into his little room, where he told him he was now in favour of the Serbo-Bulgarian coalition. '"What a world to live in!" he kept repeating. "What an extraordinary state of events!"'[6] But Grey was not the man Newbolt had known. 'Year by year he becomes ever more powerful. He has learnt to drive conversation where he likes, like a football.'[7] Newbolt confided his feelings about Grey to Alice: 'Dearest, I was really rather sad about EG. I comforted my sad heart with thinking of a friendship that is very wonderful to me – passing the love of men. My heart is unquiet, but it rests in thee.'[8]

5. *NL* HN to MEN, 25 Feb. 1911
6. *NL* HN to MEN, 4 Nov. 1912
7. AHL, 25 Feb. 1912
8. ibid.

CHAPTER 38

The Royal Society of Literature

In 1912 Newbolt was elected to the Athenaeum Club. He explained to Emily, that 'the Committee is empowered to select a certain number of persons of distinguished eminence in Science, Literature, the Arts, each year. I am one of these. In future please address my letters "His Eminence" and do not be surprised if I go bald or grow a long white beard and a double waistcoat! For the first time I have done something that will please my father-in-law.'[1] The rewards of fame included sitting on committees and giving lectures, and Newbolt now began to do a good deal of both at the Royal Society of Literature (to which he had been elected in 1902). The RSL had been founded in 1825 but had now become 'a society no-one ever heard of.' It was revived by Maurice Hewlett who was eager for a British Academy, the equivalent of the *Academie Française*, to uphold and preserve the purity of the language. Why

1. *NL* HN to MEN, 9 Apr. 1912

not form a committee to be called the Academic Committee? Hewlett put all this to Newbolt on Salisbury railway station. Newbolt agreed. 'Literature,' he wrote, 'is suffering from a lack of public consideration. Literary men don't influence the course of affairs, because they hardly seem to be a recognised and united profession, even as actors are now.'[2] The problem was how to select the 40 eminent writers who would form the committee. It was the task of Edmund Gosse and a lawyer called Pember to nominate members for election, and it was suspected they were favouring their friends. Newbolt had it out with Gosse over a lunch at the Savile. 'Gosse was nervous, blushed like a lobster at meeting me, and entered upon a long explanation of the circumstances of his own election'.[3] The outcome was that several famous writers refused to stand. Max Beerbohm drew a cartoon of the committee when it was finally agreed upon. Newbolt, with his greyhound profile, is clearly recognisable in the middle of the group on the left.[4] It was then decided that Associates of the Society should become professors, and Newbolt was created Professor of Poetry. His duty was to give a series of lectures on poetry. (These lectures were collected in *A New Study of English Poetry* in 1917.) Professor Newbolt's lectures 'all drew crowded audiences and were fully reported in *The Times*.' In one of them he introduced the Georgians, a group of young poets which included Rupert Brooke, Walter de la Mare, John Drinkwater and John Masefield. Their work had recently been collected by Edward Marsh in the first volume of *Georgian Poetry*, published by the Poetry Bookshop. 'I even ventured to speak of them in a room where a dozen of them were standing clustered together at the back.' After the lecture, Rupert Brooke sent him a copy of his first book of poems. Newbolt met Brooke again at Cambridge in 1913. He found him 'by far the most interesting' of the young poets there, but added, 'He has a too beautiful face.'

These lectures all involved extra work. Not only was there research to be done, but extra secretarial assistance was required from Ella. On one occasion he wrote: 'Ella is black and fagged. She has just finished sending out the cards for my lecture.'[5] He

2. *NL* HN to MEN, 21 July 1910
3. *NL* HN to MEN, 1 May 1910
4. Ann Thwaite, *Edmund Gosse*, 1984
5. *NL* HN to MEN, 25 Feb. 1913

complained of being 'breathlessly hurried round the cage', one day pushing another out of the way too fast. Meetings at the Poetry Bookshop were an even worse chore. You didn't even get a dinner there. And there was Mrs Humphrey Ward and her committee demanding that he should take up arms against the Times Book Club. Sometimes the work made him positively ill. 'Three dinners, two speeches, one lecture, all successfully completed before a microbe got me by the throttle and I have been in bed these two days.'[6] Newbolt's general health was not good at this time. Besides regular bouts of 'flu, he suffered from chronic constipation. 'It is humiliating to think that so much of one's general usefulness depends on that confounded half hour after breakfast'.[7] His eyesight was also deteriorating. He had recently had an embarrassing experience with a grey hen pheasant which he had brought down against the orders of Howard Pease on his moor in Northumberland. An eminent optician could find no pathological condition, 'but my old glasses are quite wrong. With new ones he thinks all my troubles will go away, provided my general health is satisfactory! A big IF!'[8]

Newbolt's most remarkable involvement with the Academic Committee came when he presented its gold medal to Thomas Hardy on the occasion of his 72nd birthday. Yeats was to accompany Newbolt to Dorset. 'When Yeats and I reached Dorchester, we found a deserted [railway] platform and a town without any sign of public interest. At Max Gate we were received by our host and hostess, who told us our ceremony was to be without witnesses. The dinner lives in my memory as beyond all others anxious. Mr and Mrs Hardy faced one another the longer way of the table. Yeats and I sat rather too well spaced at the two sides: Hardy, an exquisitely remote figure, asked me a hundred questions about my impressions of the architecture of Rome and Venice. Through this conversation I could hear Mrs Hardy giving Yeats much curious information about two very fine cats, who sat to right and left of her plate on the table itself. In this situation Yeats looked like an Eastern Magician overpowered by a Northern Witch – and I too felt myself spellbound by the second Mrs Hardy's

6. *NL* HN to MEN, 9 Nov. 1912
7. *NL* HN to MEN, 23 Nov. 1909
8. HN to MEN, 27 Jan. 1908; *LLL*, p.139

famous pair of blue eyes. At last Hardy rose from his seat and looked towards his wife: she made no movement, and he invited her to leave us for a ceremony which was performed without witnesses. She at once remonstrated. But Hardy insisted and she made no further appeal but gathered up her cats and her train with perfect simplicity and left the room. He listened uneasily to my little lecture, "The Novels of Thomas Hardy" – but when I ended and Yeats began his much longer and more remarkable oration, the shadow on his face darkened unmistakably. Yeats ended, drew out the medal and presented it, but Hardy sat with the trophy in his hand and dismay still on his face. Then he put his other hand into the tail pocket of his coat and drew out a roll of paper. We were moved to protest that no speech of thanks was necessary but he explained he was bound to give us his speech aloud because he had already given a copy of it to the reporters from London!"[9]

9. *LLL*, p.166

CHAPTER 39

Francis' Breakdown

Francis's breakdown at Oxford came without warning in the spring of 1913. A telegram, 'one of an idiotic series', arrived from the Dean of New College to announce that Francis was in a nursing home, having been found at 6.30 in the morning 'lying on the floor and not knowing anything'.[1] Margaret hastened to Oxford, leaving Ella to look after Newbolt. She ascertained that the incident had occurred when the boy was sleep-walking out of doors. It was put down to excessive study for Mods. Newbolt wrote a strange letter to Margaret the day after he heard the news: 'He'll be intellectually a broken kneed horse, however quickly he recovers his health.' Within three days, Newbolt had recovered his sense of proportion. 'The Dean is too funny. He writes most kindly to console me for Francis failing to get a class. He seems to think *I* must be seriously disappointed at him

---

1. *NL* HN to EN, 25 Feb. 1913

missing a 2nd in Mods! Not at his being ill.[2] Francis made a gradual recovery, but insomnia remained a problem.

1913 ended with one good piece of news for the Newbolts: Celia finally became engaged to Ralph Furse. Old Arthur Coleridge was ecstatic. Three weeks before his death, he wrote 'I prophesied it years since. Ralph, a flawless youth, is thrown into constant society with our darling Miranda. Of course they love one another and we old folk look on and bless and applaud. How Mary would have skipped and rejoiced and broken into wild numbers!'[3] The ladies set about preparing the trousseau before she could change her mind, determined that Celia's engagement should not suffer the fate of Dido Chitty's. (She had abandoned her fiancé for another. 'Everyone knows about it,' wrote Newbolt. 'Even the Headmistress and all the Ladies of the Cheltenham Ladies' College.)'[4] Celia was married to Ralph on 2 June 1914. The ceremony took place at Netherhampton church. Celia wore a gown that would afterwards do for her presentation at court (this was now considered necessary because of Ralph's burgeoning career in the colonial service). Her pale beauty was perfectly set off by Pamela Glenconner's wedding present, a necklace of diamonds and aquamarines. Ralph was generally approved of, even by Mrs Tatt, the carrier's wife. She said she was glad that 'such a delicate little thing' had not married 'a rough gentleman'. Afterwards there was champagne and chicken for 80 at Netherhampton House and supper for the village in a marquee across the road. Emily entertained the older ladies (including Mrs Duckworth) in a separate room. Looking back on that sunny day, Newbolt declared it 'the happiest in our lives'. Nine weeks later, Celia (now the mistress of Halsdon) declared herself pregnant. On practically the same day the Germans invaded Belgium.

2. *NL* HN to MEN, 28 Feb. 1913
3. *NL* 7 Oct. 1913
4. *NL* HN to EN, 1 Aug. 1912

PART VIII WAR 1914–1918

CHAPTER 40

1914

War had been expected for many years, yet until Germany savaged Belgium, Newbolt had doubted the wisdom of declaring war. 'It is so big a thing and there is so little spontaneity or justification,' he wrote to Alice Hylton. By the end of July 1914, he knew that war was inevitable, and he feared it: 'These days are very like days before death. One does not know what may be the other side of Armageddon. It may well be that we shall not recover our happiness in the years left to us.[1] After the shooting at Sarajevo, an ashen-faced Lord Grey had appeared before the cabinet, bearing in his shaking hand the Austrian ultimatum to Serbia. The news arrived at Netherhampton, while A. P. Herbert (Francis's friend at Winchester) was staying for the weekend. 'We were in the middle

1. AHL, 30 July 1914; *LLL*, p.189

of a game of bowls when the telephone rang, and I was left alone. I remember thinking, "That ring was about the war." Out came Sir Henry, his lean face as calm as usual. "War has been declared," he said, "your turn!" I picked up a heavy bowl, and wondered what to do. What, I wondered, did Drake do on a similar occasion? I flung the great missile with an accuracy that astonished me, and the circle of black shining mahogany was dispersed into beds and bushes all round the compass. Only the little white jack miraculously remained. I rather feared Sir Henry would disapprove of this disgraceful throw. All he said was, "But you missed the flag-ship!"'[2]

Newbolt may have appeared calm, but inwardly the dogs of war were unleashed. The enemy were now 'godless barbarians', 'the Devil incarnate,' 'the Damned Ones'. He went forward with his crest held high and many a loud hosannah. Chivalry was at the height of its vogue in England in 1914. Two years earlier, Scott had perished like a gentleman on his way back from the South Pole and Samuel Guggenheim, dressed in his best, had gone down calmly with the *Titanic*. In that year, too, *Where the Rainbow Ends*, the play written by Clifford Mills and Reginald Ramsay, had first been staged. (It was to be repeated every Christmas until the late 1950s.) In it the hero, St George, leads four children through the realm of the Dragon King to find their shipwrecked parents. There was much talk of 'dying for England' on the way, and a lion cub was sustained with doses of 'Commonwealth Mixture'. Newbolt was ready with an ode the day war broke out. 'The Vigil', appeared in *The Times* of 5 August. 'I don't believe even "The Charge of the Light Brigade" had such a circulation,' he declared. No one observed that it had been published sixteen years earlier in *The Island Race*. Next, he came up with something new, 'The King's Highway'.[3] It was a rehash of 'Drake's Drum'. The poet imagines a ghostly Elizabethan midshipman singing 'The Song of the Larboard Berth' on board a modern cruiser. Stanford set it at once and demanded that a Royal Command Concert at Queen's Hall should include it. The performance was a huge success.

Newbolt now proposed to write a letter diary of the war, one that

2. A.P. Herbert, *His Life and Times* 1970
3. *St George's Day* (1918) Not included in *SP*

'would provide vivid contemporary notes on passing events and show how we lived on our island during those years.[4] He set about arranging sources. First he tripled his intake of newspapers, then he set up a series of lunches with people in the know. Admiral Custance was an obvious choice, and, of course there was Lord Grey who, although Foreign Secretary, was not always as well-informed as Newbolt had expected. (Sometimes Grey didn't even appear to have read the morning paper.) By the greatest of good luck, General Sir Horace Smith-Dorrien (whose exploits at Paardeberg in the Boer War, Newbolt, unlike some, had lauded), was in charge of the army headquarters at Salisbury and lived near the Newbolts, at Harnham. He was a fine figure of a man, the veteran of nearly 50 years of campaigning throughout the empire, and treated Newbolt like a younger brother and allowed 'genial little indiscretions'[5] to drop his way. He had no hesitation about giving Newbolt permission to read his war diaries (subsequently published in book form). It was arranged that Lady Smith-Dorrien (also a charmer) would come over to Netherhampton and read these diaries aloud every two months.

Smith-Dorrien was slower to join the British Expeditionary Forces than had been expected. After he should have left, Newbolt hurried over to Harnham to console Smith-Dorrien's wife ('she feels things with such intensity, that's why I like her')[6], only to find her husband 'sitting quite placid at his table, sending off his will to his solicitors.' Disappointingly, Smith-Dorrien declined to divulge 'where Ours are going to strike'.[7] A recipient for the letter diary now had to be found. Newbolt had been writing daily (sometimes twice daily) to Alice Hylton for several years. (The ultimate count of his letters to Alice runs into thousands.) He decided he would now feed the war to her along with matters of a more intimate nature. The letter diary was eventually typed but never published. After Newbolt's death, Margaret had doubts about whether the letters should be made public. She finally decided to include a suitably proper selection (made with Alice's assistance) in the second volume of his autobiography, *Later Life and Letters*

4. *LLL*, p.183
5. *AHL*, 14 Aug, 1914
6. *AHL*, 19 Aug.1914
7. *AHL*, 20 Aug,1914

(published posthumously), because of the 'wonderful record' they gave of her husband's daily thoughts.

Meanwhile, British troops had reached German-occupied Mons. Newbolt wrote to Alice: 'I long for the moment when 80,000 Britons will get in on the flank of the Godless huns. If only they could score the first innings.'[8] As he wrote, von Kluck attacked from Mons with overwhelming success, killing and wounding 20,000 allied soldiers. Even Newbolt was taken aback. The scale of the disaster became more real when he saw the wounded being unloaded into Harrods' motor-vans at Waterloo. But then came a visit from Lady Smith-Dorrien. Her husband's diary revealed that Mons had not been a defeat at all, but a brilliant retreat in the face of superior force. The British had divided into two corps under Haig and Smith-Dorrien, with Sir John French as Commander-in-Chief. Smith-Dorrien's men, in an unofficial rear-guard action at Le Cateau, had fired their Lee-Enfield rifles so rapidly that the Germans were deceived into thinking they were machine guns. 'That stand against the odds is the biggest thing since Waterloo,' declared Newbolt. 'And to get off with 6,000 killed and wounded is simply splendid.'[9] Smith-Dorrien was later severely criticised by French for this waste of lives. Robert Bridges' son, Tom Bridges, had been on the retreat from Mons. Newbolt struck up with 'The Toy Band'[10] 'Dreary lay the long road, dreary lay the town' as the defeated army straggled through the night. The 'big Dragoon' (Tom Bridges) dreamed of a band to hurry his soldiers along. Then he spied a toy shop selling drums and penny whistles and improvised his own.

Naturally, Francis and Ralph Furse were vying with each other to be the first into a good regiment and first at the front. Francis had the advantage, being already in the Territorials and, by 22 August, he found himself a second lieutenant in the famous Oxford and Buckinghamshire Light Infantry. 'Too late for the big battle,' lamented Newbolt. Meanwhile his equipment had to be bought. Newbolt was determined that everything should be of the best. Fully-equipped (indeed over-equipped, in the opinion of Ponsonby, his commanding officer), Francis went to Parbrook

8. *AHL*, 22 Aug. 1914
9. *AHL*, 31 Aug, 1914
10. *SP*, p.133

Camp above Portsmouth, where he enjoyed himself 'in his own rather serious fashion'.[11] He wrote excited letters home about the heroic deeds of his comrades already in the trenches. 'Our men actually held their fire until the enemy were only twenty yards away, masses of them: and not one of them fired until the order came. One realises pretty soon what it is to be in a crack regiment.'[12] At moments like these, Newbolt could overlook the risks that his son was about to run. 'It will do him good. It will develop him both physically and morally in a way that Oxford never could have.'[13] With Celia's help, he set about writing the story of the 'Ox and Bux' for the Country Life Series of regimental histories. Ralph, meanwhile, had enlisted in 'a sort of territorial cavalry'[14] called King Edwards' Horse. Almost at once, he was promoted to the rank of captain, which was irritating for Francis, but then it was discovered that he had poor hearing so Francis might yet be first at the front. Celia faced dangers of a different kind. Her baby was due. It would obviously be impossible for her to be alone at Halsdon, so she moved back to Netherhampton.

Meanwhile there occurred the 'Miracle of the Marne'. Just when the allies looked like being swept westwards into the sea, they made a successful stand. Paris was saved, and the tide of battle began to flow the other way, the Germans retreating towards the Aisne. A wave of optimism swept over Britain. Newbolt read what he called 'the Armada psalm' at family prayers: 'The Lord will arise and scatter his enemies.' 'The very sound of that verse is like a shell bursting.'[15] A man from the War Office told Newbolt he expected 'the Damned Ones to "crack" in a few days'[16]

Throughout this period Newbolt complained bitterly about the shortage of hard news. The War Office Press Bureau was 'the Devil that tells nowt'.[17] Repington's war reports in *The Times* were inadequate and depressing, and Newbolt preferred Hilaire Belloc's optimistic weekly journal *Land and Water*. At least Belloc knew something about France. With so few facts available, rumour

11. *AHL*, 18 Aug. 1914
12. *AHL*, 20 Nov. 1914
13. *NL*, 18 Aug. 1914
14. *AHL*, 11 Aug, 1914
15. *AHL*, 14 Sept. 1914
16. *AHL*, 16 Oct. 1914
17. *AHL*, 20 Nov. 1914

moved in to fill the gap. Perhaps the strangest one was that 20,000 Russian soldiers from Archangel had landed in England. People claimed to have seen them (with snow on their boots) at Portsmouth and Southampton simultaneously. Evie Duckworth was told definitely that 44 night trains with whitewashed windows had been through Castle Cary on their way to Weymouth. Finally, Francis Acland, a senior government official, told Newbolt that 'there's not one Russian in England or France', and that was that.

Fortunately, Newbolt had an alternative source. His nickname was 'Tom', an abbreviation for 'the automatic mind', sometimes referred to as 'the man in the basement'. 'Tom' was a version of Freud's 'unconscious', although Newbolt never referred to Freud. He did, however, refer to Havelock Ellis, Freud's contemporary, although it is doubtful whether he read all seven volumes of *Studies in the Psychology of Sex*, which were banned in Britain. For Newbolt, as for Freud, the chief manifestations of the automatic mind were in dreams. But these dreams Newbolt did not interpret as disguised manifestations of sexual desire. They had a more practical application: they foretold the future of the war. In October 1914 'Tom' predicted a final victory. The Germans would be driven back beyond the Aisne. 'The next few days will show that they are beat.'[18] In fact, of course, the Germans could not be dislodged from the heights north of the Aisne. The allies dug themselves in on a line that stretched from the Belgian coast to Switzerland, and for the next four years neither their line nor that of the Germans shifted more than half a dozen miles.

Newbolt nevertheless continued to long, like so many others, for the Big Smash. At the first Battle of Ypres, the Germans made an attempt to break through the line at the Ypres salient, an attempt which failed after the most desperate fighting. 'It's a wonderful story,' Newbolt declared on 15 November. Then on 5 December he read that the casualty list was 25,000. For the first time he admitted 'the terrible volcano one lives over'. It appeared that at Ypres the regular army had practically ceased to exist. The loss of 'boy officers' had been appalling. Newbolt had heard a rumour that the War Office was going to restrict their number at the front. 'They are too brave and not hard enough.'[19] There had already been

18. *AHL*, 11 Oct. 1914
19. *AHL*, 6 Oct. 1914

fatalities among the sons of his friends. Charles Longman's son had died on the Aisne, having already received five bullets on the Marne. Maurice Hewlett was almost insane with worry about Cecco, a Flight-Captain in command of an airship. He had disappeared after a 'very secret' attack on Kiel.[20] 'It is rather sad to think of all that bright young Round Table dissolved for ever. Francis in any event will never go back to Oxford. It seems years since he wrote waltzes for his College Ball and took me up the Cherwell in a punt: and I sat in Chapel and saw all his friends. In three months' time half of them will be under the soil of France.'[21] Henry Chitty had almost been the first casualty of the war. He was shot while still in training at Hemel Hempstead. Newbolt wrote to Alice 'I've just heard a very hard bit of news. My nephew and godson, Henry Chitty, who only left Oxford last year and has just got his commission as a Gunner in the London Artillery, was shot, on Thursday, by a friend, a fellow subaltern, with a revolver which the idiot was fooling around with. He was shot through both lungs. He was possibly saved by the fact that, being fired at within six feet, the bullet went clean through him and out again.'[22] (It was found that night in Henry's hospital bed.) 'Even if he recovers it is fearfully hard luck, for although he's a born soldier, his father made him go to the Bar. He was overjoyed at the chance of slipping away into the army.'[23] Henry lost the use of one lung. He was never able to join his battery at the front. By way of consolation, neither was he considered fit to return to the Bar, and eventually he founded his own prep school.

Newbolt considered himself too old to volunteer for active service (he was 47). Yet he had friends who did. Calderon went to France as an interpreter. He was wounded at the first Battle of Ypres and went back for more. Sandy Wollaston, the son of old Woolly Bear, was a naval surgeon on an armed P & O liner. Sir Victor Horsley (Milly's doctor) was to die tending the wounded in Mesopotamia at the age of 59.

Life at Netherhampton, however, continued as usual: 'The larkspurs like a forest of blue-tipped spears, the rose borders a

20. *AHL*, 30 Dec. 1914
21. *AHL*, 25 Aug. 1914
22. *AHL*, 16 Aug,1914
23. *AHL*, 13 Aug. 1914

Persian pattern of pink and red rosettes.'[24] On the downs, sheep grazed amid poppies and charlock while behind the house swans floated on a glassy river. At the end of September the Newbolts had celebrated their seventh year at Netherhampton House and the final departure of Henry Furse. 'The Devon Yeoman is going to retire to his yeomanism in Devon, and we are going to try and live on here without him. But he seems to be quite off his head at present and may change his mind.[25] The only visible sign of war was the soldiers who filled every train with their 'jolly good humour' and rested between trains in the cathedral close. 'All the maids brought them tea!'[26]

Margaret meanwhile put her energies into war work on the home front. She proposed to supply the folk of Netherhampton with cheap bread in case of a siege, and persuaded her husband to invest in sacks of flour. 'The trouble is that there's no bakery [and] I don't yet know how much flour will be needed! How much *does* go to a loaf?' The scheme was not a success. The authorities suspected the Newbolts of hoarding! Housing Belgian refugees was a more successful venture. There had been a wave of sympathy for the victims of Liège, and landed neighbours vied with each other to accommodate them in unwanted estate cottages. Margaret resurrected a dwelling as overgrown by brambles as the Sleeping Beauty's. Walls were whitewashed and old clothes collected, but still the Belgians did not come. Finally, at the end of November, they arrived. Alphonse, a bicycle-dealer from Bruges, his wife Albertine and their small daughter. No sooner had they arrived, than Alphonse fell ill. 'Margaret rushing in and out with thermometers and castor oil. Poor Albertine weeps. But if anyone could pull them through, it would be Margaret.'[27] After Alphonse had recovered, Newbolt paid a call. 'Their French is very bad. Their genders are all anyhow. Little Marie Louise is a perfectly happy and confiding creature; we shall all probably weep when she goes.'[28] But go she shortly did. The Belgian's were not replaced.

The war at sea was, of course, of the greatest interest to Newbolt. Though Custance, the Little Admiral, had unfortunately retired, he

24. *AHL*, 3 and 4 July 1915
25. *AHL*, 18 Sept. 1914
26. *AHL*, 9 Aug. 1914
27. *AHL*, 17 Dec. 1914
28. *AHL*, 18 Dec. 1914

would now be able to see other admirals, like Sturdee, in action. He was confident in the navy they commanded. Britain had twenty of Fisher's Dreadnoughts at sea, each more state-of-the-art than the last. In 1914 most of this Grand Fleet was stationed on the East Coast, prepared for any German attack from the North Sea. Newbolt waited confidently for the clash of the giants. It was not to be. Admiral von Tirpitz had quickly concluded that a confrontation with his opposite number, Jellicoe, should be postponed indefinitely. The way to defeat the islanders, he reasoned, was to starve them out, and this involved sending out raiders to sink merchantmen all over the Empire. These would include Germany's most effective sea weapon, the U-boat. On 23 September 1914, the U-9 sank three armoured Cruisers, *Hogue*, *Cressy* and *Aboukir*, with a loss of 1,600 lives, the biggest submarine disaster of the entire war. Newbolt blamed it on 'the *braggadocio* of that swollen idiot Churchill'[29] As First Lord of the Admiralty he had failed to take the Germans' 'damned machines' seriously. 'Winston, they say, has lost all interest in the Navy and is bent on conducting the land campaign, with the assistance of Joffre![30] Only in the Pacific could Newbolt find the kind of action that would inspire him to verse. 'A Chanty of the Emden' was a rollicking shanty about a bold sea-captain who sent merchantmen to the bottom. Unfortunately, this captain was a German. Captain Müller met his match under the guns of the Australian ship, *Sydney*, but not before putting up a gallant fight. The captain of the *Sydney* also displayed gallantry. Part of the last verse runs:

> They knocked her guns and funnels out,
>   They fired her fore and aft:
> They fired her fore and aft, my lads,
>   And while the beggar burned
> They salved her crew to a tune they knew,
>   But never had rightly learned—[31]

That tune was Chivalry. Müller had always treated his prisoners with respect, and now he was respected in turn. When he surrendered, the Australians allowed him to keep his sword.

29. *AHL*, 28 Sept. 1914
30. ibid.
31. *SP*, p. 131

When Sturdee set out for the Falklands, leading the largest squadron ever to be commanded by a British admiral, Newbolt's hopes of a battle were raised at last. He was not disappointed. On 9 December he picked up an evening paper on leaving the theatre. 'What a joy it was last night to buy an authentic Naval success for a penny!' The success was no less than the sinking of *Scharnhorst* and her sister ship *Gneisnau* at the Battle of the Falklands. 'My never-too-much-admired Sturdee, who has swooped 7,000 miles, since I was with him five weeks ago, has brought his quarry down.' Newbolt did admit that the British vastly outnumbered the Germans. The historian, Cruttwell, says: 'The honours in so ill-matched a contest must go to the defeated. Sturdee was anyway merely the fortunate instrument of the greater designer at Whitehall (Churchill), who had so quickly and cunningly forged his plan of annihilation.'[32] Newbolt invited Custance down to Netherhampton and as they sat up late before a crumbling log, they talked about U-boats. One had met an unusual fate. She had been discovered off the Scottish coast by a trawler which promptly 'rammed her. She dived, too rapidly, and hit the bottom. Two leaks couldn't be stopped, so she came to the surface and was captured. Since then there are 400 trawlers all out looking for submarines to ram. I'm delighted because it bears out what I wrote to Fisher, that the way to hunt them is with boats of small value.'[33] This was not the only suggestion that Newbolt put to Fisher, now reinstated as First Sea Lord. His was also the idea of 'the Mosquito', a torpedo launched from a bathing machine with a man astride it in an inflatable rubber suit, who would abandon ship at the last minute.

Newbolt's chief contribution to the war was as a propagandist. Propaganda was in its infancy at this time. The government's first move had been to invite distinguished writers, including Newbolt, to a meeting at Wellington House on 2 September. Their task was to put the British case to neutral countries. Thomas Hardy left an account of that meeting. To him, the September sun, coming in from the dusty street, gave a tragic cast to the faces round the great table. 'All were filled with misgivings about an unknown future.'[34] Newbolt now set about writing propaganda in the form of an adventure series for boys, known as Longman's Venture Library.

32. C.R.N.F. Cruttwell, *A History of the Great War*, (1934)
33. *AHL*, 18 Dec. 1914
34. *Life and Work of Thomas Hardy*, Ed. Michael Millgate (1984)

The books were to come out each Christmas for eight years. The first was entitled *The Book of the Blue Sea*. It aimed to arouse a warlike spirit in boys of a nautical disposition and told the true stories of five heroes (boys to begin with) of the Napoleonic wars. By far the most interesting was 'Charles', in fact Newbolt's grandfather. Newbolt had access to his letters, and took the opportunity to include a good wad of family history in the book. Young Charles was one of the ten children (six of them boys) of a doctor who eventually practised in Belgium. His letters gave a vivid account of life on one of Nelson's ships. As a midshipman, aged thirteen, he slept in the cockpit of a frigate with a mob of fellow midshipmen, his hammock slung a foot from the deck-head so that, in a high sea, his nose frequently bumped it. One morning the gunner took him to the powder-magazines in the ship's hold. He was made to put on felt slippers before he went down the ladder; the floor and walls of the magazines were lined with felt too, lest anything should accidentally strike a spark. 'Only then did he realise that he was standing exactly underneath the cockpit where he slept. The gunner saw him glance upwards. "Ay" he said, "there's enough there to take ten ships' companies to heaven."'[35] It was Charles Newbolt's greatest sorrow that he missed Trafalgar. His ship, *L'aimable*, was escorting a convoy to Malta at the time. Charles later distinguished himself on 'The Bright Medusa'.[36] *Medusa* was at the siege of Monte Video, where she captured more than one enemy ship, and young Charles became a prizemaster for the first time, with the responsibility for sailing a captured Spanish merchantman through stormy seas. His naval career ended less gloriously. By 1817 the navy had almost ceased to exist. There were only 114 ships on the Navy List and the only chance for 'derelict officers' was to get a place in a merchant fleet. Charles became captain of the West Indiaman *Hamilton* and made regular voyages to Jamaica until 1827 when, on a journey home, he died of yellow fever. He was 33 when his last hammock was sewn up and slung into the Sargasso Sea.

Newbolt also spread propaganda by travelling the country, delivering a lecture entitled 'Poetry and Patriotism'. Much of it was extemporised around his most rousing poems. These lecture

35. *The Book of the Blue Sea*, p,7
36. *S.P.*, p.93

tours were not without their share of hardship. Audiences could consist of a thousand or of a handful of people 'mostly knitting'. In Newcastle he was obliged to stay with Mr Barnes, an architect who was '*decidedly* middle-class. The maid talked to me as an equal, deposited my boots and hot water outside my door and refused my repeated invitations to "come in". It's odd that these trifles should seem so large!' By way of consolation, his posh Northumbrian friends came to support him in Newcastle. 'It was jolly to see parties of Nobles and Hodgkins, who had forgone their good dinners and come miles in the storm.'[37] The proceeds from these lectures went to the Prince's Fund.

After the disaster at Mons, Newbolt found a secret country to which he could escape. It was called Aladore, the title of a new book. The word was composed half of Ammerdown and half of door. In the story, the door led to an enchanted garden where lived Aithne. To win her love, Ywain had to perform acts of knightly valour at the command of the evil Prince of Paladore. He first saw Aithne (who of course represented Alice) in her garden: 'Her face was turned away from Ywain: but his blood moved by the sight of her, and by her ear that was like the hollow of a shell. Her skin was as white as the swans of Aengus, and her eyes grey like the dawn'.[38] The pair became airborne, and so they reached the magical city of Aladore. There they were married in a secret chamber and lived content for many a season, but Ywain always longed to see Aithne as she was in her youth. To rediscover her youth he visited her birthplace, the Castle of Kerioc (none other than Bamburgh Castle). It was from Kerioc that Ywain and Aithne were summoned to do battle with Paladore. After the battle, Ywain and Aithne were never seen again. Those who came to seek their bodies found only two figures 'fashioned of black bronze' upon a tomb.[39]

'Tom', Newbolt's newly discovered 'automatic mind', had a new and useful role to play. He supplied the series of vivid dreams on which *Aladore* was based. Newbolt would sit up late, writing the book in the Ark. 'The lights on the Downs last night were quite Aladorable. It is good to know that even in war and tumults there are silent spaces left, in which the deepest and most lovely things

37. *AHL*, 17 Nov.1914
38. *Aladore*, p.60
39. *Aladore*, p.362

still hold.'[40] Then he would go to bed and dream up new chapters, and 'they were the best bit'.[41] In one dream, he saw Ywain on the eve of his final battle, in a dark chapel before a candlelit bier: 'And Ywain put forth his hand and took hold on the edge of the pall, and he drew back the pall upon the bier and looked and saw the face of him which lay thereon ... The face was his own face.'[42] This dream was so vivid that he could not shake it off for days. The body on the bier represented not only himself, but 'all the pilgrims he had ever known, everyone walking by the light that was in him'.

Newbolt always referred to Alice as the co-author of *Aladore*. In fact, she was not. She did, however, criticise each chapter as it came from the typist, sometimes sternly. She wanted the final battle to be bloodier, but Newbolt protested that 'too much realism of that kind would be a great mistake, this being an allegory.'[43] She also illustrated the book with fifteen tiny drawings, many featuring fauns. Newbolt described these as: 'Naked and manlike to the middle, in their flesh fat and in their countenance all merry babes: but below they were of another fashion, for their hams were wool-begrown and they were goat-kneed and goat-footed.'[44] Newbolt was enchanted with Alice's drawings, but often distraught at her slowness in producing them. The illustrations were due with the publisher at the end of September. On 15 September Newbolt wrote 'We are still short of three. This I say not to worry you, but only by way of talking to my dear partner.'[45] A placatory letter followed on 25 September. 'I send you the proofs. How charming they are! They will do more than any words to give the tinge of sunset colour which I desired.'[46]

The book was serialised in *Blackwell's Magazine* without illustrations. There was then a *de luxe* edition of 200 copies, as well as an ordinary one. Some of these were to be a gift to Alice (since a lady could not be paid). Alice had 'precise and decided views' on the binding of the *de luxe* edition.[47] So had Newbolt. He wanted 'plain white vellum with the title in gold.' She did not. The production even of the standard edition proved difficult.

40. *AHL*, 14 Aug. 1914
41. *AHL*, 31 July 1914
42. *Aladore*, pp.356–7
43. *AHL*, 1 Oct. 1914
44. *Aladore*, p.185
45. *AHL*, 13 Sept. 1914
46. *AHL*, 25 Sept. 1914
47. *AHL*, 3 Nov. 1914

Blackwood was a Scottish publishing house and there were constant failures of communication between Sir Andrew Blackwood (in London) and the headquarters in Edinburgh. To add to this problem, Sir Andrew was senile. On one occasion, he mislaid one of Newbolt's telegrams. 'Sir Andrew put the wire in his pocket and forgot it. But Providence ordained that he should fall on his head on the way to lunch and when they undressed him they found *my* wire and telephoned it to me!'[48] Then Bliss, the printer, defected to the army, leaving a note saying: 'I am now Private Bliss, 020360 [and] hope soon to be on a lorry in France. My boy will see to your book.' Newbolt was speechless with fury. '"My boy" is a little dunderhead incapable of taking in a telephone message.' There was also a shortage of paper. And then Carl Henschel, Newbolt's plate maker, was persecuted for being a German. (He was eventually obliged to change his name to Knight.) Finally *de luxe* copies, jointly signed, were sent to close friends. 'Yes, of course we must send one to the Ingenious One,' wrote Newbolt.[49] (The 'Ingenious One' was Alice's friend, who had arranged meetings for the couple.)

It remained only to see what the critics made of Aladore. 'I expect no kind of success,' Newbolt confessed.[50] He had none. The only good review was in the TLS but it was 'unbearably insipid. No doubt dull little Dalton wrote it in his lunch hour.'[51] What 'dull little Dalton' actually said was: 'Just at present a book about a place called Aladore and people called Ywain and Aithne, written in the Morrisian style, is likely to be received with imperfect sympathy.'[52] Alice's illustrations, surprisingly, won some praise. Newbolt told Alice: 'You have conquered the critics. If you were a poor church mouse you would now be earning quite good crumbs of bread and cheese!'[53] A few friends found kind things to say about Newbolt's contribution. Canon Skrine wrote to say he had enjoyed his trip to Aladore, but added: 'It is not everybody's luck to go to Aladore.'[54] Newbolt sadly concurred. And yet, he added, what joy there was in

48. *AHL*, 23 Oct. 1914
49. *AHL*, 11 and 12 Dec. 1914
50. *AHL*, 30 Nov. 1914
51. *AHL*, 12 Dec. 1914
52. *TLS*, 10 Dec. 1914
53. *AHL*, 14 Dec. 1914
54. *AHL*, 23 Feb. 1915

it 'until the heathen began to rage furiously. I am wishing I could begin another *Aladore* at once.'[55]

At the end of 1914 Newbolt had an honour to lay at Alice's feet. He had been declared Sir Henry in the New Year's honours list. Pamela Glenconner, acting for Lord Grey, had asked him whether he was willing to accept a Knighthood. At first he had demurred. The honour was for services to poetry, and Newbolt did not feel that writing poems was a 'proper job', nor did Margaret, who wrote: 'It seems a slight insult to poetry to give it worldly prestige'[56] Nevertheless, Newbolt accepted 'the little illumination'.[57] Now there was the rig to get together. Normal evening dress would have done for the visit to the palace but Newbolt was determined to wear the velvet knee-breeches and ruffles of the Nelson era. 'Imagine me in the act of choosing swords, buttons, cocked hats and shoe buckles. Also solemnly debating the merits of various kinds of lace for my worship's ruffles!' he wrote to Alice.[58] George V was disappointing. 'Such a queer, shy, abrupt-moving, small-headed person he is. [But] when I had kissed hands and got up, he looked me very straight in the face with those curious dark eyes and bowed with an odd look of meaning something.'[59]

55. *AHL*, 20 Dec,1914
56. *NL* MEN to HN, 14 July 1914
57. *NL* HN to EN, 15 Jan. 1915
58. *AHL*, 11 Jan. 1915
59. *AHL*, 13 Jan. 1915

CHAPTER 41

1915

At last it was Francis's turn to join his comrades in France. He was to serve under Smith-Dorrien at the northern end of the line. He had only been in the trenches three weeks when he was wounded at the Second Battle of Ypres, during a new German attack. This was the campaign in which they used gas for the first time. But the damage done to Francis was of a more insidious nature. At first he could remember nothing. 'When he came to again he was hanging up near the roof of a hospital train in England. He heard one RAMC officer say to another, "Then here we've got a bad case of shell concussion – out of his mind, I think.' He wished to say that he was all right, but no word came.'[1] Margaret visited Francis at Queen Alexandra's Hospital for officers at Highgate and reported that he was suffering from 'ghastly nightmares of shells and

---

1. Henry Newbolt, *Tales of the Great War*, 1916

fighting. He can't remember which day he was knocked over, but has a very vivid recollection of seeing everyone else killed and himself remaining untouched.' What in fact had happened was that Francis was ordered to occupy some farm buildings in front of the Germans. He had succeeded in getting his exhausted and unwilling men to the isolated position, where they were shelled throughout the night. At dawn a bullet flattened itself in his knapsack, knocking him over. Immediately afterwards, the blast from a shell lifted him into the branches of an apple tree. Newbolt's comment was 'he played the game in a very tight place.'[2] By an amazing coincidence, these events had taken place on 23 April, St George's Day.

Francis was actually suffering from severe shell-shock. His condition when he returned to Netherhampton remained distressing. 'I wish his hands wouldn't shake so,' commented Newbolt.[3] In August he was granted a two-month extension of leave. Newbolt's reaction was surprising. 'I'm sorry that he isn't doing more for his country.'[4] Only to Margaret did Francis admit that he dreaded returning to France without his dead friends. 'Now that the Johnner and Ponsonby and Vidal have all gone, I feel so alone in this war.'[5] Gradually he took up his old occupations, particularly music. 'Francis is downstairs today and I can hear his accustomed tread on the piano! When I went to his room this morning, he was sitting up against his pillows and making sandbags at a great pace. But he looks so thin and pale.'[6] By November Francis had cheered up sufficiently to buy a small car called a Peugeot 'Pram' with his wound gratuity. 'The wretch came down from London in it, the first time he had ever driven any car! He succeeded in putting it into a ditch on arrival. After that it would only go backwards. This morning he unscrewed most of its outer anatomy, and Celia and I attended as consultants. Celia, with great acuteness, diagnosed the trouble and I operated with complete success.'[7]

Newbolt did not waste the first-hand information supplied to him by Francis. The first chapter of his boy's book for Christmas

2. *AHL*, 30 Apr. 1915
3. AHL, 5 June 1915
4. *AHL*, 1 Aug. 1915
5. *AHL*, 13 Oct. 1915
6. *AHL*, 16 Oct. 1915
7. *AHL*, 15 Nov. 1915

1916, *Tales of the Great War*, was entitled 'Adventures of a Subaltern' and was based on Francis's experience at Ypres. 'I get too excited to write it at times,' Newbolt told Alice.[8] Newbolt also wrote a poem about Francis. It was entitled 'St George's Day: Ypres 1915' and spoke of the stricken orchard.

> Where a boys's voice and a boy's hand
>   Close up the quivering rank,
> Who under those all-shattering skies
>   Plays out his captain's part.[9]

Francis was now the schoolboy who had played the game.
The Great War spawned a mass of games-playing war poems. Newbolt had many imitators, as the critic E.B. Osborn remarked: 'I cannot understand why this stout old nation persists in thinking of war as sport. Sportsmanship is our new homely name for the *chevalerie* of The Middle Ages.'[10] The young officers at the front joined in the game, in one case literally. There was Captain Neville who acquired footballs for himself and his platoon comrades to kick ahead of them when going over the top. He died instantly, but one ball is preserved and the exploit was commemorated by a certain 'Tomahawk':

> 'On thro' the hail of slaughter.
> Where gallant comrades fall,
> Where blood is poured like water,
> They drive the trickling ball
> The fear of death before them
> Is but an empty name
> True to the land that bore them
> The SURREYS play the game.'[11]

Captain Neville was not alone. The sons of Newbolt's friends went to war with school songs in their hearts. There were the Grenfell twins, Julian and Billy, who died in May and July 1915 – 'two lads galloping into Valhalla on their ponies.' Their mother, Lady Desborough, wrote a memorial volume about them to which

8. *AHL*, 19 Feb,1916; *LLL*, p.233
9. *SP* p.129
10. E.B. Osborn, *The Muse in Arms*, quoted in Girouard p.283
11. Paul Fussell, *The Great War in Modern Memory*, 1975 p.27

friends contributed. In the photograph at the beginning, Billy stands in the position of Watts's *Sir Galahad* beside his horse. As for Julian, someone wrote 'of all men, he *is* the Happy Warrior!' At this time Pamela Glenconner's son Bim was also killed, to the enormous distress not only of his mother but of Newbolt.

Celia's baby was born in April, the same month that Francis was wounded. Netherhampton was in turmoil, with Margaret and the servants going in all directions and the local doctor in attendance. 'Tom' was at work again. Newbolt found he had an uncanny ability to read people's thoughts. 'I stood by the doctor while he was writing, and I suddenly knew he was anxious and out of his depth. Then when I sat on the sofa by Margaret I distinctly heard her thinking, first of a world with a babe and no Celia, then with Celia childless, and then of ourselves alone.' In the event Barbara, always known as Jill, arrived safely. It was three weeks before Newbolt was allowed to visit her mother. Only an occasional female visitor was permitted to go up to Celia's room. One of these was her pretty friend Imogen (of the poem 'Imogen Dancing'). 'They must have made a pair for Perugino,' commented Newbolt. He had to content himself with shouting up to the bedroom window from the lawn. He was, however, allowed to see little Jill. 'She was a lovely thing, perfectly human, with long hair and brown intelligent eyes wide open.'[12] When she was two months old, Jill was christened in Netherhampton church, and a week later an unknown 'Monseigneur L'Evêque' came to stay at Netherhampton and say a mass in the church giving thanks. Celia appears to have been flirting with Catholicism. 'A bishop on that scale is of course a handful – it's like nursing a playful mammoth. Still he is enormously amusing. Gave us last night a hugely dramatic account of his interview with Northcliffe, whom he castigated'.[13]

Ralph was ordered to the front almost on the day Jill was born. He was known to be absurdly reckless. 'If the cautious Francis was a Roundhead, Ralph was a Cavalier. He is just the old English idiot, the cavalryman born, who doesn't care what happens to the army, while he for the moment is careering wildly over the field.'[14] By the end of 1915 Newbolt was struggling to keep up his spirits. The ill-

12. *AHL*, 4 Apr. 1915
13. *AHL*, 28 May 1915
14. *AHL*, 13 Apr. 1915

fated invasion of the Turkish peninsula of Gallipoli had failed. Calderon had died there.

The next patriotic book to encourage boys to the front was due but, not surprisingly, Newbolt's attitude to war was changing. 'I write about heroic deeds and hairsbreadth escapes as if they were children's games, with no real pain or danger in them,' he admitted to Alice.[15] But the rent of Netherhampton had to be paid. *The Book of the Thin Red Line* was a military version of *The Book of the Blue Sea*. (The title of course referred to the stand made by the Highland Brigade at Balaclava). Like its predecessor, it was addressed to a hypothetical boy – 'My dear Man' – and was lavishly illustrated in colour with Highlanders charging, sporrans abristle. The heroes were again boys (at the beginning of the story). 'Stonewall' Jackson of Virginia was the most famous. It was he who said, after being mortally wounded at the Civil War Battle of Chancellorsville in 1863, 'Let us cross over the river and rest under the shade of the trees.' Newbolt was deeply moved by his Nelson-like death. 'Though he was not of the Thin Red Line, he came of the same race and made war after the same chivalrous fashion.'[16] The other soldier to whom much space was allocated was an Indian army officer called simply 'George'. He was none other than Newbolt's great-uncle, George Newbolt. Just as the story of Charles Newbolt had been told in the *Blue Sea*, so was that of his much younger brother told in the *Red Line*. But Newbolt was hard put to make a hero out of George. George was an administrator first and a somewhat cantankerous soldier second. At the age of eighteen, 'a slim youth with a long face and brown hair,' he joined the private army of the East India company. He quickly transferred to the staff of the Governor-General at Lucknow and was put in charge of supplies. Here he had a hard time with the army wives. When troops had to be moved in bullock carts, 'they shouted all day long, in Scotch and Irish mostly, at the native bullock-drivers, who invariably shouted back that their bullocks were tired and could go no faster than $1\frac{1}{2}$ miles in an hour. Then they all agreed in cursing the engineer who had made the road.'[17] Even at native banquets George found reason to complain. He was usually placed at the

15. *AHL*, 25 Mar. 1915
16. *The Thin Red Line*, p.viii
17. George Newbolt's diary, *Red Line*, p.172

bottom of the table. 'The great people helped each other to the dishes, the smaller ones looked on, except when the king picked out some individual guest and sent him down a portion of some native delicacy of which good breeding obliged him to partake.' George had an excellent command of three native languages, but conversation on these occasions was impossible, 'seeing that the discordant sounds of native music and the screeching of nautch-girls would effectively drown every ordinary voice.' It was during this period, when not yet 21, that George married the first of several wives and was converted to an extreme form of dissenting Protestantism which forbade even writing letters on a Sunday.

In the Second Sikh War George saw action for the first time. It was at Chillianwallah, when the rebellious Sikhs of the Punjab defeated the British. George, as Field Commissariat Officer, should have been spectating comfortably from an elephant, but suddenly the tide turned and Sikhs, brandishing their *tulwars*, pursued the 56th Sepoys almost between the legs of his beast. Raising his rifle, George attempted to pick off a few, but did little damage, for he was slow to reload. Then he was violently sick and his *mahout* wisely retired his elephant to behind the lines.

There is a strange little sequel to the story of George's adventures in India. He did not go home on leave until he was past 50. When he landed at Southampton he dined with an officer of 19, who was sailing next day for India. That officer was young George, his only son, who had been sent to England at the age of two. (This was the George who Francis had cared for at Bilston vicarage.) While researching Colonel Newbolt's story, Newbolt turned up material about Charles and George Newbolt's father, the doctor who had moved to Belgium. Dr Newbolt, it seems, had moved in the best circles, becoming physician to King Leopold; other famous patients were the Emperor Ferdinand of Austria and Mrs Fitzherbert. These people he mostly treated at the resort of Spa, where he used to set up his practice during the season.

CHAPTER 42

1916

The Battle of Jutland was the only occasion on which the two main fleets clashed. On 31 May 1916, British ships under Jellicoe 'came out to hit' (Newbolt's expression) from Scapa Flow and surprised the reluctant Germans on the high seas. Battle was never fully joined, the enemy eventually escaped into the mist, and both sides claimed victory, although each had lost 5,000 men. Newbolt, like many people, considered Jellicoe had been too cautious at Jutland. He now set about putting his views into *A Naval History of the War* (not to be confused with his later two volumes of the official history). Hodder and Stoughton had offered him an advance of £500, he told Margaret. A month later he added 'The military censor is trying to spoil my book.'[1] The censor did. The book was not published until 1920, but Newbolt continued to add chapters throughout the war.

1. *NL*, 20 Sept.1916

In July his attention turned to the allied offensive on the Somme, where Kitchener's New Army was being destroyed. With Smith-Dorrien out of the picture, Newbolt's chief informant was General Bill Furse, a brother of Henry. General Furse had fought on the Somme, where Haig had now replaced French as Commander-in-Chief. 'Uncle Bill' was a bluff, hearty fellow whose visits to Netherhampton were sudden and (to Margaret) alarming. 'Celia and I had just finished tea when a motor drew up and a male figure advanced towards the door. Celia fled, from some notion that she hadn't got the right frock on. The male figure didn't ring, but burst in with a "Hullo!" He wanted Henry [Furse] but he put up with Celia and Jill and me in a kind, noisy, distracted sort of way, and had tea and went round the garden. He was in high spirits, uttering with a loud and genial tone of confidence the most pessimistic and even desperate opinions about the war.'[2] Newbolt persisted in believing that, if we had lost much, the enemy had lost more: 'The German war machine is strained to breaking point.'

Ralph survived the Battle of the Somme, waiting in vain for a cavalry charge. Afterwards he was granted a short leave. Newbolt described Celia's preparations for joining her hero: 'She spent *hours* in her room, surrounded by a vast pile of clothes and trunks! Went off this morning very severe and pretty, in black frock and ermine hat and tippet.[3] Ella and Newbolt were left in charge of the two-year-old Jill (Margaret being away). He took a fairly casual attitude to nursery duties. 'This morning I found it quite easy to read my *Times* while she played *alone!*'[4] Often there were longer separations from Celia, when she went away with Jill to Halsdon. 'That child has too many grandparents,' Newbolt commented gloomily.[5]

By September, Newbolt was concerned about his health. 'My ticker thumps at times,' he told Margaret[6] and he was suffering from headaches and tiredness. He took a week off to walk with Ella in the Malvern hills. Ella's mother came too (she did not walk) and so did *The Times* journalist Clutton Brock. 'He simply carries you

2. *NL* MEN to HN, May 1917
3. *NL*, 26 Nov. 1916
4. *NL* HN to MEN, 24 Nov. 1916
5. *NL*, 22 July 1916
6. *NL*, HN to MEN, 7 Sept. 1916

along like an aeroplane.' But Ella kept up quite well. Newbolt was now revisiting the scenes of childhood holidays. He wrote to Emily that he was amazed she had not returned to so lovely a landscape. 'The farms of black and white timber, the stooks all standing among the hanging fruit. Of course it's a place for people with good legs, but donkey chairs can take you right to the top. From West Malvern you can see the ridge of the hills receding like the spine of a gigantic lizard.'[7]

While at Malvern, Newbolt saw something of Stanford, who wished him to write the libretto of his new opera, *The Travelling Companion*. The tale of *The Travelling Companion* was one of Hans Andersen's most gruesome: John, an orphan, comes upon a corpse in a church and replaces it in its coffin. Then he meets the mysterious Travelling Companion who leads him to a city whose princess slays suitors who cannot answer her questions. The Travelling Companion gives John the answers and he marries the princess. The Travelling Companion turns out to have been the corpse in the church. Harry Plunket Greene claimed to have initiated the collaboration: 'I was sitting at home one evening smoking a pipe and reading Hans Andersen. I came presently to *The Travelling Companion*. and when I had finished it I got up and telephoned Stanford. I told him I had something to show him and would he came along at once. We sat down then and there and wrote a joint letter to Henry Newbolt.[8] By the time Newbolt saw Stanford in Malvern, the 600-line libretto was complete. The opera won a Carnegie Trust medal that year, but it was not to be staged until after Stanford's death. It was put on in 1926 at the Theatre Royal, Bristol and, according to Plunkett Greene, was considered 'one of their best cards'.[9] The general opinion of the critics was that the opera was poorly structured and that the author of the libretto lacked a sense of theatre. The opera was recently re-staged by courtesy of the John Lewis Partnership.

While Newbolt struggled to make a living in these ways, Frank's income increased. He was now Recorder of Doncaster, and Newbolt was to see him earn £500 in the Law Courts in an afternoon in 'a most refined manner'.[10] He owned a country

7. *NL*, 4 Sept. 1916
8. Henry Plunket Greene. *Charles Villiers Stanford* (1935) p.194
9. [ibid.]
10. *NL* HN to EN, May 1917

232

house, Mattocks, on the edge of a wood above Lyme Regis. He later published a book of etchings of this wood, *The Enchanted Wood* (1925), introducing naked nymphs among the tree trunks. Unfortunately, the prints were accompanied by his own verses. In the summer of 1916 Frank laid on a splendid wedding for Molly to John Medley, ADC to Tom Bridges, at Southwark Cathedral. Newbolt was impressed by the wedding presents which 'were numerous and costly and included a cheque for £200.'[11] At this stage, Henry Chitty became engaged. He had recovered from his wound and was on garrison duty in East Anglia. 'We saw in *The Times* that Henry Chitty is engaged to Violet Becher, daughter of Major and Mrs Becher. Clearly he is the Major of Henry's battery. Henry writes but says only that she is perfect, and that he proposes to live in British East Africa for his health. All this makes me fear that Tom Chitty is not pleased and that the marriage is considered an imprudent one.' On 6 October Henry married Violet. 'It was a queer thing of Henry not to write to me even a p.c. when he made up his mind to jump overboard. I'm not annoyed but I feel much less inclined to help him.'[12] In fact, the marriage ended in divorce and Henry married Ethel Gladstone in 1922. The eldest of their children, my husband Thomas, was in his twenties before he discovered that his father had been married before.

The Christmas party at Netherhampton in 1916 was a small one. Ralph, Celia and Jill were at Halsdon. There was only Francis, 'my poor damaged hero'.[13] Francis had been posted to Oxford as an instructor. There he had 'the fun of examining his cadets in New College hall where only two years ago he was himself doing a paper on Catullus!'[14] But he was still far from well. 'He is only fit for the lightest duty. He had some trout fishing near here, and even that was too much of strain on his nerves.' Emily was of the party. She arrived cold and cross because the driver of her hired car had lost his way and she had left her knitting behind. Then she exhausted herself by going to church too much. Newbolt had insisted that there should be no presents – 'But if you *should* wish to give me anything, will you bring a little old snuff box that used to be in

11. *NL* HN to EN, July 1916
12. *NL* HN to EN, n.d. 1916
13. *AHL*, 21 Dec. 1916
14. *NL* HN to EN, 28 June 1916

Grandmamma's house? I can remember her explanation, that it was made of Shakespeare's mulberry tree and that Shakespeare had been dead some years.'[15] (Peter and Marcia Newbolt still have this little box.) Newbolt looked back on yet another year of war. Even near Netherhampton the human cost was visible. In Salisbury Newbolt had seen an ambulance from Southampton 'with 4 wounded officers lying on shelves quite straight and flat, like dead men in a family vault. A gruesome sight but wonderful to think that they were probably fighting only 2 days ago!'[16]

15. *NI*. HN to EN, 17 and 30 Dec. 1916
16. *NL* HN to MEN, 19 July 1916

CHAPTER 43

1917

1917 was the year of the German submarine, when U-boats, in defiance of international law, made unrestricted warfare on merchant shipping. The Kaiser planned to starve Britain into submission in six months. In April nearly a million tons of allied shipping were sunk, and there was only six weeks' supply of wheat left in Britain. It was Lloyd George, now Prime Minister, who suggested the ancient and traditional method of convoy. The hierarchy at the Admiralty at first opposed it, but was eventually persuaded, and by October the tonnage being lost was almost halved. At this stage, Newbolt at last managed to land some war work. He infiltrated himself into a kind of part-time propaganda position at the Admiralty . 'You'll be amused to hear,' he told Emily, 'that I am now an officer of the Secret Service Department.'[1] Corbett (now Sir Julian) had been at the Admiralty

1. *NL*, 17 July 1917

since the beginning of the war. Newbolt was liaison officer between the Admiralty and the War Cabinet. He was also required to write a pamphlet on the history of the British submarine, or E-boat 'to counteract the belief abroad that the Submarine is a German invention'.[2] He enjoyed reading previously unpublished submarine exploits of the present war in his cramped little office. 'For 2 hours I've been lost at sea, looking on at one fight after another. It is all just the "same old game". I haven't read a word that would have made Nelson stop to think.'[3] The problem was publication; Admiral Brownrigg, the Chief Censor, preferred to tell as little as possible about any episode. 'Not for nothing are they called the Silent Service.' Many times Brownrigg told Newbolt, 'You must write not for your readers but to confuse the enemy.'[4] Another of Newbolt's tasks was to present to the War Cabinet a monthly account of British tonnage lost. The total was still disappointingly high, but Newbolt felt the public should be told the truth. In this he disagreed with Sir Eric Geddes, the new First Lord of the Admiralty. Newbolt's Christmas book for boys that year was entitled *Submarine and Antisubmarine.* Besides tales of heroic exploits, he included a vivid description of what it felt like to dive in a submarine: 'The light of day gives place to a green twilight full of small bubbles. Mentally you feel a slight chill', and so on.[5] There is no evidence that Newbolt ever dived. But he had spent a long time in Room 105 at the Admiralty.

At the end of October Newbolt travelled to the Orkneys to inspect the Grand Fleet at Scapa Flow. He boarded Admiral Sturdee's flag-ship *Hercules* in the teeth of a gale. 'Squalls of hail rattle on the tin walls of my cabin, and white horses go galloping past without a pause'.[6] Life on board, as usual, was a round of dinners with admirals. 'If they don't overfeed me I shall make a great success of it.' As before, there were hazardous invitations to dine on neighbouring ships. '*Colossus* was only four cables off but we bobbed like a cork on a boiling saucepan.' There was also a chance to mix with some of the junior officers. One of Katharine Furse's two naval sons, Peter, was a midshipman on board *Hercules.*

2. *NL* HN to EN, 20 Sept. 1917
3. *NL* HN to MEN, 10 Sept. 1917
4. *HN* to AH, 23 Oct. 1922; *LLL*, p.289
5. *Submarine and Antisubmarine*, p.38
6. *NL* HN to MEN, Oct. 1917

'After tea I got him in from his watchkeeping and took him off to my cabin and had a good hour's talk. He was perfectly natural and easy.' Newbolt helped the boy with the spelling of ships' names. But best of all were the long chats with Admiral Sturdee himself. After each of these Newbolt hurried to the Flag Officer's cabin to make notes. (There was no fire in his own.) The climax of the visit was a day of manoeuvres on the Flow, 'which you book in advance, like a tennis court.' Sturdee was taking out a division of four battleships and Newbolt was up on the bridge. By 4.30 he admitted to being 'frozen fairly solid'.[7] Young Peter was at a voice pipe, repeating orders 'in a very seamanlike voice. I dug him in the ribs but I couldn't talk to him of course.'[8] As before, Newbolt felt perfectly well at sea. He had arrived on board with a heavy cold and 'a small disturbance in the innards.' He left with neither. To Margaret he wrote: 'I feel quite as if I were *really* away at sea. It seems years since I parted from you dearest.' He decided to return to London after four days because he felt he had garnered all the information he could process. He had hoped to find a fire lit in Ella's house, but none of his letters had arrived. Somewhat disgruntled, he retired to the Athenaeum and awaited the weekend at Netherhampton which he feared would be equally cheerless. 'I hope the house will feel less damp this time. Last time it was like a cold nutmeg-grater on my skin!'[9]

Newbolt had now moved into Ella's house almost completely. He spent only his weekends at Netherhampton, and even these were often curtailed. But he did not have his alternative wife entirely to himself. Her siblings continued to give trouble. Hew had married the wrong Ethel. 'He's lucky,' declared Newbolt, 'to have drawn a prize at all after all his gambling.'[10]

It was at the party to celebrate Hew and Ethel's engagement that Newbolt came under enemy fire for the first time. There was an air raid. 'Such a funny scene when the whistles and maroons went. All our guests arose and ran. In two minutes Ella and I were left alone. Only one bomb was dropped. It sounded as if it were a gun being fired in the garden opposite, but it was really down near the

7. *NL* HN to MEN, 24 Oct.1917
8. ibid.
9. *NL* HN to MEN, 5 Nov. 1917
10. NL HN to MEN, 18 Feb. 1918

Chelsea Pensioners' Hospital. It destroyed the house where Dr Barnes used to live and all in it.'[11]

Newbolt was now able to appreciate Ella's character to the full. She was strangely restless and unpredictable. 'She arrives and elopes at a moment's notice and she doesn't tell me where.'[12] When her sister Anna went into a local nursing home Ella became calmer. She 'is not a bit in rags. It's rather good for her to have [Anna] to occupy her.'[13] Sitting in the audience of his lecture at Bedford College one evening, Ella looked her best. 'Bright and handsome, a class above the Grey Ladies.'[14]

For the first time in his life, Newbolt now became acquainted with kitchen matters. Food shortages were a constant problem in 1917. Food was begged from Netherhampton. 'A little present of bacon and vegetables would be very soothing to Ella's mind.' he told Margaret. When Ella had a Netherhampton egg for breakfast, he declared, 'she almost wept.' Ella herself was not above a little hoarding, and had a number of packets of tea hidden away and lived in terror of being apprehended. During this period, Newbolt entered a food shop for the first time. Food rationing had been introduced and he was eager to see it in action. 'Ella and I for a lark went shopping with cards to Barkers,' he told Emily. 'I stood in a queue of six people and got a chicken for 3 coupons! *But* it cost 10/6!'[16] While waiting in that queue he deplored the 'lady customers who hadn't thought out their purchases beforehand and took up time by long and very stupid conversations over the counter.'[16]

Inevitably there was occasional domestic friction between Newbolt and Ella. Usually it was about punctuality. 'Ella came in very late for dinner having been down to tea with Mrs Rye at Wimbledon. She was fit for nothing. But after a mouthful of dinner and a lie down on her bed she reappeared and read aloud a rattling good book about a transport which was eventually torpedoed. Most refreshing!'[17] Newbolt sinned just as frequently in the matter of punctuality. He often dined at his club, but was

11. ibid.
12. *NL* HN to MEN, 18 April and 4 May 1917
13. *NL* HN to MEN, 23 April 1917
14. *NL* HN to MEN, 12 Oct. 1917
15. NL HN to EN, 2 Mar. 1918
16. *NL*, 1 Mar. 1918
17. *NL* HN to MEN, 20 Feb. 1918

expected home at a reasonable hour. Once, after a public dinner, he came home too late to see the New Year in with Ella. He had got talking munitions on the Underground and was carried on to Hammersmith. There was a silence at breakfast. Nevertheless, on the whole, the arrangement with Ella worked well, and Newbolt missed her in the summer when she left for her annual holiday. Alternative accommodation was seldom satisfactory. On one occasion Margaret's Aunt Minna suggested he should move into her London house while she was in Bournemouth. 'You'll be amazed to hear that I was totally defeated by the maids. They had moved into the best bedroom because of the air raids, leaving the top floor for me!'[18]

Besides working at the Admiralty, Newbolt was now touring the country with a lecture on the League of Peace, forerunner of the League of Nations. At Walsall he met his most 'rough hewn' audience. The lecture was held in the new Town Hall and the proceedings began with an hour's singing by the Glee Society. Afterwards old friends crowded round, including one 'who had been the librarian at the Free Library in my youth and had handed out books to me across the counter. He said, "I remember fetching *Daniel Deronda* for you in 5 or 6 volumes!" I was astonished to find I could now see clean over his head!'[19] Another lecture was delivered at the old Shakespeare Memorial Theatre in Stratford. Here George Otto Trevelyan, father of the historian, was Newbolt's host at Welcombe, his country house. 'Welcombe was the real bonus. It is like a much less ugly Orchardleigh, and Sir George called me " my dear boy" and asked me to come to his room at every opportunity. He was keener on the war than anyone but me!'[20] On the way back in the train there was another treat: Newbolt travelled with Gervase Elwes, 'who has six splendid looking boys, four of them in the war. He showed me their photos, one so like Francis when he came out of hospital that I said "Has that one been wounded?" and he said, " How did you know?" It greatly comforted me to talk to a real Roman Catholic. So sensible and English and patriotic.'[21] Another of Newbolt's lectures in 1917

18. *NL* HN to MEN, 6 Sept. 1917
19. *NL* HN to MEN, 4 Mar. 1917
20. *NL* HN to MEN, 24 Apr. 1917
21. *NL* HN to MEN, 24 Apr. 1917

was entitled 'Patriotism, Pigs and Potatoes', and was about food production at home. 'If the war goes on much longer, I shall become nothing better than a tap, being turned on by all the Movements of the Day!'[22]

Newbolt also wrote poems to raise funds. 'Comrades of the Great War' consisted of a hundred lines written for a concert to raise money for the King's Naval Fund. Newbolt frankly declared, 'it has every quality except poetry but it may be amusing – even to the Navy! Irene Vanbrugh spoke the piece splendidly and George Robey, Prime Minister of Mirth, gave £100 for it and put it up for auction again. In the end £510 was raised.' Newbolt also contributed to the war effort with a Masque performed on May Day 1917 in the garden of Whitelands College, Chelsea. Mary, the Princess Royal, was present. She was disappointing. 'It was her first public function and she was very nervous. When she put the gold cross and chain on the Queen of the May she was much the most embarrassed of the two. You would have thought she was the commoner. But she is evidently a thorough Englishwoman.[23] The grandest fund-raising occasion of all was the Commemoration Concert for seven of the divisions that had seen action. It took place at the Albert Hall at Christmas, and was arranged by Arthur Somervell with Gwen Herbert, wife of A.P. Herbert, acting as secretary ('she really is magnificent'). London society fought for tickets and Newbolt had difficulty in securing one even for Ella (who then decided not to come). Alice was stranded in Wiltshire and had to make do with a written account. Newbolt described the balconies hung with regimental shields: 'It was a really blood beating sensation to realise there was not one of them that did not mean a thousand heroic deaths.'[24] The climax was reached when Somervell's 'silver trumpets "gan to chide"' and Plunkett Greene's voice rang out. Newbolt read one of his poems and brought the house down.

Sitting on eternal committees was less fun. Worst was the committee for *entente* between the great writers of Europe. The 'tomahawks' were soon out as to who these were, and Gosse was a nuisance as usual. 'He really is a tiresomely feminine cat!'[25]

22. *NL*, 19 Feb. 1917
23. *NL*, 13 May 1917
24. *AHL*, 17 Dec. 1917
25. *NL* HN to MEN, 31 Jan. 1917

Newbolt proved a skilful chairman of a committee on books. When Charles Longman opposed the report of the Departmental Committee on Books 'I got everyone's opinion before I let [him] loose to reply, [and then] said that I was sure he could not mean that, from the beginning, our terms of reference were objected to by him. It worked! He stuck to only two minor points. I finished him off by telling him he ought to have been at the Bar, he had been so skilful in getting his own way!'[26] The committees multiplied as the war went on; sometimes he had three in an afternoon. He responded unevenly to the burden of work. Occasionally, he declared, 'it is the only thing that keeps me alive';[27] at other times, he announced, 'I would rather be under fire than under committee! I would like to spend the whole day on the sofa and speak to nobody.'[28] On this particular occasion, he was suffering from piles. Eventually he wrote 'Epitaph on a Public Man' about himself:

> Stranger if you desire to know
> What End was his who lies below,
> In far too many Chairs he sat
> And died worn out by merely that.[29]

Meanwhile, back on the farm, Margaret laboured. She was determined that Netherhampton House should be self-sufficient. Two pigs were acquired and named 'Lenin' and 'Trotsky' (Lord Hylton thought these names amusing).[30] The village was now to be saved from starvation by the Great Bread Scheme. Margaret ordered the lawn to be dug up and a ton of Irish seed potatoes to be planted in January. 'We think of nothing nowadays but food and farming', Newbolt told Emily.

The local St George's Society was converted into a share-holding potato growing society under the War Agricultural Committee. Ruffell, the gardener, became the Business Manager, with the responsibility of paying out dividends. Newbolt did the accounts for him. He instructed him 'to pin them on the toolshed door

---

26. *NL* HN to MEN, 19 Mar. 1918
27. *LN* HN to MEN, 20 Jan. 1916
28. *NL* HN to MEN 2 Jan. 1918
29. *A Perpetual Memory* (1939) Not in *SP*
30. *NL* HN to EN, 18 Mar. 1918

which is the procedure laid down in the rules.'[31] There was a moment of panic when conscription was brought in and Ruffell was called up. Margaret could 'neither dig nor market the potatoes without him' but she managed to get him off for a year on the grounds of a double hernia. There was then an anxious moment six months later when Ruffell was called before a tribunal at Wilton Workhouse, but Newbolt's skill as a pleader got him excused once more.

As the war ground on, Margaret's sense of isolation at Netherhampton increased. For the first time she began to feel jealous of Ella. Newbolt constantly entreated her to visit London, but she was less and less inclined for it because her hearing was worse than ever. 'Will a lecture *and* a dinner be too much for you?' Newbolt enquired. Occasionally they had lunch together and one, at least, of these was pleasant. 'If I had not had two committees immediately afterwards I might have bought a toothbrush and gone away with you!'[32] Sometimes her visits were less satisfactory. After one, Newbolt wrote : 'Will you go on very regularly taking Sanatogen or Boots' equivalent? You need it badly. Your happiness, mine and Celia's depend on it.'[33] At Christmas 1917 the pipes froze at Netherhampton and Margaret went down with pneumonia. 'There's a dismal suitability about everything this winter. We seem to be living in exile from all our old joys and ways. I don't feel *anxious* about the future, but I have a sense of holding the breath.' There were rumours that the Germans were planning a massive bombing attack on London and that the British Museum Library might be destroyed.

31. *NL* HN to MEN, 27 Feb. 1918
32. *NL* HN to MEN, 28 Apr. 1917
33. *NL* HN to MEN, 8 Jan. 1918

CHAPTER 44

1918

In March 1918 came a massive German offensive on the Somme, its aim to capture the railway junction at Amiens and end the war. The Germans did indeed break through, but Newbolt preferred to concentrate on the heroic British defence of Arras, which turned the war in our favour. These were, nevertheless, tense days. 'Armageddon is in full swing,' Newbolt wrote.[1] Francis's spirits now took a turn for the better. (He was on coastal defence at Dover.) His letters began to express patriotic optimism of the best sort. 'He has the one thing I feared life hadn't given him – the resilience and the joy of courage, not merely in the fight but in the dark hour. He has come through that horrible battle and made a man of himself again.'[2] In July the allies, now including the Americans, began their offensive, and the German line was breached all the

1. *NL* HN to MEN, 22 Mar. 1918
2. *NL* HN to MEN, 31 Jan. 1918

way from Ypres to Verdun. The first great success came when Foch (now in command of all the allied armies) penetrated the Marne bulge. 'The news from France is breathless. At the Marne, Foch had to use all the troops he had. He used them with perfect nerve and won.'[3] In such circumstances, Foch could be forgiven for not being an Englishman.

Newbolt now joined the new Ministry of Information, at the request of Beaverbrook, who had just become the first Minister of Information. (The head of what had previously been the Department of Information had been John Buchan). Beaverbrook required Newbolt to take control of the All-world Cable Department, and 'get the world in accord with British Policy.' Newbolt was delighted. At last he would have news of the War first-hand 'The work includes knowing all about everything.'[4]

On 3 September 1918, British tanks under Haig made a corridor two miles wide through the Wotan Sector of the German line south of Ypres. Newbolt had the news the same day, but did not dare rejoice until the morrow. 'We couldn't be sure the Boche would not retake his line. But apparently our Generals have found out how to hit and hit, and he simply broke'.[5] On that day also, Uncle Bill Furse exploded on Netherhampton to tell Margaret the same news. She described how, striding round the sundial garden he 'spread his arms in a kind of expansive gesture of *détente*. I shall recollect as a piece of Netherhampton history [that] heavenly September morning. All "the old September" seemed in it.' Suddenly Margaret had a memory of past happiness. 'I longed to run on to the Orchardleigh terrace and down the avenue with you,' she wrote.[6]

The rejoicing at Netherhampton the next weekend was universal. Both Francis and Ralph were there. 'What a weekend! When comes another such? Never I think till the sun drops dead from the signs. It was a culmination of joys, to, be laid by for a "Perpetual Remembrance".'[7] Thus Newbolt described it to Margaret when he returned to London. The signing of an armistice now depended on how long the starving people of

3. HN to EC, 13 Aug. 1918; *LLL*, p.252
4. HN to EC, 13 Aug. 1918; *LLL*, p.252
5. *NL* HN to MEN, 3 Sept. 1918
6. *NL* MEN to HN, 4 Sept. 1918
7. *NL* HN to MEN, 9 Sept. 1918

Germany would hold out. Buchan predicted they would hang on till the spring, but Newbolt said that they would not enter another winter in 'paper clothes'.[8] The British too were heartily war-weary, and that included Emily. She was tired of being short of money. When Newbolt pointed out that 'we all live on less nowadays,' she wrote: 'I should think so!' in the margin of his letter. She had no housekeeper and only a lady gardener. To Newbolt's alarm, she even threatened to sell the family china.

Naturally, Newbolt knew about the armistice days before anyone else. On 31 October he wrote to Alice: 'Buchan and I are going to Heligoland to see the German High Canal Fleet come in.'[9] This trip unfortunately had to be cancelled because of pressure of work, but there was a consolation. Three months later Newbolt received the following letter from Admiral Luce of the *Ramillies*: 'On the occasion when the Grand Fleet put to sea to meet and bring in the surrendered German High Sea Fleet, the Captain of one of our newest battleships noticed a peculiar sound of a drumming nature. It was described as a drum beat of a ceremonial or stately sound. Nothing could be found to which it could be attributed. Was this Drake's Drum?'[10] Meanwhile, Newbolt celebrated 11 November from his office chair. 'I can hear as I write the cheers rolling along Fleet Street and the Strand,' he told Margaret. 'The sound of the guns over London this morning was thrilling, and ever since then, the cars go by with flags, and bugles. The crowd cheer every bit of khaki they see.'[11] At Netherhampton Ruffell rang the church bell. Newbolt was exhausted by the time he returned there at the weekend. 'I took to falling asleep in the middle of conversations, even in the act of walking. On Sunday afternoon I curled up in my Ark and slept.'[12]

Christmas 1918 was the feast of Ralph and Celia. He was fresh from galloping after Uhlans (German cavalry) in Belgium. She had just produced Newbolt's first grandson. Patrick 'the slit-eyed little ruffian', was born on 8 December. On Christmas Eve, Ralph sprawled before the fire 'like a giant puppy, a handsome, clumsy,

8. *NL* HN to MEN, 3 Sept. 1918
9. *AHL*, 31 Oct. 1918
10. Admiral Luce to HN, 16 Feb. 1919; *LLL*, p.408
11. *NL* HN to MEN, 11 Nov. 1918
12. *AHL*, 17 Nov. 1918; *LLL*, p.259

comfortable thing that dreams his hunting over again'.[13] On Christmas morning, young Jill went to church with her father, 'the prettiest thing I ever saw. She all in white fur. Her little bare legs contrasted with his great leather gaiters like Cupid with Mars. These tiny wise old elves. In seven years they vanish.'[14] Newbolt felt strangely excluded by Ralph and Celia. 'The young are too happy to form part of anyone's life.'[15] The post-war years were to be theirs.

13. *AHL*, 24 Dec. 1918
14. *AHL*, 26 Dec.1918
15. *AHL*, 24 Dec. 1918

PART IX TWENTIES 1919–1929

CHAPTER 45

St George's Day

The Great War effectively ended Newbolt's career as a war poet. Mass-produced massacre did not inspire him. 'I spent most of the years of my life under the certainty of war,' he wrote, 'the conviction that my country must pass through the trial.' Now there remained the memory of that war, but it was a memory not of glory but of too many friends dead. 'I cannot sever myself from them'.[1] Worst of all, there was Francis. Francis who woke screaming in the night because he dreamed he was treading on the faces of his friends buried in mud, Francis who started in fear at any loud noise as if it were a shell exploding. There had been a grisly moment when his knapsack was returned from the front.

1. *LLL*, p.187

The one that had stopped the bullet. The family unpacked it one morning in June. 'An amusing assortment of clothing and trench-sodden boots was spread on the lawn,' Newbolt wrote. It was not entirely amusing. 'There was always the thought of masterless kits being unpacked on other lawns.'[2]

In September 1920, Newbolt visited the battlefield at Ypres with Francis. Dame Katharine Furse, the gaunt old war horse, and her other sailor son, Paul,[3] came too. The whole area around the town was like 'a Highland moor, a vast green bog full of holes and every hole filled with bullrushes and other huge weeds. In some there were green pools into which frogs leapt, splash, as you came up. Everywhere there were shells, some still alive, piled in rusty heaps. Also old broken rifles, tins for water, petrol, ammunition and barbed wire all about in grass two feet high so that you can hardly lift your feet through it.'[4] Francis, still carrying the old broken pipe he had on *that* night, was their guide and remained remarkably calm and unemotional. 'It was a marvel to see him pick his way from point to point like a dog. We followed exactly all his movements on each of those extraordinary days and nights. We staggered and struggled over the field of the Second Battle of Ypres for four and a half hours, in which time we covered exactly five miles!'

It was a vivid moment when they topped the ridge, and saw the whole wide valley, with the stiff slope up the far side to the enemy's position. Like Francis, they climbed as far as Foch's Farm, where Francis had dug in for the final bombardment. 'It was painfully interesting to trace the advance of the big shells towards Foch's Farm, hole after hole, till at last they found it and settled down to obliterate it.'[5]

The closest Newbolt ever came to a real battle was in the cinema. In 1916 he saw a silent newsreel: 'Men marching into action, long, long columns of them winding away up an endless road, going by with broad grins at you. The effect was to make me love them passionately.' It also resulted in a poem, 'The War Films', which bore little resemblance to a patriotic ballad:

2. *AHL*, 16 June 1915
3 *NL* HN to MEN, 3 Sept. 1920
4. ibid.
5. *NL* HN to MEN, 7 Sept. 1920

> O living pictures of the dead,
> O song without a sound,
> O fellowship whose phantom tread,
> Hallows a phantom ground[6]

These farm labourers in tin hats had taken the place of St George on his white horse. Newbolt had met one quite recently at Orchardleigh – 'quite vulgar, a Tommyish sort of Tommy (I don't mind if I never see him again) who said 'when you've seen two-thirds of your pals knocked over, you love 'em like your own brother. You know sir, you do *love* 'em.'" The belief in chivalry was still there, but it was a chivalry far from Will Threlfall pounding down the touch line with the rugger ball or Julian Grenfell rejoicing that he had been born 'at just the right time'. It was a chivalry that was based on the foot soldier rather than the knight. Jan Morris rightly saw in that poem the sounding of the trumpet for the imperial retreat. 'Even the imperialist balladeers were muted now, and it was Sir Henry Newbolt himself, who spoke for them all in 'The War Films'.[7]

Yet never at any point in the war had Newbolt openly denounced the awful waste of life, although in letters to Alice he admitted to moments of discouragement. In October 1915 he wrote 'It is hard to avoid these waves of depression that seem to swamp everyone, with all the papers bleating like a pack of frightened sheep. *Enfin*, I refuse to despair – in my waking hours. Of course at 4.00 a.m. it is a bit ugly.'[8] His friends remarked on his cheerfulness. Walter de la Mare said, 'Throughout the War, however dark the day and louring the prospect, he remained a steadfast optimist.' Percy Lubbock, writing to Ella, agreed: 'The only person I wanted to hear talking about the war was H.N. There was something about his tone (I can still hear it plainly) so perfectly just and sane.'[9]

There had been a scandal in 1917. An officer in the Royal Welsh Fusiliers and a holder of the Military Cross had refused to return to the front. He published pamphlets against the war. His name was Siegfried Sassoon and he claimed that the war was being

6. *SP*, p.118
7. James Morris, *Farewell the Trumpets: An Imperial Retreat* (1979), p.210
8. *AHL*, 11 Oct. 1915
9. Vanessa Furse Jackson, *The Poetry of Henry Newbolt* (1994) p.159

misreported in the press and needlessly prolonged by politicians. As one who 'had seen and endured the suffering of the troops I could no longer be a party to prolonging those sufferings for ends which I believe to be evil and unjust.' The pamphlet was much discussed and found sympathy in many quarters. Newbolt ignored it.

St George's Day, a collection of a dozen war poems by Newbolt, appeared in 1918 under the John Murray imprint. It was the last book of his poems to be published in his lifetime. At the beginning of the war he had planned a set of martial ballads for Stanford to set to music, to be entitled *Songs of the War*. 'Something for the Tommies to march to, vulgar but effective'.[10] But only three were ever written: 'The King's Highway', 'The Toy Band', and 'The Chanty of the Emden', and all these were written before the end of 1916. With the final victories of 1918 Newbolt's heart had risen briefly, but his lyre remained silent. 'My pulses are full of poetry but I can't find time to reduce them to tranquility.' In the same letter he gave the true reason: 'I don't even feel the joy of victory as wildly as I should have done three years ago. To win a game makes the pulse leap; but to massacre.'[11]

St George's Day was not a resounding success. Martial poetry was out of fashion. 'There is a concerted movement among the young critics to boycott all who write military or naval poems. Perhaps that might account for their treatment of me in these last years!'[12] No doubt Newbolt was smarting under a peculiarly unkind parody of 'Drake's Drum' that J. C. Squire had published in 1917.[13]

It was eight bells in the forenoon and hammocks running sleek
(It's a fair sea flowing from the West)
When the little Commodore came a-sailing up the Creek
(Heave Ho! I think you'll know the rest)
Thunder in the halyards and horses leaping high,
Blake and Drake and Nelson are listenin' where they lie,
Four and twenty blackbirds a-bakin' in a pie,
And the *Pegasus* came waltzing from the West.

10. *AHL*, 14 Dec. 1914
11. *AHL*, 6 Oct. 1918, *LLL*, p.255
12. *NL* HN to MEN,1919
13. *Tricks of the Trade*

Now a new school of war poets had arisen led by Rupert Brooke, Wilfred Owen and Siegfried Sassoon. Newbolt appreciated them, but with reservations. He even published *New Paths on Helicon* (1927) a critical anthology of the poetry of the first quarter of the twentieth century. But of the war poets he only chose those who saw the conflict, however ugly, as having some meaning. Owen was firmly excluded: 'I don't think these self-pitying, shell-shocked poems will move our grandchildren greatly,' he declared. Siegfried Sassoon on the other hand, was approved. In his poem 'All Souls Day', a soldier stands on the battlefield of yesterday where 'shapes like windblown shadows pass', but the poem concludes on a note of hope: 'in Thee, O ultimate power, who art our victory and our vision.' Newbolt wrote; 'In the colossal futility of modern war, the refuge of indignation, of satire, of fierce contempt, was no longer tenable. An Order of Nature there must be and a moral order.'[14]

A four-line poem, 'A Perpetual Memory: Good Friday, 1915'[15] was found among Newbolt's papers after his death. It strangely echoed the mood of the young war poets:

> Broken and pierced, hung on the bitter wire,
> By their most precious death the Sons of Man
> Redeem for us the life of our desire –
> O Christ how often since the world began!

14. *New Paths on Helicon*, p.399
15. *S.P.* p.137

CHAPTER 46

John Buchan

At the end of the war Newbolt and his department were given twenty-four hours' notice to leave the office in Norfolk Street and move downmarket to South Kensington. It was all the fault of Bonar Law, the new Conservative Prime Minister, 'that champion muddler who proves as silly as his face'.[1] More immediately, it was the fault of Sir Arthur Durrant, who did not have the guts to stand up to a certain Mr Mond at the Office of Works.

> There is an official called Durrant
> Who resembles a common black currant
> Being under the hand
> Of a monster named Mond
> Though he'd like to be decent he durren't[2]

1. *NL* HN to MEN, 9 Jan. 1919
2. *NL* HN to MEN, 15 Jan. 1919

'Such,' declared Newbolt, 'is Government by business men, coal-heavers and grocers.[2] He briefly succeeded in securing an office further along Norfolk Street. 'They were under the impression that we are the Ministry of Information which is being wound up. They had no idea that we were a department of the Foreign Office and on a permanent footing.'[3] But Cecil Harmsworth, the new under-secretary at the Foreign Office, abolished the department in the interests of economy. Newbolt departed on 1 April, commenting, 'My schemes for serving my Country have been defeated by the brute stupidity of officials'.[5] John Buchan wrote a comment on Newbolt's career as a civil servant: 'In the last year of the War I found him a most able colleague. But although he did well by his generation he never quite belonged to it. Providence had cast him for a bard, a companion of men-at-arms and the chronicler of their deeds. He found his niche in letters in a kind of half-lyric, half-ballad, but for him that was only half a life. He would have liked to live in the thick of great deeds. Yet he was not quite at home in the world and, apart from his poetry, he never found work which wholly satisfied him.'[6]

No sooner was one 'official stamp' removed (this was the phrase that John Betjeman used in connection with Newbolt), than a new one was applied, this time by H.A.L. Fisher, at that time President of the Board of Education and in the process of steering his Education Acts through Parliament. Newbolt used to meet Hal at The Club (founded by Dr Johnson). After a dinner there, Fisher (a younger man) had invited Newbolt to walk home. He needed advice on a lecture on the history of London. A few days later a letter followed, 'Hal has paid me the high compliment of asking me to be Chairman of his new Committee on the teaching of English in Schools.'[7] After two years of hard work, the report came out and had a good reception. (It was in use in teacher training colleges until 1942.) For financial reasons Newbolt now needed a book to write. 'I was asked to do John Percival's Life but I am *not*

2. *NL* HN to MEN, 14 Jan. 1919
3. *NL* HN to MEN, 10 Jan. 1919
5. NL HN to MEN, 18 Jan. 1919
6. John Buchan, *Memory Hold-The-Door*, p.218
7. *NL* HN to MEN, May 1919; *LLL*, p.264

going to do biographies.'[8] So he settled for *An English Anthology of Prose and Poetry* (1921) published by Dent. This book was a quirky, self-indulgent affair. Much space was allotted to Newbolt's personal friends like William Cory, Robert Bridges and Mary Coleridge. The prose excerpts (sometimes pages in length) included such personal favourites as Drake's request for reinforcements before the Armada and Holinshed's account of the trial of Richard II. Meanwhile Newbolt plodded on with the boys' Venture Series. There were three volumes yet to go. *The Book of the Long Trail* (1919) was about explorers. Naturally, Newbolt brought in the adventures of his friend Frank Younghusband in Lhasa, and Sandy Wollaston in the mountains of Rwanda-Burundi. The last volume, *The Book of the Grenvilles* (1921) ended with an account of the heroic deaths of Julian and Billy Grenfell. On the last page, a boy enquires; 'How are we to go on after this war [in] such an empty world?' He is told, 'the pain of beauty is what we have gained by war. We used to get it from great poets, but now thousands have seen it even nearer.'

At Christmas 1921, John Buchan appointed Newbolt editor-in-chief of Nelson's Teaching of English series. Here was a permanent satisfactory escape from officialdom. 'My forces had been somewhat overdrawn on the Government account during the last four years,' declared Newbolt. 'Now I am going to sail like the Theban Eagle.'[9] Little did he guess what a wearisome task would fill the rest of the decade. Introductions to the great poets began to pour from his pen. (It would be almost as tedious to list them as it must have been to write them.) Then more anthologies followed: *The Time and Tide of English Poetry* and the lengthy *Noble English* (four volumes, of prose selections). At first the work seemed mild and pleasurable: 'I am enjoying myself over two new volumes of my Noble English series. I am in the age of Swift, Steele, Addison. It takes a lot of reading and counting up the pages but it is a good work to do in a garden chair.'[10] Then the pace began to tell, and the Theban Eagle's wings began to droop. 'This week I've written notes on over seventy poets and prosers,' Newbolt told Margaret.

John Buchan now became a close friend. They had liked each

8. *NL* HN to MEN, 18 Feb. 1919
9. *HN* to MEN, 25 Dec.1921; *LLL*, p.285
10. *HN* to EC, Aug. 1923; *LLL*, p.303

other since they met in 'the queer subterranean world of the Secret Service.' Certainly, two men can seldom have been better matched, although Buchan was thirteen years younger than Newbolt. Newbolt visited Elsfield Manor, Buchan's Oxfordshire mansion, for the first time in February 1920, after lecturing to undergraduates at Oxford. He was immediately enchanted by Buchan's wife Susan and her happy family of children ranging from one to eleven years old. He was sure Margaret would like her too. 'She says the village is in need of your instruction,' he told her. 'She has a Mother's Union but hankers after a Women's Institute. I think I have found a real friend for you.'[11] He had in fact found a real friend for himself. Susan Buchan was the kind of well-born, intelligent woman he admired, and he wrote her several letters, one of them suggesting material for her book on Wellington. On later visits to Elsfield she took him on 'pleasing forays round the library', and he was gratified to find that 'my old friend Ronsard' was as familiar to her children 'as A.A. Milne to most young people today.'[12]

When the Buchans made a return visit to Netherhampton, Newbolt finally rebelled against Margaret's tattered curtains and threadbare carpets. 'We must get something down in the corridor upstairs. I positively hate that old carpet,' he told her.[13] During the visit, Newbolt took the Buchans to see Thomas Hardy. Fortunately the Grand Old Man was 'amazingly full of talk though he looked very old.' If Buchan considered Newbolt 'not quite at home in the world of men and affairs', Newbolt considered Buchan not quite at home in the world of letters. 'I wish I were as free as John Buchan from the fatal scholar's habit of trying to know all about a subject before you write about it. He always seems able to call his secretary and dictate an article on anything at a moment's notice.'[14]

11. *NL* HN to MEN, 10 Feb. 1920
12. *NL* HN to Susan Buchan, 19 April 1931
13. *NL* HN to MEN, 15 Feb. 1927
14. *NL* HN to MEN, 15 June 1926

CHAPTER 47

Naval Operations

Few people (and this includes eminent historians) realise that Henry Newbolt was part-author of the official *History of Naval Operations in the Great War* put out by the Committee of Imperial Defence. Corbett had written the first volumes, but had died within hours for putting down his pen at the end of Volume III. In Margaret's opinion, writing the last two volumes hastened Newbolt's death. The two volumes are a solid, competent piece of work. They are still a vital source for naval historians, yet they can be enjoyed by the general readers, despite the shortage of battles. (Unfortunately for Newbolt Jutland had already been covered by Corbett.) There was left for him the submarine campaign, the convoy system and the final blockading of German ports. He succeeded, however, in playing up the surrender of the German Fleet, the one he had so unfortunately missed. 'It was typical of the navy that the

Commander-in-Chief regarded it as hardly worth describing.'[1]

Writing the book presented many problems. The first was the sheer volume of source material. (Newbolt envied Gibbon, who based his *Decline and Fall* on a mere ten thousand pages of manuscript.) There were enough official documents available to him to fill a library. In 1917 alone, three hundred telegrams a day passed between the Admiralty and naval ships in home waters. Over and above these there were records of War Cabinet proceedings, memos between government departments and so forth. Newbolt did not, of course, work unaided at the office of the Committee for Imperial Defence in Whitehall Gardens. He had five assistants (two of them military) as well as an archivist and his indispensable secretary Edith Keate. He was also assisted by the German Admiral von Mantey.

The second problem was censorship. As usual, the Admiralty did not want to make public anything that might help the Germans in a future war. When near the end of the first volume, Newbolt wrote: 'I am weighed upon by tons of official secrets – horrible corpses which are just now heaving up the mounds and seem likely to burst their coffins.'[2] Sometimes he was tempted to take a line that was not the official one. In this matter he had learned a little cunning from Corbett, who used to slip in his own views by implication, 'thus avoiding the blue pencil'. Even so, the following official disclaimer was printed at the beginning of Newbolt's book: 'The Lords Commissioners of the Admiralty have given the author access to official documents in the preparation of this work, but they are in no way responsible for his reading or presentation of the facts as stated.'

The third problem was individual admirals and cabinet ministers. Each was a *prima donna* fiercely defending his version of what happened during any particular engagement. (It was Churchill who had sent Corbett's blood pressure soaring to fatal heights when he insisted the Jutland volume should be rewritten in his favour.) Although Newbolt had missed the Battle of Jutland, he had the unenviable task of summing up between Jellicoe and Beatty in a chapter entitled 'After Jutland. Professional Opinions'. The accusation that Jellicoe had turned away from the enemy at

1. *Naval Operations*, vol V, p.381
2. *NL* HN to MEN, 16 Feb.1927; *LLL*, p.350

6.15 a.m. on the fatal day and had only turned to face him at 9.00 a.m. still stood. With supreme tact, Newbolt excused Jellicoe on the grounds that there was still plenty of time left for him to join battle. But as the present day historian Captain Stephen Roskill points out: 'His about-turn can hardly be described as an endeavour to engage the enemy'.[3] As a result of Newbolt's tolerant attitude, he found Jellicoe remarkably compliant throughout the progress of the book.

> When all around are bellicose,
> And bent on saving face,
> I think how ten just Jellicoes
> Might save the whole damned race.[4]

Beatty was another matter. He privately referred to Jutland as 'the terrible day when we might have accomplished so much'[5] It was he who, on that day, fought the hardest naval action of the war. Newbolt liked Beatty, now First Sea Lord, even more than he liked Jellicoe. He was young, he was handsome, he was well-bred, he was literate. According to Roskill, Newbolt admired him because he was in the Nelson mould, one of those supermen to whom Carlyle had considered power should be entrusted unconditionally. Beatty was the last in Newbolt's long succession of heroes. Yet sometimes Newbolt felt that all the admirals, even Beatty, were against him. In 1927 he wrote: 'Admirals All are writing to Editors All'.[6] He used his charm to disarm them. He has left an account of a speech he gave at the Navy Club, when he was the only civilian among 'hundreds of officers of all ages'. He excused himself as 'a Poor Pavement Artist', and told them how Brownrigg used to say, 'I've sent your tripe down to Admiral Hall.' They loved the joke, but he asked himself whether there was not some truth in it. '*Am* I just a balladmonger who loves the sea and seamen?'[7]

3. Stephen Roskill, *Admiral of the Fleet: Earl Beatty* (1980)
4.*NL* HN to AH, 24 Sept. 1926; *LLL*, p.347
5. Stephen Roskill, *Admiral of the Fleet Earl Beatty* (1980) p.323
6. HN to MEN, 16 Feb. 1927; LLL, p.350
7. HN to AH, Oct. 1922; *LLL*, p.289

CHAPTER 48

Private Lyrics

Emily died well into her eighties. On her eightieth birthday, she wrote: 'Nobody loves me, no not one.'[1] A few days after writing that letter she suffered a severe stroke. Now it was too late for Newbolt to tell her how much he had loved her. 'How can it be so impossible for a son to tell his mother that he loves her so profoundly that to part from her finally is a mutilation of his earthly existence?'[2] Emily was moved to a nursing home in Salisbury. 'Yesterday the doctor came to tell me that this was the day, and I went and was alone with her for seven minutes during which I could not keep from whispering my name through the empty chambers of her senses. She only sighed three times and then lay still as if she had fallen asleep.'[3] He addressed a six-line

1. *NL* EN to HN 21 Feb. 1919
2. HN to EC, 31 Aug,1919; *LLL*, p.265
3. *HN* to AH, 6 Mar. 1921; *LLL*, p.278

poem to her entitled 'March 5th, 1921.'

> 'Me at the dawn's first breath
> Thee in the dusk of death
>   Thy love and my love tended:
> We shall be mother and son
> After all days are done
>   All darkness ended.'[4]

It was left to Margaret to clear up the house in Winchester where Emily had lived for nearly twenty years. 'The worst job was clearing the kneehole writing table. Multitudes of little woven boxes containing mostly rubbish, but here and there a treasure such as the baby shift your father wore. One thing has helped me through, the recollection of the care and trouble your Mother took over buying every mortal thing for my kitchen and linen cupboard in 1889.'[5] Margaret too had lost both her parents. Mrs Duckworth had died in 1916 and Mr Duckworth followed her a year later after a day's skating on the lake (assisted by a chair). Campbell and his wife Viola were now enthroned at Orchardleigh, and soon some rather odd people began to appear at shooting parties. Newbolt found an ally in the old keeper, Sigsworth, out shooting for the first time for twenty years 'without my master'. Newbolt too was close to tears. 'I see him everywhere,' he told Margaret, 'and hear his voice as clearly as I hear the cock pheasants getting up. (But I have to admit it was the first time I've ever felt *safe* at an Orchardleigh shoot!)'[6] There were other deaths during this period. Woolly Bear was gone: 'I had only one mother and one Wollaston'[7] and Bernard Holland : 'He was so much more than just a Civil Servant of the orthodox kind.'[8] The motor-car was beginning to take its toll too. Smith-Dorrien had been run over in Bournemouth and Alice Hylton's mother had succumbed in Bristol. Admiral Fisher had fallen out of an aeroplane without a parachute. 'It is incredible how they fall – suddenly and quietly, like September apples into deep grass. Loneliness begins to show as a deadly chill. What would the world be like for the last of his

4. *SP*, p.136
5. *NL* MN to HN, 18 Feb. 1920
6. *NL* HN to MEN, 21 Dec. 1919
7. *AHL*, 27 Jan. 1926
8. *NL* HN to MEN, 26 May 1926

generation, with all the boughs bare and all the birds silent?'[9]

The Victorian era had now truly been laid to rest. 'We have come a long way from the changeless days of our youth when everything and everybody from Queen Victoria to the butler and the shooting season seemed to be fixed immutably in their places.'[10] The twenties now came in with a rush. Newbolt would live to see Jill do the party circuit with Laurence Whistler in a sports car, but she would by then be inhabiting another world.

Meanwhile the London life with Ella continued. Number 29 had become increasingly dear, as he told Ella: 'Not because of its convenience, but because it is your setting and your making and the symbol of our life together. You fit me like a fur tippet.'[11] He was glad of a comfortable home during the tube strike of 1919, when thousands of travellers stood outside underground stations in the snow. The strike also caused him problems, particularly on an occasion when he nearly missed a deadline. 'Ella had ordered breakfast in bed for both of us at 9.30 when the phone rang about the article for the *Weekly Despatch* which I hoped they had forgotten. I got it done by 1.20 and pretty good rubbish I must have written. My old brougham came in quarter of an hour later with a decayed old grey horse and a driver in his early seventies. But I got there just in time'.[12] It was a relief that evening to get back to a warm fire. But even Ella could not protect him from the effects of the evil weather that year. His annual attack of 'flu threatened to turn into pneumonia and Dr Gray came over on his bicycle.[13] Margaret was summoned from Netherhampton, bearing long woollen underpants, but was warned, 'that bedroom on the top floor' would be too cold for her. 'You had better stay at Frank's.'

Alice Hylton also needed comforting at this time. Her son Toby had been killed in a shooting accident. 'She poured out her sad heart – at least her salt tears, as she does every time I see her. I wish she could write verses. That would relieve the pain perhaps. Of course she is very lonely.' Lord Hylton continued to be a cold and distant figure. Even at this time he seemed more concerned about

9. *AHL*, 8 May 1925
10. *NL* HN to MEN, 26 May 1926
11. *NL* HN to EC, 28 June 1922
12. *NL* HN to MEN, 7 Feb. 1919
13. *NL* HN to MEN, 5 Feb. 1919

his position in the Royal Household than about his wife. Newbolt recorded a conversation:

Government Official: We would like to offer you the position of lord in waiting.

Lord Hylton: What about my appointment as Captain of the Yeoman of Guard?

Government Official: Oh! Someone else, Lord Jersey I think, is Captain of the Yeomen of the Guard.

Lord Hylton: But he resigned it more than nine months ago!!!
Exeunt Omnes

Francis was also far from happy. He had failed to get into the Foreign Office and had to make do with a poorly paid post in the Colonial Office. When Ralph and Celia moved to Hanover Terrace, Holland Park, in the early twenties, he moved in with them. He wrote a play about the war, for which Newbolt held out little hope. 'The plot, I think, no audience could stand: it is an ingenious combination of horrors.'[14] Meanwhile, Celia had published a volume of poems. Francis also had difficulty in finding girls to take to dances. 'Poor old Francis,' said Newbolt, 'he has no little foxes with whom to trot.'[15] Then he bought a bigger Peugeot, and suddenly there were lots of girls. One of these was Nancy Triffitt to whom he proposed marriage. Newbolt did not at first appear to approve, possibly because of her social status. Nancy was an art student who had been a fellow lodger at Francis's digs at 12 Leonard Place, W8. Indeed, it was to separate him from her that Newbolt had moved him in with Ralph and Celia. Francis wrote the following letter (on St George's Day), begging Newbolt to relent: 'This is the great adventure of my life, comparable only to that of St George's Day 1915. I pray to God that you and Mother may share this St George's Day with me.'[16]

After one more week of resistance, Newbolt gave in and the couple were married at the end of the year. Newbolt wrote them an affectionate letter after the wedding, and Margaret wrote an even more affectionate one. She assured 'my great darlings' that they reminded her of her first dawn as a married woman when she

14. *NL* HN to MEN, 2 Nov. 1927
15. *NL* HN to MEN, 7 Mar. 1919
16. *NL* Francis to HN, 23 Apr. 1921

turned to her husband in bed and thought. 'He is here!'[17] Peter Newbolt was born two years later, on Trafalgar Day. He was the first and only grandson to bear the name of Newbolt. Francis and Nancy continued to live at Hanover Terrace for another four years, until Peter's sister, Anne, was born. Then Newbolt rented a house for them at a cost of £600 a year. It was in the same street as Ralph and Celia's. 'From now on,' Newbolt declared, 'grandchildren must be our luxuries.'[18]

The number of grandchildren eventually increased to seven. Francis had another daughter, Mary, in 1932, Celia and Ralph started a second family with Nicholas and Theresa. Jill was by then an enchanting teenager, excelling at Christmas charades, and Pat a typical English schoolboy with a nice turn of phrase. When Newbolt tipped him five shillings, he remarked, 'Why this sudden outbreak?'[19] Newbolt has left a picture of Peter Newbolt's sixth birthday party, 'the dark big heads' of Peter and Anne contrasting strongly with the 'small honey-coloured heads' of Nicholas and Theresa Furse: 'Peter is enormous and looked amazingly handsome in his laurel wreath with his fine red colour and vividly expressive face – a picture of a young Roman Emperor.' (It was the custom of the Newbolts to crown the birthday child with laurel.) From that party, Newbolt went to Celia's house, and was not allowed to leave until they had given me "Drake's Drum" and "The Old Superb" on their new gramophone. Too loud, of course, and the singer not a patch on Harry Greene.'[20] Newbolt was a greatly loved grandfather because he had the art of conversing with children. They would say, 'Talk, Creamer!' and he would. ('Creamer' had been Jill's version of 'Grandpa' and it had stuck.) Children outside the family loved him too. Buchan's daughter Alice, writing her memoirs, picked him out as the only one she clearly remembered of all the guests at Elsfield Manor. She said he treated children as equals, and listened to them with real attention.

Newbolt always felt that it was a mistake to revisit the places where he had been happy, and he proved it on his own last visit to

17. *NL*, Jan. 1922
18. *NL* HN to MEN, 18 Mar. 1926
19. *NL* HN to MEN, 15 Apr. 1931
20. *HN* to MEN, 22 Oct. 1929; *LLL*, p.360

Italy with Margaret in 1929. It was not a success. Throughout the holiday he fretted about work left undone. He was happier at Aisholt, in the Quantocks, where Evie, Margaret's unmarried sister, had bought a cottage. 'I enjoyed myself there more than among all the vintage of Italy and I felt as if I were getting to know you quite well,' Newbolt told Margaret.[21] Aisholt had become Margaret's secret home. Newbolt always felt himself a guest there. He once asked if he should tip Lizzie, the old servant. 'Of *course* you don't tip. That would make me feel you had divorced me!' replied Margaret. Her deafness was probably part of the cause of this retreat into a lonely Somerset valley. She read a great deal down there and she was well up with the new generation of female novelists, including Naomi Mitchison and Rose Macaulay, whom Newbolt also admired. She was deeply moved by Kathleen Mansfield's diaries. Both of them thought Rebecca West 'a bit of a show off.'

Cures for Margaret's deafness were continually sought. In 1925 she underwent a painful treatment at the Clinique Raymond in Freibourg. It involved 'the enforcement of electrified tubes into the ear and of a burning liquid up the nose.' After that, she could not even read for a while.[22] To add insult to injury. Newbolt had abandoned her for the Alps with Ella. Margaret wrote to him, 'I am glad you found the company good. I knew how happy Ella would be to get you. My self company becomes deadly and I don't know how to get through the evening without reading.'[23]

Theories of Time started Newbolt on a second career as a poet in the twenties, not a public poet but a private one. He was much taken by the books of his tubby Cliftonian friend, the philosopher McTaggart. To Alice, he wrote: 'Time and Space are illusions and will pass away: our lives in Time will end, Time ends, but not our life, our personal life, which is of the substance of the Eternal.'[24] 'I ask people to receive me in a new spirit.'[25] The new poems were short lyrics. There were never enough to fill a book and those there were, were published posthumously in a volume entitled *A Perpetual Memory* (1939). Earlier, T. S. Eliot had recognised their

21. *NL* HN to MEN, 1 Oct. 1929
22. *NL* MEN to HN, 21–24 Aug. 1925
23. [ibid.]
24. *AHL*, 19 Jan. 1925, *LLL*, p.322
25. *AHL*, 29 Oct. 1926; *LLL*, p.344

charm and printed two of them in Faber's Ariel Series (which consisted of individual poems printed in pamphlet form with illustrations.) It was unfortunate that Newbolt did not return Eliot's admiration. He explained in *New Paths on Helicon* that he enjoyed Prufrock, but found 'The Waste Land' excessively depressing.

It was Margaret who, on 1 May 1925, finally catapulted the best of the new poems into orbit. Newbolt had written to her, boasting of the money he had earned by a lecture for the Florence Institute at Burlington House. She replied: 'I admire your wonderful money-making success ... but, even admitting that you speak at the rate of £20,000 an hour ... a first class poem is more valuable to the world than 20,000 Institutes. It is a very small mind that cannot appreciate that fact!' Beneath the stinging rebuke was Margaret's sense of deception and isolation. She had married a poet and he had turned into a public figure. The man she longed to live with quietly in the country preferred to live with Ella in town.

On this occasion her barb hit home. Within days of receiving the letter, Newbolt. wrote 'The Nightjar',[26] a poem about a bird found dying in the orchard at Netherhampton. The poem has left a tear in the eye of all his recent admirers, including Patric Dickinson, John Betjeman and Kingsley Amis. The last six lines ran

> So wonderful she was – her wings the wings of night
> But powdered here and there with tiny golden clouds
> And wave-line markings like sea-ripples on the sand.
> O how I wish I might never forget that bird
> Never!
>> But even now, like all beauty of earth,
> She is fading from me into the dusk of Time.

26. *SP*, p.139

CHAPTER 49

Public Acclaim

The honours kept rolling in long after Newbolt had ceased to write the ballads that made him famous. In 1922 he was made a Companion of Honour for 'conspicuous service of national importance.' 'I hardly know what a CH is. It is limited to fifty. Its good points are that it was founded for Jan Smuts. He didn't want other things.'[1] A year later Newbolt embarked on one of those ventures that normally crown a successful career, a trans-Atlantic lecture tour. He went to Canada, as the guest of the Canadian Council, who had founded a Travelling Imperial Lectureship in his honour. He was to speak on culture and Christianity and the tour was to conclude with a grand conference at Toronto. The bookings were organised by a Major Ney. He was a hard taskmaster, arranging for Newbolt to travel from coast to coast, visiting and delivering eighty-one addresses.

1. *HN* to AH, 20 Dec. 1921; *LLL*, p.287

Newbolt sailed in January 1923, on the Canadian Pacific *Marloch*, accompanied by Alice Hylton who, quite by chance, was on a visit to the Governor-General at Ottawa with her daughter Betty. (Margaret chose to follow later.) The voyage was not what Newbolt had hoped for. The weather was appalling – 'waves right over the decks and cabins flooded', and he was seasick. 'Alas!' he told Margaret. 'Your good wishes about Alice were hardly fulfilled. We had some walks on deck at first, and some sitting in the sun, but it was a very public sun! Then my liver went wrong, and the storms came. Still, she was a ministering angel when pain and anguish wrung my brow, and I'm sure she quite enjoyed that section of the voyage, even if *I* did not!'[2]

The tour itself was a resounding success. The Canadians loved Newbolt's speeches, whether from podium or pulpit. But he found they lacked culture. The only one of his poems they seemed to have heard of was 'Play up!' 'It's a kind of Frankenstein's Monster that I created thirty years ago and now I find it falling on my neck at every corner! In vain do I explain what is poetry: they roar for "Play up": they put it on their flags and on their war memorials and their tombstones: it's their National Anthem.'[3]

Undoubtedly, Newbolt was a mesmeric speaker. Sir Michael Sadler, writing to de la Mare, described him giving an address 'to crowded thousands in Toronto – a darkened church with lights on him in his scarlet university gown. Absorbed in his subject, he spoke for an hour after Evensong. But no one stirred.'[4] Newbolt did not deny his powers: 'When I preach on the Bible they really do cry. They say, "it's your English voice."'[5] The climax of his success was reached at a concert where an American tenor called Barclay sang the 'Songs of the Sea'. After endless curtain calls, Barclay spied Newbolt in the audience and waved to him. 'Then, when the audience caught on, they roared like the Atlantic. After they dispersed the performers got me back (in my furs) onto the stage and the Orchestra and Choir and Singers and Conductors, and every kind of official fell upon me and nearly suffocated me.'[6] Buoyed up by acclaim, Newbolt's health survived remarkably well. But towards the end, the pace was

2. *NL* HN to MEN, 11 Feb. 1923
3. *NL* HN to MEN, 1 Mar. 1923
4. Sadler to de la Mare, 26 Apr. 1923; *LLL*, p.300
5. *NL* HN to MEN, 15 Feb. 1923
6. *NL* to HN to MEN, 19 Feb. 1923

beginning to tell. The weather was bitterly cold and there were vast distances to cover. Certainly the trains were comfortable. In one letter he wrote: 'I must get the nigger to rig up my sleeping berth for me for the night. It is most luxurious having the whole drawing room to myself.'[7] But he often had to travel by horse-drawn sleigh through the frigid air. The contrast between arctic exteriors and overheated interiors was trying, and Newbolt began to suffer from asthma and nose bleeds. 'I get so tired of hiding soaking handkerchiefs in my pockets.'[8] Fortunately, Milly's daughter Dido, now married to the Canadian lawyer John Read and settled at Halifax, took him in hand and found a doctor to cauterise his nostrils. Dido wrote to Margaret: 'Uncle Harry was so jolly. Halifax fell at his feet and demanded a great deal more of him than the schedule announced. Of course he was too generous and I'm afraid got a little tired. We kept him in bed for breakfast every day.'[9]

There were times when Newbolt wished that Margaret had agreed to accompany him. 'I am only a poor disembodied spirit,' he wrote, 'travelling far beyond the bounds of Space and Time.'[10] He spoke of his physical longing for her. 'I have so much to tell you that can't be put on paper. What fun it will be, that meeting of ours. Two wandering stars coming to nest in the same bed. The beds here are of the old family kind you like, vast and comfortable – room for three at least!'[11] In fact, Ella appeared more concerned for him than Margaret. She suggested a throat spray for the asthma and it worked.[12] 'It is wonderful how her detail-loving mind works out our salvations,' commented Margaret.[13] But Ella herself did not write. 'She hasn't written me one real letter. Only laborious and devoted copies of other people's letters have arrived.'[14] Newbolt was particularly concerned because Ells's mother 'the Duchess' had died suddenly. Margaret wrote: 'The whole weight of the family is [as] always on her shoulders and Hew mends a boiler while she does all the horrid undertaker arrangements.'[15]

7. *NL* HN to MEN, 11 Feb. 1923
8. *NL* HN to MEN, 11 Feb. 1923
9. *NL* Diana Read to MEN, 11 Feb. 1923
10. *NL* HN to MEN, 11 Feb. 1923
11. *NL* HN to MEN, 2 Mar. 1923
12. *NL* HN to MEN, 23 Feb. 1923
13. *NL* MEN to HN, 23 Feb. 1923
14. *NL* HN to MEN, 15 Mar. 1923
15. *NL* MEN to HN, 23 Feb. 1923

Government House, Ottawa was Newbolt's base, the address to which letters were sent. The Governor-General, Lord Byng, was a friendly bear of a man, a fellow member of the Athenaeum . 'He walked me about with his long arm round my neck, like a chimpanzee with one of the smaller apes.' Lady Byng, by contrast, 'looks much more than half Hebrew. She addresses His Excellency as "Old Towzer". In return he calls her "The Woman".'[16] Newbolt warned Margaret about The Woman. 'If *you* get on with her it will be because she is very keen about birds and animals. So you mustn't be so autocrabbish as you sometimes are and say you know next to nothing about the robin or the thrush!'[17]

Margaret finally arrived in Canada at the end of March, having endlessly prepared a wardrobe in London. She had rightly concluded that she should wear very light dresses for indoors, and very warm outdoor clothes. She had her fur coat altered by 'your little Jew in Bishopsgate'. She travelled out with the Baden-Powells (they were on a tour of Scout rallies), whom she already knew because of Katharine Furse's recent passionate friendship with Olave, which had followed upon Katharine's appointment as Assistant Chief Commissioner of the Guides. (Katharine's relationship with Olave ended in tears, but not before she had succeeded in loosening the stranglehold of the Baden-Powells on the Guide movement). Baden-Powell was already an admirer of Newbolt. In *Scouting for Boys* (1908) he included Newbolt's 'Play up' in the form of a play.

Back in England, Newbolt continued to be fêted. He now moved in the highest social circles, being frequently invited to dine both at the Palace and at Mansion House, and to share boxes at the opera with persons of importance. And, in spite of Margaret, the committees continued to multiply. There was the Speaker's Committee on the Decoration of St Stephen's Hall. The Speaker of the House of Commons had commissioned a series of frescoes for the chapel building through which the visitor must pass to reach the central lobby. It was Newbolt's duty to select eight historical episodes appropriate to a chamber where the Commons had sat until the rebuilding of 1834. Speaker Whitley had hoped

16. *NL* HN to MEN, 28 Feb. 1923
17. [ibid.]

for a series to be entitled 'The Story of our Liberties', but Newbolt changed it to 'The Building of Britain'. Thus he could include 'King Alfred Beats the Danes', 'King Richard I Departs for the Crusades' and 'Queen Elizabeth orders Raleigh to Sail for America'. One of the painters selected was Sir William Rothenstein, now far from well and only able to complete the commission with the aid of a sling on a pulley to support his arm. The paintings were officially unveiled by Stanley Baldwin in 1927, but King George V and Queen Mary were allowed a sneak preview. (It was the first time royal feet had trodden that floor since Charles I prorogued Parliament) 'The King was in boisterous good humour, but I don't think he was much interested in the pictures,' Newbolt told Margaret. The Queen recognised a good friend in one of the frescoes and cried, 'Here's Katie Cromer! But has she really gone lined like that?'[18] Bryan Fell's current *Guide to the Palace of Westminster* omits Newbolt's part in the planning of the frescoes, although Newbolt published a guide to them. Another two years of Newbolt's time were spent on the Sub-Commission on the Monuments in Westminster Abbey.[19] 'Today I have been sitting with about forty Diocesan dullards in the Jerusalem Chamber. I saved half an hour by going dead off to sleep – not being in the line of Cosmo Lang's eye.'[20] (The Archbishop of York was notoriously fond of the sound of his own voice.) 'You can imagine how endlessly flowed the silver stream of his words and how he smiled with enjoyment of the sound.[21] Newbolt was also a member of the Central Council for the Care of Churches.

Now there was the subject of the Clifton memorial for the recent war to consider. Newbolt pointed out that the Public Schools 'to a large extent had saved the country'[22] by supplying 30,000 officers. An appropriate monument must be built for those who came from Clifton, and this time symbols of chivalry were avoided. The Memorial took the form of a massive entrance arch carved with the names of the fallen. It was opened by Earl Haig in 1922, the year when Newbolt was elected president of the O.C. Association. Haig made a speech with which Newbolt no doubt fully concurred,

18. *NL* HN to MEN, 27 June 1927
19. *LLL*, p.245
20. *NL* HN to MEN 12 Jan. 1927
21. *LLL*, p.245
22. Winterbottom, p.70

declaring 'clean living and honest dealing' to be more important than 'Cleverness in Arts and Sciences'.[23] John Percival would have concurred, but he had lain for three years lay in a great marble vault beneath the High Altar of the Chapel.

At the end of the twenties, Newbolt suffered from a strange fit of euphoria, brought on by the newly fledged BBC, He had suggested a series of literary broadcasts to Sir John Reith. One was to be done in conjuction with Kipling. Reith invited the two poets to lunch. 'It was a medium success,' commented Newbolt, 'but R.K. said he wasn't "learned enough".[24] Working alone, Newbolt completed one series of talks first on poetry and one on prose. He also conducted an Empire Day broadcast on the occasion of George V's recovery from illness, and is said by Patric Dickinson to have written the King's first Christmas broadcast. (Peter Newbolt questions this.) These successes suggested a new venture: 'I've had the happy inspiration of giving up all my jobs and setting up a salon in London. We'll make the Sitwells green with jealousy. We'll have a Publishing Gang of our own like Virginia and Co., and a miniature Play House like Masefield.'[25]

Miss Edith Oliver was probably responsible for this aberration. She was the daughter of the rector of Wilton and had written a novel about a phantom child, which Newbolt described as 'The best first book I ever read. Better than David Garnett's *Lady into Fox*'. She conducted a salon at the rectory, which was attended by a surprising number of the bright young artists of the day. She was Rex Whistler's older woman, 'delicious Edith whom I adore.' He painted her in the garden at Daye House and brought his London friends down to disport themselves in it. One of the friends was a pretty boy called Cecil Beaton who was in love with an even prettier one, Stephen Tennant (Pam Glenconner's son). They attended a fancy dress ball at Wilton House wearing too much makeup and too little else, and Cecil fell into the river afterwards. When things got out of hand Edith would go and pray for the boys in the rectory turret.

It was through Edith Oliver that Newbolt came to know Siegfried Sassoon, now rising forty and still a bachelor. Sassoon was

23. Derek Winterbottom, *Henry Newbolt and the Spirit of Clifton*, 1986, p.71
24. *NL* HN to MEN, 20 Nov. 1928
25. *HN* to EC, 15 Sept. 1930; *LLL*, p.370

Newbolt's type. He had a distinguished head with bold features . He was both a good cricketer and a witty talker. He normally preferred to mix with younger men but made an exception for Newbolt. He was invited to tea at Netherhampton and Newbolt described the party sitting in a circle on the lawn with Sassoon shouting into Margaret's ear trumpet. Sassoon attended a gentleman's dinner at Netherhampton on the occasion of the tenth anniversary of the outbreak of War. Raymond Mortimer, George Trevelyan and Walter de la Mare were also there, and the talk naturally turned to the subject of the war. Sassoon declared that 'he would go again, and if he, then everybody.' 'That alone is enough to make friends on, isn't it?' said Newbolt to Margaret afterwards.[26] Newbolt was equally keen to please Sassoon, almost too much so. A few months earlier, the two men left a meeting of the Royal Literary Society together. 'Henry Newbolt walked with me as far as Westminster Abbey, talking all the time, telling me what Lord Grey told him about August 1914, etc. Newbolt is a continuation of Victorianism. His kindness was a little oppressive. But gratifying – very gratifying.'[27]

It was the Victorianism in Newbolt that attracted John Betjeman, a younger admirer. They also met at Daye House. 'I found a young couple invited to meet each other.' Newbolt wrote. 'Margaret, not having overheard the demoiselle's name, spoke to each of them about the other, saying "your wife says" and "your husband thinks", which caused, at first, consternation and then geysers of laughter. They are engaged in their own view, but not at all in her father's! He is Chetwode, the General. The young man is a charming lad, though handicapped by poverty and the name of Betjeman. His strong suit is his taste for the poets of the 18th and 19th centuries. He quoted yards of them. Afterwards he came back to see this house and fell quite in love with it. I should like to cultivate him, but of course it would be dull for him to stay with septuagenarians, especially as he seems to spend his time motoring his young contrabandista about from visit to visit. It amused me to think what a bore he must be to his distinguished father-in-law Sir Philip, Seventh Baronet!'[28]

26. *LLL*, p.320
27. Rupert Hart-Davies (ed.), *Diary of Siegfried Sassoon 1923–25*, 1985
28. *NL* HN to MEN,18 July 1932

Betjeman had a high opinion of Newbolt as a poet and was delighted when his own poems appeared under the John Murray imprint in 1937. 'I have the great consolation of knowing that Murray's other poet is SIR HENRY NEWBOLT,' he wrote. 'T.S. Eliot wanted my poems for Faber but he was too late and how infinitely more horrible to appear uniform with STEPHEN SPENDER & MACNEICE.'[29] Betjeman was eventually to publish a selection of Newbolt's poems in 1940. In the introduction to this, he wrote: 'To appreciate Newbolt one must understand that he stood for the England of Empire Builders, country gentlemen, high moral Christian values and English scenery. He was one of a generation which is passing but which is, with all its faults, loveable and honest.'[30]

Betjeman and Newbolt had something else in common besides poetry. They were united in their determination to save England from the developers. After Newbolt's death, Betjeman praised his attempts 'to preserve the beauty of English scenery from the rapacity of speculators and the ignorance of local officials.[31] The landscape round Netherhampton was of special concern. It saddened Newbolt to see the thatch of local cottages replaced by 'chocolate-painted tin'. He also objected to the planned erection of pylons within view of Netherhampton House. 'If they come, we won't come back.'[32] Newbolt felt equally strongly about the preservation of Georgian London. When Carlton House Terrace was threatened by 'buildings of a commercial class', he wrote to Betjeman, then editor of the *Architectural Review*.[33] Then he signed an application for Waterloo Bridge (which was, of course, Victorian) to be scheduled an Ancient Monument. 'What a Brobdignagian Lark!'[34] In the last year of his life, when he was very ill, he found the strength to protest against the Bressey Plan for the better circulation of traffic in the capital 'to the detriment of everything else'.

With the death of Robert Bridges in 1930 at the age of 85, a 30

29. Betjeman to Edward James, 1 Jan, 1937. John Betjeman Letters, Volume One: 1926 to 1951 (1944)
30. *Selected Poems of Henry Newbolt* (John Betjeman (ed.) (1940))
31. ibid.
32. *AHL*, 4 Apr. 1934
33. *John Betjeman Letters*, vol. 1:, 16 Dec. 1932
34. *AHL*, 22 June 1934

year friendship ended. The laureateship was now vacant but Newbolt knew that he had little hope of it. 'One look into *Poems New and Old* would convince Ramsay MacDonald that I am the last man on whom his choice could fall: "you belong to the wrong generation!" he would say . To the generation that was prepared to defend the country – which is now a crime.' Newbolt consoled himself with the thought that he had in effect been laureate for the last twenty years: 'I've written in *The Times* all the commemorative verses that were wanted. Even now they're asking me for an inscription on the great monument on Helles Point in Gallipoli – the monument to which all nations dip their flag in passing.'[35] Newbolt had guessed right. When *The Times* published a list of possible laureates his name was not among them. John Masefield, with whom Newbolt was on good terms, got the job.

35. *NL* HN to MEN, 29 Apr. 1930

PART X THIRTIES 1930–38

CHAPTER 50

Eclipse

It is not often that a portrait painter fortells the future of his sitter, but Meredith Frampton appears to have done just that when he painted Newbolt in 1930. The subject sits at a desk in Furse's studio at Netherhampton against a fake classical background, but he is not writing. He stares into the distance, pale and dignified but immensely withdrawn. People remarked on his pallor when the picture was hung in the Royal Academy the following summer. The picture now hangs in the National Portrait Gallery. The painter, MacColl, insisted Newbolt had indeed looked white and papery.[1] Frank, with his usual frankness, said 'some friends think your portrait makes you look worn and ill. You have changed so

1. *NL* HN to MEN, 2 May 1931

275

much.'[2] Newbolt himself did not like the portrait. He had already had the unnerving experience of unveiling his own memorial a year or two earlier. The Mayor of Bilston had decided to honour a famous son while he was still alive. The occasion was the centenary of St Mary's Church. The memorial was a small bronze tablet set into the wall of the vicarage, merely stating that Newbolt the poet was born there.[3] Revisiting the vicarage had been a moving experience. 'What place could be so strange to a man of sixty-five as the house where he was born – the house which he left when he was not yet four years old, and which he had never since revisited?'[4] Newbolt spent a night at the vicarage. 'I was astonished, from the first moment of entering the house to find it correspond so closely with my old memories. It was even more spacious than I had believed it to be.' The night nursery overlooking the railway line, the parental bedroom (where he all but dashed his little brains out) were exactly as he remembered them, but best of all was the long, book-lined study. 'There I seemed to have an impression not only of my father's words but of his appearance – his face and gesture.'

The visit to Bilston inspired Newbolt to take up his own writing again. The last volume of *Naval Operations* had been published in 1931 and he now retired to Netherhampton to write his autobiography. *My World as in my Time*, which brought him to the brink of the First World War, came swiftly from his pen. For the childhood chapters Frank was helpful and there were lengthy sessions at Kensington Park Gardens (round the corner from Ella's) 'You were so astoundingly precocious – I was so disastrously backward,' wrote Frank,[5] 'It was you that Wollaston liked. It was you to whom he sent a wedding present.' When the manuscript was complete, Frank was asked for his comments. 'There is no reference, as in the photographic *Twymans*, to early love affairs. At 12, you say, you fell in love. Was that the Whitby enchantress? I love her still – Eleanor Slater, most ill fated of her sex.' The love affair with Margaret was sketched almost as lightly. Celia also urged Newbolt to be indiscreet but he disobeyed her.[6] Ella's part in the love triangle was of course omitted completely.

2. *NL* FN to HN, 4 Oct. 1932
3. *My World*, p.1
4. *My World*, p.5
5. *NL* FN to HN, 4 Oct. 1932
6. *NL* HN to AFN, 23 Apr. 1932

The autobiography, although discursive, is full of delightful humour. It met with well-deserved praise when it came out in 1932, except from the Ruskin Society, which was outraged by Newbolt's passing comment that Ruskin's marriage was never consummated (a fact not as generally known then as it is now). Legal action was even considered. By that time Newbolt was into the second volume. Working at his normal rate this would have been completed by 1933, but by 1934 it was less than half written. He had reached 1914. 'Now I must stoop my shoulders to the burden of war,' he told Alice on 18 March 1934, and added a week later, 'I am trying to work. I am interested in the chapter but I am suffering from the shivers and restlessness. I almost wish we had visitors coming to stay!' Two months later, on his 72nd birthday, he wrote 'I cut off heads of withering iris, I prune my old dying fig tree, I write to you, and to my bank and to the rate collector, but I do not *get on*.'[7]

Newbolt never did finish the second volume of his auto-biography. It was completed for him after his death in the form of letters, collected by Margaret under the title *The Later Life and Letters of Sir Henry Newbolt* (1942) He could not bring himself to fight all over again the war to end all wars, particularly in view of the fact that a new war was threatening. 'The Boches, after all, are as bad as ever,' he had told Alice in 1933.[8] At first he had tried to persuade himself that Hitler was but a paper tiger, 'a string of barrels with an engine in his chest and a spare head in front. Perhaps Lord Monsterbrook finds his circulation needs stimulating.' The Nazi purge of 1934 changed his mind. 'Germany makes me quite sick. The bloody-minded ways of Adolf Hitler are even worse than those of the Kaiser Wilhelm.'[9]

There was another cause for Newbolt's inability to complete his autobiography. He did not tell Alice of the early symptoms of the mysterious illness that was eventually to kill him. It first manifested itself at the Bemerton pageant in the summer of 1933. The pageant was to commemorate the death of George Herbert in 1633. At first Newbolt had refused to help dramatise 'such an undramatic man!'[10] but eventually he repented. According to

7. *AHL*, 5 June 1934
8. *AHL*, 3 Mar. 1933
9. *AHL*, 3 July 1934
10. *AHL*, 3 Mar. 1933

Theresa Whistler, during a rehearsal, when the weather was hot and thundery, George Herbert took his revenge. Newbolt became suddenly 'very ill, even astray in his memory.'[11] The seizure passed but thunder in future was to bring on similar seizures. A year later Newbolt described a dizzy spell during a storm 'which almost persuaded me I had Bats in the Belfry'.[12] He also began to suffer from exhaustion. 'Tireder and yet tireder,' he wrote. Sometimes he could only manage the first mile of his 'post-breakfast tramp' along the Salisbury road. He began to feel the cold excessively and found Margaret's regime of open windows intolerable. He spent more time in the Ark where he had a fire and where 'I can shut all the windows when I like!'[13] 'I am on the downward slope,' he told Alice. 'I am put away in a corner of the dusty past like Nelson in the Abbey.[14]

Margaret, at first, refused to admit that Newbolt was ill, accusing him of wrapping himself 'in a napkin of old age'. Certainly he had good days. Only two weeks after complaining that he could not walk the first mile to Salisbury he strode all the way there and back, carrying a bag of apples over his shoulders on a stick like Dick Whittington.[15] In an attempt to cheer him up, Margaret took him to stay with new friends in Northumberland. There, she told Alice, he showed 'some hope, and even talked of reading aloud his poems one evening. But then there was music!'[16] Newbolt gives a different picture of that visit. 'Those people in their sixty mile an hour cars are like will o' the wisps. They move with the swiftness of starlight and they seem omnipotent until something happens, as it does to ordinary mortals, and then their world goes hollow.'[17] Back at Netherhampton the fear of an approaching international conflict cast murderous shadows across the garden. The very birds were at war. 'Jays kill the smallë foulës right and left. It is real Hitlerism. The walled garden is wild with scurrying chases. Disjointed members and little shiny feathers lie on the grass paths. I am sick and bilious with gold and purple before my giddy eyes.

11. *Whistler*, p.359
12. *AHL*, 21 May 1934
13. *AHL*, 3 April 1934
14. ibid.
15. *AHL*, Feb. 1934
16. *AHL*, 13 Oct. 1934
17. *AHL*, 5 Sept. 1933

Inwardly I am full of ravening wolves.'[18]Newbolt's last poem appeared in the Christmas 1932 number of *The Listener*. It was entitled 'The Star in the West'.[19] In the last verse Newbolt looked into a future of utter hopelessness:

Dare not to ask! – unless ye dare also to hear
The story of his cross, his first and second death –
That men have murdered Night, and made stars of their own,
And flung them down from heav'n, and Peace has died by fire.[20]

The time for leaving Netherhampton had come. The reasons for this were at least in part financial. Newbolt had already been obliged to resort to such money-making devices as selling his letters from Hardy for £700. The subject of moving house had been under discussion since 1931, but he had then changed his mind. 'We can afford ourselves another half year. I refuse to be pushed out of our way of life without making a fight to keep it.'[21] Eventually he informed Lord Pembroke's agent that he would leave in September 1934. 'I can't believe it,' he told Alice. 'It is so great and final a decision.'[22] That summer was one of leave-taking. There were last visits from the grandchildren, 'fleeting about the lawn and making lovely entrances and exits from behind the yew hedge'.[23] There was a final game of bowls. 'We played till dark and the lawn is still animated by our games.'[24] (The pain of that occasion was increased by Newbolt dropping a wood on his toe, an unusual act of clumsiness.) He found some consolation in the fact that the new tenants were childless: 'so there will still be room for our little ghosts.'[25] A single artistic gentleman, the Hon. David Herbert, Lord Pembroke's younger son, had briefly considered taking the house. 'It was lucky I was at home, so that Margaret did not have to take him round with her Radio-Aid Box,' commented Newbolt.[26] (In the end, Herbert preferred Tangier, where he still lives with a parrot.)

18. *AHL*, 9 Aug. 1934
19. *SP*, p.140
20. *SP*, p.140
21. *NL* HN to MEN, 24 Mar. 1931
22. AHL, 26 Mar, 1934
23. ibid. 23 July 1934
24. ibid. 7 Aug. 1934
25. ibid. 21 Oct. 1934
26. ibid. 19 July 1934

It is said that moving house is inadvisable after the age of seventy. The Newbolts certainly found it so. They had planned to move into a small London house, but small houses proved even more expensive than large ones, and in the end it was decided to extend Ella's house backwards into the garden and move in with her. Even with the extension they would only have one third of the space they had had at Netherhampton. Newbolt reminded himself that 'the "paw" have to accommodate their necessities to tight quarters'.[27] But the poor did not own bronzes ('where does one *put* bronze busts?'[28] or portraits by Meredith Frampton. ('Shall I raffle it at the Albert Hall? Would you pay half-a-crown to be exempt from all risk of finding yourself the owner?') Fortunately, Siegfried Sassoon was in need of furniture. At the age of 50 he had ended his long love affair with Stephen Tennant and married Hester Gatty. They had moved into Heytesbury House, near Warminster. The marriage did not last, but Sassoon remained in the house, increasingly solitary. It is possible that the bedroom carpet, on which J.R. Ackerley's alsatian Tulip had an unfortunate accident, came from Nether-hampton House.

There remained the problem of 'about a million books. It will be like moving the earth in a donkey cart.' Parting with his books all but broke Newbolt's heart. Why did people write so many? Why had he bought so many? Which must be condemned to execution? 'I am calling them out and drilling them in thousands,' he told Alice. 'Finally some few of them will be ordered to London. I am not happy and how should I be? I shall always be expecting them at my elbow, long after they have been sold for the defrauding penny.'[29] Margaret did not help. She kept rescuing volumes from the condemned pile behind his back and putting them back in the shelves. Going through letters was, even worse. 'I seem to be in a long dream of the dead. They haunt me and I ache and tremble.'[30] The newly dead concerned him particularly. There was Roger Fry, 'the best talker at the Vienna Café' and the most successful of his discoveries for the *Monthly Review*. He keenly regretted that he had lost touch with him when he joined the Bloomsbury Group. And

27. *AHL*, 22 June 1934
28. *AHL*, 16 June 193428. *AHL*, 16 June 1934
29. *AHL*, 16 and 17 July 1934
30. *AHL*, 11 Sept. 1934

there was Helen Holland who had also just died, leaving seven cases of letters. Margaret was at that moment on the studio floor with the earliest ones, 'thinking sadly of Orchardleigh and the girlhood of Helen Virgin.'[31] Maurice Hewlett had died ten years earlier, after writing his epic poem about the working man, *The Song of the Plough* (1916). Newbolt found his letters particularly painful to read. 'I wish I could have my Maurice back. He was difficult with his lifelong scrapes and his wild opinions but it was so easy to love him.'[32]

Then there were the Netherhampton farewells to endure. 'Margaret entertains her blessed Women's Institute for the last time at 6.30 tonight in the garden. Ping pong table and whist drive chairs encumber the lawn already. Cakes and teapots. And I have dressed all in white to please and honour Dame M. All will admire her garden, her furniture (and, if not her husband) her husband's portrait and her daughter's dog. All the time I shall be groaning inwardly.'[33] There was a problem about what to do with Ruffell, but he solved it for himself. He dropped dead while loading the furniture van. Newbolt declared it was a fine end, 'for a true friend whose sole desire had been to serve me with dog-like devotion.'[34] He wished he could do likewise. 'How I wish we could make up parties for the journey to the Continuing City, and book our passage in a ship of the old world type, flitting under white canvas.'[35]

Newbolt never recovered from the loss of Netherhampton. He persisted in referring to 29 Camden Hill Road as 'Margaret's doll's house' and took no interest in the running of the place, beyond remarking that a couple had been taken on to work for them, the man a Canadian war veteran and the woman 'all furs and henna'.[36] When spring came round he wrote to Alice 'You are in the sun where you have your own flowers within reach. Here May does not feel like May'.[37]

Margaret was less unhappy. The countrywoman had lost her countryside but she had gained her Ella. After a lifetime of living

31. ibid. 6 Feb. 1934
32. ibid. 18 Mar. 1934
33. ibid. 18 July and 9 Aug. 1934
34. ibid. 26 Oct. 1934
35. ibid. 14 May 1934
36. *AHL*, 14 June 1934
37. ibid. 13 May 1935

apart, as convention demanded, the two women were at last united under one roof. And thus they were to remain for the rest of their long (in Margaret's case, very long) lives.

But there was little happiness for Margaret in the sudden deterioration of Newbolt's condition after the move. He was turning into a ghost. 'It is some evil enchantment keeping him under lock and key'.[38] Theresa Whistler writes 'a pane of glass seemed to slide between us. His mind remained perfectly clear behind it, but he lost all impulse to respond. He became a parchment shadow of himself'.[39] Peter Newbolt, too, remembers him as 'very pale and silent. As a boy I was a bit overawed by the strangeness of the atmosphere at Number 29.' Friends stayed away. Even de la Mare avoided his old master, unable to bear the overthrow of a personality. Margaret understood his feelings . 'I know how sad it makes you to see Harry and *not* to see him'.

But although Newbolt did not speak, he listened and he thought. Theresa has told me of an occasion when Margaret and Ella were at a loss for a word in a crossword. 'Ask Harry,' said Ella, and Harry, sitting in a corner of the sitting room, gave them the answer. Margaret spoke of his resignation. 'It is difficult for me to write of the astonishing patience with which he bore these clouded years. His interests had always been ardours, and now the flame of his vitality burned low.' Perhaps Newbolt longed for death, but knew that neither Margaret nor Ella would hand him the fatal draught. Perhaps he remembered a letter he had written to Ella during an idle hour at Lincoln's Inn when he first loved her. 'When I'm old and bedridden, you'll put something in my tea won't you? No, you won't. You'll sit in my room and look into the garden that was our life and think thoughts longer even than the thoughts of youth. I know you women.'[40]

No none could give Newbolt's disease a name. The symptoms were not those of Parkinson's, for his hands did not tremble and his face was not masklike. Of course there were visits to different doctors and Margaret claimed there was a temporary improvement after each new treatment.[41] In the last year at Netherhampton

38. Vanessa Furse Jackson, *The Poetry of Henry Newbolt*, 1994
39. Whistler, p.359
40. HN to EC, 13 June 1893. Private Collection
41. *LLL*, p. 403

Newbolt had consulted Francis's 'shellshock man', Rupert Reynell. 'He said I was a perfect example of normality, and only a little out of order (but that little how much!)' Reynell recommended daily insulin injections by the village nurse (Newbolt saw to it that Margaret gave them to him) but insisted that he was not suffering from diabetes. The injections were to improve his appetite.[42] Nevertheless, a letter of 30 July 1933 from Newbolt to H.G. Wells enquires about a cure for diabetes.[43] Newbolt referred to keeping to a sugar-free diet as early as 1928. 'It appears I have for a long time been living habitually on a diet almost entirely composed of bread, jam, cakes, porridge and potatoes'.[44] Great had been his rejoicing when he discovered a sugar-free white wine. Now Newbolt began to have difficulty in walking. Theresa recalls how, as a small child, she used to walk "Creamer" up and down the corridor at Number 29. Outings became increasingly burdensome. Jill, now an actress with 'great natural aptitude'[45] was in a West End comedy in the autumn of 1935 and Newbolt said he would attend the first night 'if I can summon up the pluck'.[46] A week or two later he equally unwillingly attended the London production of his opera *The Travelling Companion*. 'We will all go in a huge Bodge to make the pot boil,' he told Alice.[47] Harry Plunkett Greene sang the lead. Newbolt left no record of the performance, but Frank was ecstatic. 'Before I sleep, my old one, I must say one per cent of what I feel about the most thrilling evening ever. My heart is too full of it to write. And Harry Greene!'[48] More often, Newbolt's outings were confined to 18 Hanover Terrace, round the corner, now full of a breed of dog called an Elkhound. Celia's dogs were abominably behaved, and in Newbolt's opinion she cared for them more than she did her children. Little Theresa he found enchanting. He described her looking like a Holbein in an Elizabethan dress, handing round the cheese biscuits at a sherry party, 'utterly absorbed in her task.' Even Newbolt's lifeline, the correspondence with Alice, was beginning to fray. After twenty-

42. *AHL*, 14 June and 3 July 1934
43. *HGW, Illinois*
44. *NL* HN to MEN, 18 July 1928
45. *AHL*, 3 Mar. 1933
46. *AHL*, 22 Oct. 1935
47. *AHL*, 22 Oct, 1935
48. *NL*, 1 Nov. 1935

seven years he could still tell her, 'Your letters are all my meals and most of my dreams.' 'When you write my fingers unfreeze and my memory unfolds a bit',[49] but often he could not answer the letters and on one occasion begged her to come and visit him urgently. Then 'the Old Ladies' made her visit impossible. They had invited a distant Canadian cousin to stay. Frank, now retired and widowed and living at Mattocks, also complained of receiving no letters and said that those he did receive were in minute handwriting.

Newbolt was certainly now suffering from loss of memory. He wrote to Alice, 'People come and go, days go by. In the evenings I feel I am getting on. In the morning I cancel that and say I'm not getting on. Last night, between eight and eleven, (just what they tell me) I was perfectly well: but waking, no such matter.'[50] In one of his last letters to Alice, he wrote: 'Today is the Day of Doom. I go to Major Nesfield, the war doctor, at 97 Harley Street. It is butting against the wall. I don't expect a long lease. I have so much still to say to you.' Newbolt died three years later at the age of 76 on 19 April 1938. A stroke had put an end to his suffering.[51] After his death Margaret found a scrap of paper in a silver box beside his bed. On it was faintly pencilled the Latin grace of Corpus Christi College that begins: '*Nos miseri et egentes homines pro hoc cibo*'.[52]

49. *AHL*, 13 May 1935
50. *AHL*, 13 May 1935
51. Newbolt's death certificate gives as causes of death: I (a) Cerebral Haemorrage, (b) Arterio-Sclerosis; (c) Acute oedema of lungs. According to Vanessa Furse Jackson, his doctor at the very end diagnosed post-encaphalitic Parkinson's disease.
52. *LLL*, p.404

SECONDARY SOURCES

Amis, Kingsley, *Rudyard Kipling*
Thames & Hudson 1975

Amis, Kingsley, *The Amis Anthology, A Personal Choice of English Verse*
Hutchinson 1988

Archer, C., *William Archer, Life, Work and Friendships*
George Allen & Unwin 1931

Archer, William L., *Poets of the Younger Generation*
John Lane, The Bodley Head 1902

Baden-Powell, Robert S.S., *Scouting For Boys*
Horace Cox 1908

Ballard, C.R., *Smith Dorrien*
Constable & Co. 1931

Bede, Cuthbert, *The Adventures of Verdant Green, an Oxford Freshman*
Nathaniel Cooke 1853

Betjeman, John (ed.), Selected Poems of Henry Newbolt
Nelson 1940

Betjeman, John, *Letters 1926 to 1951*
Methuen 1994

Binyon, Laurence (ed.), *Letters of Maurice Hewlett*
Methuen 1926

Blow, Stephen, *Broken Blood, The Rise and Fall of the Tennant Family*
Faber 1987

Brown, Jane, *Gardens of a Golden Afternoon, The Story of a Partnership, Edwin Lutyens and Gertrude Jekyll*
Allen Lane 1982

Buchan, John, *Memory Hold-the-Door*
Hodder & Stoughton 1940

Buchan, William, *John Buchan: A Memoir*
Buchan & Enright 1982

Carrington, Charles E., *Rudyard Kipling, His Life and Work*
Macmillan 1955

Chisholm, Anne & Davie, *Michael Beaverbrook, A Life*
Hutchinson 1992

Christie, O.F., *Clifton Schooldays 1879–1885*
Shaylor 1930

A History of Clifton College 1860–1934
Arrowsmith 1935

Churchill, Winston S., *The World Crisis 1911–1914*
New English Library 1964

Cobett, Julian, *The Campaign of Trafalgar*
Longmans Green & Co. 1930

Cruttwell, C.R.M.F., *A History of the Great War*
O.U.P. 1930

De la Mare, Walter, *The Return*
Edward Arnold 1910

Dickinson, Patric, *The Non-Combatant: A Study of the Poetry of Sir Henry Newbolt*
BBC Third Programme 1956

Dickinson, Patric (ed.), *Selected Poems of Henry Newbolt*
Hodder & Stoughton 1981

Fink, V.P.S., *Queen Mary's Grammar School: 1554–1954*
Queen Mary's Club, Walsall 1954

Fowler, T., *The History of Corpus Christi College*
Oxford Historical society 1893

Franklin, Arthur Ellis, *Records of the Franklin Family and Collaterals*
Routledge 1935

French, Patrick, Younghusband, *The Last Great Imperial Adventurer*
HarperCollins 1994

Fuller-Maitland, J.A., *The Music of Parry and Stanford*
Heffer 1934

Furse, Dame Katherine, *Hearts and Pomegranates: The Story of Forty five years: 1875–1920*
Peter Davies 1940

Furse, Ralph, *Aucuparius, Recollections of a Recruiting Officer*
O.U.P. 1962

Furse, Ralph (ed,), *A Perpetual Memory and other Poems by Sir Henry Newbolt*

Fussell, Paul, *The Great War in Modern Memory*
O.U.P. 1975

Gathorne-Hardy, Jonathan, *The Public School Phenomenon*
Hodder & Stoughton 1977

Girouard, Mark, *The Return to Camelot*
Yale University Press 1981

Green, Roger Lancelyn, *Andrew Lang, A Critical Biography*
Edmund Ward 1946

Greene, Harry Plunkett, *Where Bright Waters Meet*
P. Allen & Co. 1924

Greene, Harry Plunkett, *Charles Villiers Stanford*
E. Arnold & Co. 1935

Grey of Falloden, Lord, *Twenty-five Years 1892–1916*
Hodder & Stoughton 1925

Grosskurth, Phyllis, *The Memoirs of John Addington Symonds*
Hutchinson 1984

Hackwood, F.W., *Staffordshire Worthies*
Staffordshire Press 1911

Haig, The Countess, *Haig, The Man I Knew*
Moray Press 1936

Hammond, N.G.L. (ed.), *Centenary Essays on Clifton College*
Bristol 1962

Herbert, A.P., *His Life and Times*
Heinemann 1970

Hillier, Bevis, *The Young Betjeman*
John Murray 1988

Hough, Richard, *Admirals in Collision*
Hamish Hamilton 1959

Howarth, Patrick, *Play up and Play the Game*
Eyre Methuen 1973

Inglis, Brian, *Roger Casement*
Hodder & Stoughton 1973

Jackson, Holbrook, *The Eighteen nineties, A Review of Art and Ideas at the Close of the Nineteenth Century*
Pelican 1938

Jackson, Vanessa Furse, *The Poetry of Henry Newbolt, Patriotism is Not Enough*
ELT Press, University of North Carolina, Greensboro, 1994

James, William, *Naval History of Great Britain Vol. 5 1793–1820*
R. Bentley & Son 1886

Jeal, Tim, *Baden-Powell*
Hutchinson 1989

Larkin, Philip (ed.), *Oxford Book of Twentieth Century English Verse*
O.U.P. 1973

Laski, Marghanita, *From Palm to Pine, Rudyard Kipling Abroad and at Home*
Sidgwick & Jackson 1987

McGarvie, Michael, F.S.A., *Orchardleigh House*
Reprinted from the Ancient Monuments Society, Vol 27, Frome Historical Research Group
1983

Sir Henry Newbolt and Orchardleigh, An Investigation into the Origins and Background of his local ballad 'Fidele's Grassy Tomb'.
Frome Society for Local Study 1985

Mackay, Ruddock, F., *Fisher of Kilverstone*
Clarendon 1973

Manton, Jo, *Sister Dora*
Methuen 1970

Marsh, Edward, *Georgian Poetry*
Poetry Bookshop 1914

Meyer, Bernard C., *Joseph Conrad, A Psychoanalytical Biography*
Princeton University Press 1967

Millard, Kenneth, *Edwardian Poetry*
O.U.P. 1991

Millgate, Michael (ed.), *Life and Work of Thomas Hardy*
Macmillan 1984

Morris, James, *Pax Britannica*
Penguin 1980

Newbolt, Sir F.G.,   *Clifton College Twenty five Years Ago, The Diary of a Fag*
      Robinson 1904

                        Clifton College Forty Years Ago, The Diary of a Praeposter
      Philip Allen 1924

                        The Enchanted Wood
      Philip Allen 1925

                        Out of Court
      Philip Allen 1925

Newbolt, Henry (ed.), *Poems of Mary Coleridge*
Elkin Mathews 1908

Newbolt, Henry, *My World as in My Time*
Faber & Faber 1932

Newbolt, Margaret (ed.), *Later Life and Letters of Sir Henry Newbolt*
Faber & Faber 1942

Olivier, Edith, *Country Moods and Tenses*
Batsford 1941

Origo, Iris, *Images and Shadows, Part of a Life*
John Murray 1970

Oltewill, David, *The Edwardian Garden*
Yale University Press 1989

Paget, Lady Walburga, *In My Tower*
Hutchinson 1924

Parker, Peter, *The Old Lie, The Great War and the Public School Ethos*
Constable 1987

Philips, Catherine, *Robert Bridges, A Biography*
O.U.P. 1992

Quiller-Couch, Arthur, *Memories and Opinions*
Cambridge 1944

Roskill, Capt. Stephen, *Admiral of the Fleet Earl Beatty, The Last Great Naval Hero. An Intimate Biography*
Collins 1980

Rothenstein, William, *Men and Memories: Vol. 3. Since Fifty*
Faber and Faber 1939

Sassoon, Siegfried, *Diary, 1923–1925*
Rupert Hart Davis 1985

Schurman, Donald M., *Julian S. Corbett 1854–1922. Historian of British Maritime Policy from Drake to Jellicoe*
London Historical Society 1981

Sichel, Edith, *Gathered Leaves from the Prose of Mary Coleridge*
Constable 1910

Smith, David C., *H.G. Wells, Desperately Mortal, A Biography*
Yale University Press 1986

Smith-Dorrien, General Sir Horace, *Memories of Forty Eight Years of Service*
John Murray 1925

Stevenson, Robert Louis, *Letters From Samoa, Vol XVII. The Works of Robert Louis Stevenson*
Chatto & Windus 1911

Temple, William, *Life of Bishop Percival*
Macmillan 1921

Thwaite, Anne, *Edmund Gosse, A Literary Landscape*
Secker and Warburg 1984

Trevelyan, G.M., *Grey of Falloden, Being the Life of Sir Edward Grey, Afterwards Viscount Grey of Falloden*
Longmans 1937

West, Anthony, *H.G. Wells, Aspects of a Life*
Penguin 1985

Whistler, Laurence,   *The Initials in the Heart*
    Rupert Hart-Davis 1964
                        The Laughter of the Urn
    Weidenfeld and Nicolson

Whistler, Theresa, (ed.) *The Collected Poems of Mary Coleridge*
Rupert Hart-Davis 1954

Whistler, Theresa, *Imagination of the Heart, A Life of Walter de la Mare*
Duckworth 1993

Wilson, James M., *An Autobiography 1861–1931*
Sidgwick and Jackson 1932

Winstone, Harry V.F., *Gertrude Bell*
Jonathan Cape 1978

Winterbottom, Derek, *Newbolt and the Spirit of Clifton*
Redcliff 1986

Woolf, Virginia, Roger Fry, *A Biography*
Hogarth Press 1940

Younghusband, Capt, F.E. & Capt. G.J., *The Relief of Chitral*
Macmillan 1895

INDEX

sister): birth, 6; childhood, 8, 12, 15, 19, 31; Mary's death, 24; education, 42; social life, 63, 64, 67, 76, 85, 86; appearance, 64, 158; brother's engagement, 81, 82, 85; marriage, 86; niece's visit, 93; brother's illness, 107; depression, 118; illness, 156–8; death, 155, 156, 158–9

Chitty, Thomas (Henry's son), 233

Chitty, Tom (HN's brother-in-law): legal career, 72–3; HN's work with, 72, 73–4, 118; marriage, 86; Swiss holiday, 98; wife's depression, 118; HN's visit, 120; wife's illness and death, 156–7; remarriage, 159–60; son's marriage, 233

Chitty family, 182, 233

Churchill, Winston, 146, 153, 217, 218, 257

Coleridge, Arthur, 81, 100, 126, 175, 207

Coleridge, Mary: ancestry, 80, 105; education, 80; love affairs, 80–1, 90; Celia's childhood, 92; Settee, 94–5, 100; work, 95, 100, 105, 109, 125, 126–7, 148, 254; reviews, 132; death, 175

Collingwood, Lord, 102, 164

Colomb, Philip Howard, 164

Coltman, Anna, 188, 189, 238

Coltman, Ella: appearance, 79; relationship with Margaret, 79–80, 81–2, 88, 90, 99, 194, 242, 264, 281–2; family background, 79–80; Lorbottle Hall, 80, 97, 129; Grecians, 80–1; relationship with HN, 82, 88, 91, 128–9, 189–93, 203–4, 206, 237–9, 240, 261, 264, 265, 268, 282; HN's letters, 85; position in Newbolt marriage, 90–1, 99, 122, 173, 276, 280–2; relationship with Newbolt children, 92, 96, 122, 183, 206; Settee, 94–5; HN's writing, 95;

Italian holiday, 98–9; *Monthly Review*, 124–5, 128, 150; health, 128–9, 192; relationship with de la Mare, 130–1; correspondence, 176, 249; family problems, 188–9, 191; religion, 190; London house, 191, 280; Malvern holiday, 231–2; Swiss holiday, 264

Coltman, Frank, 79–80, 97–8, 188

Coltman, Hew, 188–9, 237, 268

Coltman, Hilda, 188, 189, 190

Coltman, Mrs ('the Duchess', Ella's mother), 188, 191, 231, 268

Conrad, Joseph, 134–6

Conybeare family, 62, 67

Cookson, Geoffrey, 125

Corbett, Julian, 145–6, 164–5, 235, 256, 257

Cory, William, 80, 111, 254

Curzon, Lord, 115

Custance, Sir Reginald, 164–5, 178, 179, 211, 216, 218

Davies, Walford, 181

de la Mare, Walter: relationship with Ella, 79, 129, 130–1; Newbolt's influence, 131–3, 282; cake-making, 184; *Georgian Poetry*, 203; on HN, 249; correspondence, 267; Netherhampton war dinner, 272; HN's old age, 282

Desborough, Lady, 226–7

Dickinson, Patric, 265, 271

Dixon, Canon, 100, 109

Drake, Sir Francis, 102, 210, 250, 254

Drinkwater, John, 177, 203

Duckworth, Revd Arthur: family, 78, 84, 85–6; Orchardleigh, 78, 85, 116, 167; relationship with HN, 79, 85–6, 89, 96; Newbolt wedding, 87; grandson's death, 117; death, 260

Duckworth, Campbell, 85, 86,

193–4, 260
Duckworth, Edina, 78, 79, 168, 184, 207, 260
Duckworth, Evie, 193–4, 214, 264
Duckworth, Helen, *see* Holland
Duckworth, Margaret, *see* Newbolt

Eliot, T.S., 264–5, 273
Elwes, Gervase, 239
Evans, Winifred (Fred), 182

Fisher, H.A.L., 187, 253
Fisher, John Arbuthnot (Jackie), Lord, 145–6, 217, 218, 260
Fitzgerald, Edward, 30, 33, 67
Frampton, Meredith, 275, 280
French, Sir John, 212, 231
Fry, Roger, 52, 119, 126, 280
Furse, Bill, 127, 231, 244
Furse, Celia (*née* Newbolt, HN's daughter): birth, 91; childhood, 92–3, 96, 121, 148, 158, 168; dogs, 173, 283; education, 182–3; coming-out, 183–4; Oxford balls, 184, 187; Rome holiday, 186; engagement, 207; marriage, 193, 207, 245–6; motherhood, 207, 213, 227, 231, 245–6, 283; brother's car, 225; wartime, 231, 233; Halsdon, 193, 233; brother's marriage, 262–3; autobiography, 276
Furse, Charles, 127, 170
Furse, Henry, 127, 170–3, 183, 193, 216
Furse, Jill (Barbara, HN's granddaughter), 227, 231, 233, 246, 261, 263, 283
Furse, Dame Katharine, 127, 236, 248, 269 Furse, Nicholas (HN's grandson), 263
Furse, Patrick (HN's grandson), 170, 245, 263
Furse, Ralph (HN's son-in-law): courtship of Celia, 184, 187; engagement and wedding, 207;

wartime experiences, 212–13, 227, 231, 233, 244; marriage, 245–6; London home, 262–3
Furse, Theresa (HN's grand-daughter), 263, 283
Furse family, 127, 236–7, 248

George V, King, 223, 270, 271
Glenconner, Pamela, Lady: Newbolt friendship, 176–7, 183, 186; family, 177, 227; Ella's dinner party, 189; Celia's wedding, 207; HN's knighthood, 223; son's death, 227
Gordon, Eliza Jane (*née* Stubbs, HN's aunt), 3, 18, 21, 85
Gordon, Robert, 21, 67, 85
Gosse, Edmund, 104, 134, 203, 240
Green, T. H., 25, 60
Greene, Harry Plunkett, 102, 180, 232, 240, 263, 283
Grenfell twins, 226–7, 249, 254
Grey of Falloden, Edward, Lord: Co-efficients, 137; wife's death, 139–40, 199; *Monthly Review*, 150–1; second marriage, 177; friendship with HN, 199–201, 211, 272; Sarajevo, 209; HN's knighthood, 223

Haig, Douglas, Earl, 40, 212, 231, 244, 270
Haldane, R.B., 137, 200
Hardy, Thomas, 127, 204–5, 218, 255, 279
Harrison, Dr Alfred, 18, 33, 117
Harrison, Selina (*née* Stubbs, HN's aunt), 3, 18, 117
Hedgecock, Walter, 105
Henschel, Carl, 222
Herbert, A.P., 209, 240
Herbert, Gwen, 240
Hewlett, Maurice: friendship with HN, 176; work, 176; home, 184; son, 184, 215; on Coltman family, 188; Ella's dinner party,

relationship with Ella, 79–80, 81–2, 88, 90–1, 189, 194, 242, 264, 281–2; Grecians membership, 80–1; engagement, 82, 85; househunting, 86–7; wedding, 87–8; married life, 89–90; daughter's birth, 91–2; relationship with mother-in-law, 93, 121, 260; Settee membership, 94–5; son's birth, 96; on 'Drake's Drum' setting, 105; Venice trip, 107–8; poetry, 108; nephew's death, 117; Earl's Terrace house, 120–1; Lynton holidays, 124; Mount Grace holidays, 168; love affair with Henry Furse, 170–2; life at Netherhampton, 171–4, 191–2, 216, 241–2, 255, 261, 278, 281–2; view of Suffragettes, 177; HN's letter diaries, 178, 199; Oxford balls, 184; relationship with son, 186, 224–6, 262–3; silver wedding, 192; health, 192, 242; trips abroad, 193-4; HN's affair with Alice Hylton, 195, 197, 211; son's breakdown, 206; attitude to HN's work, 211, 223, 256, 265; wartime experiences, 216, 241–2; HN's knighthood, 223; HN's letters, 231, 238, 244, 245; death of parents, 260; deafness, 264, 272, 279; Canada trip, 267, 268; HN's old age, 278, 283; move to London, 280–2; HN's death, 284

Newbolt, Mary (HN's half-sister), 2, 5, 5–7, 12, 14, 17–23, 24–5, 32

Newbolt, Mary (HN's grand-daughter), 263

Newbolt, Mary Jane (*née* Newham, HN's father's first wife), 2

Newbolt, Milly (HN's sister), *see* Chitty

Newbolt, Molly (HN's niece), *see* Medley

Newbolt, Nancy (*née* Triffitt, HN's daughter-in-law), 262–3

Newbolt, Peter (HN's grandson), 86, 165, 234, 263, 271, 282

Newham family, 7

Noble, Sir Andrew, 147, 148

Oakeley, Edward, 40, 69, 107–8

Oliver, Edith, 271

Ollivant, Alfred, 149–50

Owen, Wilfred, 251

Parker, Sir Peter, 103

Pattison, Dorothy (Sister Dora), 15–16, 19

Pattison, Mark, 15–16, 57

Peile, Dick, 63, 169, 190–1

Pembroke family, 176, 184, 279

Percival, Dr John: Clifton headmastership, 33, 37, 40; Master of Trinity, 44, 54, 63; children, 62, 63, 97; Commem (1899), 116–17; Clifton war memorial, 144; biography, 253; death, 271

Plant, Colonel Edmund, 46, 52

Pollen, Arthur, 178, 180

Quiller-Couch, Arthur: at Clifton, 40, 48, 52; at Oxford, 60; on 'Drake's Drum', 111; *Monthly Review*, 125; son's education, 161, 185

Read, Dido (*née* Chitty, HN's niece), 93, 182, 207, 268

Read, John, 268

Reith, Sir John, 271

Rosebery, Lord, 150–2

Rothenstein, William, 119, 128, 134–6

Ruskin, John, 59, 63, 122, 277

Sassoon, Siegfried, 249–50, 251, 271–2

Scott, Sir Walter, 38, 60, 100, 123, 169
Shaw, George Bernard, 138
Sichel, Edith, 125, 175
Sickert, Walter, 119, 195
Sidgwick, Arthur, 57, 63
Smith-Dorrien, Sir Horace and Lady Olive, 211, 212, 224, 231, 260
Solari, Angelo, 22, 24
Solomon family, 3, 18
Squire, J. C., 250
Stanford, Charles Villiers, 105, 165, 180, 232, 250
Stephen, Julia, 86
Stephen, Leslie, 103
Stevenson, Robert Louis, 95
Strachey, St Loe, 111
Strang, William, 119, 196
Stubbs, Eliza (née Solomon, HN's grandmother), 3, 14, 15, 20, 21–2
Stubbs, Eliza Jane, see Gordon
Stubbs, Emily, see Newbolt
Stubbs, George Bradnock (HN's grandfather): public life, 2; attitude to Emily's marriage, 3, 5; relationship with grandson, 5, 14–15, 20; son-in-law's funeral, 9; daughter's finances, 11; wife's death, 21; death, 30
Stubbs, Heath, 70
Stubbs, Joseph (HN's great-grandfather), 14, 25
Stubbs, Selina, see Harrison
Sturdee, Sir Doveton, 217, 218, 236, 237
Symonds, John Addington, 36, 51, 57, 108, 127
Symons, Arthur, 154

Tennant family, 177, 227, 271, 280
Tennyson, Alfred, Lord, 4, 29, 49, 57, 100, 111
Threlfall, Will, 42, 249
Trevelyan, George Otto, 239

Tryon, Vice-Admiral Sir George, 101–2
Tyrrell, Father, 191

Victoria, Queen, 73, 151, 261

Walrond, Arthur, 71
Ward, Mrs Humphrey, 204
Waterhouse, Alfred, 105
Watt, A.P., 120
Watts, G.F., 144
Webb, Tom, 18, 19, 20, 21, 23
Wells, H.G., 137–40, 141–2, 154, 166–7, 283
Whistler, Theresa, 80, 85, 121, 278, 282–3
Whitehead, Rowland, 73, 125
Wilde, Oscar, 71
Wilhelm II, Kaiser, 104, 200, 235
Wilson, Revd James (Jimmy), 44–5, 51
Windle, Eliza and Mrs, 12, 13, 21
Wollaston, George: Clifton housemaster, 37–8; relationship with Newbolts, 46, 47, 79, 276; Bridges comparison, 105; son, 215, 254; death, 260
Woolf, Virginia (née Stephen), 86, 103, 135, 145
Wordsworth, William, 39, 143, 199

Yeats, William Butler, 106–7, 204
Younghusband, Frank, 40, 46, 115, 143, 254